CULTURE AND REFLEXIVITY IN SYSTEMIC PSYCHOTHERAPY

Systemic Thinking and Practice Series
edited by Charlotte Burck and Gwyn Daniel
published and distributed by Karnac

This influential series was co-founded in 1989 by series editors David Campbell and Ros Draper to promote innovative applications of systemic theory to psychotherapy, teaching, supervision, and organizational consultation. In 2011, Charlotte Burck and Gwyn Daniel became series editors, and aim to present new theoretical developments and pioneering practice, to make links with other theoretical approaches, and to promote the relevance of systemic theory to contemporary social and psychological questions.

Other titles in the series include

Hildebrand, J. *Bridging the Gap: A Training Module in Personal and Professional Development*
Jones, E., & Asen, E. *Systemic Couple Therapy and Depression*
Asen, A., & McHugh, B. (Eds.) *Multiple Family Therapy: The Marlborough Model and Its Wider Applications*
Krause, I.-B. *Culture and System in Family Therapy*
Mason, B., & Sawyerr, A. (Eds.) *Exploring the Unsaid: Creativity, Risks, and Dilemmas in Working Cross-Culturally*
Campbell, D., & Mason, B. (Eds.) *Perspectives on Supervision*
Johnsen, A., & Wie Tortsteinsson, V. *Self in Relationships: Perspectives on Family Therapy from Developmental Psychology*
Smith, G. *Systemic Approaches to Training in Child Protection*
Seikkula, J., & Arnkil, T. E. *Dialogical Meetings in Social Networks*
Baum, S., & Lynggaard, H. (Eds.) *Intellectual Disabilities: A Systemic Approach*
Anderson, M., & Jensen, P. *Innovations in the Reflecting Process*
Wilson, J. *The Performance of Practice: Enhancing the Repertoire of Therapy with Children and Families*
Bertrando, P. *The Dialogical Therapist: Dialogue in Systemic Pratice*
Flaskas, C., & Pocock, D. *Systems and Psychoanalysis: Contemporary Integrations in Family Therapy*
Groen, M., & van Lawick, J. *Intimate Warfare: Regarding the Fragility of Family Relations*
Fredman, G., Anderson, E., & Stott, J. (Eds.) *Being with Older People: A Systemic Approach*
Burck, C., & Daniel, G. *Mirrors and Reflections: Processes of Systemic Supervision*
Singh, R., & Dutta, S. *Race and Culture: Tools, Techniques and Trainings: A Manual for Professionals*
Seidenfaden, K., & Draiby, P. *The Vibrant Relationship: A Handbook for Couples and Therapists*
Seidenfaden, K., Draiby, P., Søborg Christensen, S., & Heigaard, V. *The Vibrant Family: A Handbook for Parents and Professionals*

For a full listing, see our website: www.karnacbooks.com

CULTURE AND REFLEXIVITY IN SYSTEMIC PSYCHOTHERAPY

Mutual Perspectives

Edited by

Inga-Britt Krause

KARNAC

First published in 2012 by
Karnac Books Ltd
118 Finchley Road, London NW3 5HT

Copyright © 2012 to Inga-Britt Krause for the edited collection, and to the individual authors for their contributions.

The rights of the contributors to be identified as the authors of this work have been asserted in accordance with §§ 77 and 78 of the Copyright Design and Patents Act 1988.

All rights reserved. No part of this publication may be reproduced, stored in a retrieval system, or transmitted, in any form or by any means, electronic, mechanical, photocopying, recording, or otherwise, without the prior written permission of the publisher.

British Library Cataloguing in Publication Data

A C.I.P. for this book is available from the British Library

ISBN 978 1 85575 778 3

Edited, designed and produced by The Studio Publishing Services Ltd
www.publishingservicesuk.co.uk
e-mail: studio@publishingservicesuk.co.uk

www.karnacbooks.com

CONTENTS

ACKNOWLEDGEMENTS ix

ABOUT THE EDITOR AND CONTRIBUTORS xi

SERIES EDITORS' FOREWORD by Charlotte Burck
and Gwyn Daniel xv

FOREWORD by Peter Rober xvii

INTRODUCTION by Inga-Britt Krause xxv

CHAPTER ONE
Culture and the reflexive subject in systemic psychotherapy 1
Inga-Britt Krause

PART I: THE INTERSUBJECTIVE SPACE

CHAPTER TWO
Can we tolerate the relationships that race compels? 39
David Campbell

CHAPTER THREE
What would (or can) I know? Reflections on the conditions of knowing and understanding in intercultural therapy 53
Carmel Flaskas

CHAPTER FOUR
Objectification, recognition, and the intersubjective continuum 71
David Pocock

PART II: EXPANDING REFLEXIVITY IN SYSTEMIC PSYCHOTHERAPY

CHAPTER FIVE
With an exile's eye: developing positions of cultural reflexivity (with a bit of help from feminism) 91
Gwyn Daniel

CHAPTER SIX
Cultural and family ethos in systemic therapy 115
Paolo Bertrando

CHAPTER SEVEN
Developments in Social GRRRAAACCEEESSS: visible–invisible and voiced–unvoiced 139
John Burnham

PART III: THERAPY AS A SOCIAL RELATIONSHIP

CHAPTER EIGHT
The personal and the professional: core beliefs and the construction of bridges across difference 163
Barry Mason

CHAPTER NINE
Hewing out hope from mountains of despair 181
Archie Smith

CHAPTER TEN
Engaging within and across culture 201
Rabia Malik & Philippe Mandin

EPILOGUE by Inga-Britt Krause 223

INDEX 227

ACKNOWLEDGEMENTS

The epigraph to Chapter Two is from *American Pastoral* by Philip Roth, published by Vintage Books. Reprinted by permission of The Random House Group Limited.

The extract from the poem "Warning" by Taha Muhammad Ali at the beginning of Chapter Five is reprinted by permission of the translaters, Peter Cole, Gabriel Levin, and Yahya Hijazi and Copper Canyon Press, Port Townsend, Washington.

ABOUT THE EDITOR AND CONTRIBUTORS

Paolo Bertrando, MD, PhD, graduated in medicine and specialized in psychiatry in Milan. He was trained in systemic family therapy by Luigi Boscolo and Gianfranco Cecchin in the 1980s, and initially used the Milan Approach for working with families with a member diagnosed with schizophrenia. His latest book, published in 2007, is *The Dialogical Therapist* (Karnac). His interests concern the dynamics of systemic therapy (both from a methodological and experimental point of view), the relationship between psychiatric and systemic thinking, and work with emotions within the systemic model.

John Burnham is a consultant family therapist and Director of Systemic Training, Parkview Clinic, Birmingham Children's Hospital NHS Trust, and formerly Director of Training in systemic teaching, training and supervision, KCC Foundation, London.

David Campbell was a consultant clinical psychologist based at the Tavistock Clinic in London. In addition to a clinical practice, he developed training courses in supervision, professional doctorate research, and Master's level family therapy training. He established a long-standing international practice as a management and leadership trainer and organizational consultant specializing in applying systemic models to strategic planning and team-building work with teams, services, and small organizations in both the private and public sector, including health, education, social services, and the voluntary sector. He offered role consultation, supervision, and executive coaching. He wrote extensively about consultation, including *Taking Positions in the Organization* (Campbell & Grønbæk, 2006) and co-edited *Organizations Connected: A Handbook of System Consultation* (Campbell & Huffington, 2008) and was co-editor of the Systemic Thinking and Practice Series. He passed away in 2009 before this book was published.

Gwyn Daniel is a consultant systemic psychotherapist, supervisor, and trainer at the Tavistock Clinic and in private practice in Oxford. She is the co-author of *Growing up in Stepfamilies* and *Gender and Family Therapy*, and co-editor of *Mirrors and Reflections; Processes in Systemic Supervision*.

Carmel Flaskas is a social worker and family therapist, and Senior Lecturer in the School of Social Sciences and International Studies, University of New South Wales, Sydney, where she convenes the Master of Couple and Family Therapy programme. She has published a number of books and articles on the therapeutic relationship, on psychoanalytic ideas in the systemic context, and on knowledge in family therapy. In 2006, she was awarded an Honorary Doctorate by the Tavistock Clinic in conjunction with the University of East London for her contributions to systemic psychotherapy, and in 2005 she received the ANZJFT award for Distinguished Contributions to Australian Family Therapy.

Inga-Britt Krause, PhD, is a social and medical anthropologist. She has carried out ethnographic work with high caste Hindus in Nepal and with British Sikhs. As a systemic psychotherapist she has worked for many years in the NHS and has helped set up Specialist Services for Asian Communities in London. Her publications include *Therapy Across Culture* (Sage, 1998), *Culture and System in Family Therapy* (Karnac, 2002), and papers on medical anthropology and cross-cultural psychotherapy. She is currently Training & Development Consultant in the Tavistock & Portman NHS Foundation Trust.

Rabia Malik is cross-cultural services co-ordinator and a senior systemic psychotherapist at the Marlborough Family Service. She specializes in working with South Asian and Muslim families and communities. She has also been a senior lecturer in psychosocial studies at the University of East London. Her doctorate, from University College London, was on the cultural construction of mental illness. She has trained, researched, and written on religion, culture, and mental health. Recently, she edited a special edition of *Context* on faith, values, and relationships.

Philippe Mandin is a senior social worker and systemic psychotherapist at the Marlborough Family Service in London. He is undertaking a research project as part of a Professional Doctorate in Social Work at the Tavistock, to explore complex relationships and processes at play during network meetings in childcare proceedings. He has recently edited a special edition of the *Journal of Social Work Practice*.

Barry Mason is a freelance psychotherapist, researcher, lecturer, and supervisor. He is Co-Director of the Institute of Family Therapy/Birkbeck College, University College Doctoral Programme in Family and Systemic Psychotherapy. He has published many articles on systemic psychotherapy.

David Pocock is Consultant Family Therapist, Family Assessment and Safeguarding Service, Oxford Health NHS Trust, UK and a visiting lecturer on the Bristol University Diploma/MSc Family Therapy training. He is a current assessor for *Journal of Family Therapy* and past member of the Editorial Board and previous moderator for the AFT/JFT internet discussion forum. He is a psychoanalytic psychotherapist in independent practice and a member of the Severnside Institute for Psychotherapy. His published work ranges across systems theory, psychoanalysis, and the philosophical underpinnings of psychotherapy.

Rev. Dr Archie Smith is an ordained American Baptist minister. He is James and Clarice Foster Professor of Pastoral Psychology and Counseling at the Pacific School of Religion. Since 1977, he has been a California Licensed Marriage, Family and Child Therapist. He has taught and practised in the UK, Kenya, The People's Republic of China, Germany, Poland, France, and Australia, as well as in the USA. He has published several books and many articles.

SERIES EDITORS' FOREWORD

Culture and Reflexivity in Systemic Psychotherapy is an important and timely book for the systemic psychotherapy field. Inga-Britt Krause's earlier books, which include *Culture and System in Family Therapy*, published in this series in 2002, have provided significant landmarks for systemic psychotherapists in placing culture centrally within systemic theory and in challenging therapists to examine their own unquestioned assumptions. This new edited volume will be welcomed by many therapists, of whatever theoretical persuasion.

In this book, Britt Krause continues her ground-breaking work, both in her own contribution and also through bringing together a number of experienced systemic psychotherapists whom she has invited to elaborate the ways in which they strive for cultural reflexivity in their work. Her request of these well-known writers also acts as a provocation to all of us as readers: how do we, and how could we, ourselves respond to this question, and how do our responses connect to the variety of ways in which each of these writers has sought to tangle with the task?

A significant feature of this volume is that Britt Krause has herself addressed the need for the further amplification of systemic theory, and she tackles this with characteristic rigour. Holding the tensions between anthropological lenses and systemic thinking and practice, she re-examines some familiar concepts, including the term reflexivity itself, as well as traces significant absences in our theorizing and the effects of these absences. She invites us, as readers, to become reflexive about our own use of language and its relationship to culture, with the aim of developing a "comprehensive reflexivity". She formulates the challenge as: "using our own selves to learn about others and the world presents difficult and thorny problems". This volume goes a long way towards opening up further creative possibilities for considering those processes which we find less accessible, and for acknowledging and engaging with perspectives that are very different to our own.

Having taken over this year as series editors of the Systemic Thinking and Practice series, founded by David Campbell and Ros Draper, we are particularly pleased that it is this book, initially conceived in conversation with David Campbell and containing a posthumous contribution from him, which is the first under our editorship.

Charlotte Burck and Gwyn Daniel
Series Editors

FOREWORD

The challenge of writing about culture and family therapy practice

Peter Rober

> "*Universal humanity is visible at the edges*"
>
> (Buck-Morss, 2009, p. 151)

In our Western societies, multi-culturalism is not an option any more. For some years now, it has become a reality. The time when the question "should our society be multi-cultural or not" had any relevance is long past. The relevant questions now are "how are we going to be a multi-cultural society?" and "how are we going to deal with the tensions multi-culturalism evokes?"

Although racism, colonialism, and cultural insensitivity are still present in our society, the dominant societal norm seems to promote being respectful towards others, enjoying the richness of cultural diversity, and being tolerant of differences. In practice, this societal norm is very tricky, especially when this norm conflicts with other values we hold dear. We have fought for social equality, for lesbian, gay, bisexual, and transgender (LGBT) rights, for the rights of children, for animal rights, and so on. Whenever our cultural openness collides with instances in which these values are not respected, this leaves us confused and in doubt, especially because many of us carry with us the burden of a historical debt of our colonial pasts, with their exploitation, atrocities, and genocides. Whatever the cost, we do not want to make the mistakes our ancestors have made and, if possible, we want to show ourselves being the exact opposite of a colonizer: humble, self-critical, generous, and respectful towards others. Such fears of cultural imperialism might result in an attitude of cultural relativism that makes it difficult to represent any practice or belief as oppressive or at odds with our values of equality, personal integrity, and freedom (Phillips, 2007; Žižek, 2008a). While we can enjoy cultural diversity, defend the rights of cultural minorities, and be open to difference, at the same time we cannot but reflect on areas of tensions: what about female circumcision, bull fighting, polygamy, honour killing, whale hunting, and so on?

For many years, talking about the tensions multi-culturalism evokes was not done in liberal circles. Just mentioning these tensions made you liable to be suspected of being a racist wolf in sheep's clothing. The only discourse allowed was the celebration of difference and tolerance. By now, the taboos implied in such politically correct practices have been exposed. The concept of tolerance, for instance, has been subjected to a critical evaluation (e.g., Hansson, 2007; Nehushtan, 2007), and some writers have arrived at surprising, even unsettling, conclusions. Brown (2006), for instance, writes that while in our multi-cultural society tolerance is seen as a solely benign virtue, her analysis shows that in our post-political world (Mouffe, 2005) the concept of tolerance often masks shady political agendas, inequality, injustice, and, indeed, intolerance. She gives the example of The Simon Wiesenthal Center Museum of Tolerance in Los Angeles, which hides its pro-Israel position behind the discourse of tolerance. Jews are presented as the ultimate victims of intolerance, and, as such, their voice is privileged to speak with moral authority about tolerance. Brown exposes the power relations inherent in such a discourse of tolerance: some are positioned as tolerant (the Israeli, the American), and others are positioned as intolerant. In the museum, examples are given of people taking the responsibility of fighting against intolerance (e.g., American soldiers fighting in Iraq), unmasking the tolerant as being intolerant for the intolerant. Like Brown, Žižek frames the concept of tolerance in the context of the post-ideology era we are living in (Žižek, 2008a,b). According to him, a plea for cultural tolerance is a plea for a status quo in the neo-liberal economic system celebrating freedom, globalization, and profit.

Why are today so many problems perceived as problems of intolerance, not as problems of inequality, exploitation, injustice? Why is the proposed remedy tolerance, not emancipation, political struggle, even armed struggle? The immediate answer is the liberal multiculturalist's basic ideological operation: the 'culturalization of politics'—political differences, differences conditioned by political inequality, economic exploitation, etc., are naturalized/neutralized into 'cultural' differences, different 'ways of life', which are something given, something that cannot be overcome, but merely 'tolerated.' [Žižek, 2008a, p. 660]

Žižek explains that the promotion of the virtue of tolerance fits nicely within an overall capitalist project of turning the whole world into a global marketplace in which all values are relative and in which everything has a price. By stressing the importance of tolerance, conflicts and tensions are psychologized and individualized ('if only he/she would be more tolerant there would be no problem'). Furthermore, the concept of cultural tolerance is problematic, since it seems to mask a patronizing attitude (Brown, 2006). Being tolerant to others can be read as: "We accept that you remain connected with your cultural traditions, but we—enlighted as we are—see the relativity of cultural beliefs and practices. So, we are flexible and suspend our own cultural connectedness in order to be tolerant, and respect you in your cultural traditions." A view of tolerance as a preferential way to deal with cultural differences betrays an underlying Western liberal view of culture as personalized and privatized (Žižek, 2008a): in our Western view, culture is not a public network of norms, rules, taboos, and prohibitions in which we are born, but, rather, a set of personal beliefs and practices that we are free to choose and enjoy. This view of culture is very different from the view of culture as public and binding. Implicitly, we consider our view superior and we tolerate the other's view. Could it be that exactly what we try to avoid is implicitly engendered in some of the ways in which we try to avoid colonialism and imperialism? It seems that the divisions between tolerance and intolerance, between being culturally sensitive and being colonist, between right and wrong, are not so clear-cut.

In a societal context in which questions like these about dealing with cultural differences are front of stage in the public debate, also, in the field of family therapy, more reflection is needed on how to deal with cultural differences. However, in our field, we already have an excellent track record in promoting cultural sensitivity, cultural competence, and culturally informed therapy (Abu Baker, 1999; Bean, Perry, & Bedell, 2002; Weisman, Duarte, Konery, & Wasserman, 2006). It is clear that being culturally sensitive is highly valued in our field. In a variety of ways, it has been promoted as a correction of ethnocentric ideas and practices (e.g., Di Nicola, 1997; Falicov, 1995; McGoldrick, 1998). While extremely important, nowadays this is not enough any more. In addition to the promotion of cultural sensitivity, we need a better understanding of the challenges the multi-cultural project poses for practising family therapists. To mention just one example of such challenges, we can refer to the tension a family therapist might feel between his/her cultural sensitivity and his/her resistance to patriarchal gender practices when dealing with families in which traditional patriarchal gender roles are considered the cultural norm. We need deeper reflection on the complexity of issues like this and, in particular, we need more reflection on ways to deal with it in practice. Promoting cultural sensitivity is not enough in these difficult situations, and it might even have negative consequences for the quality of the therapeutic encounter. If the therapist only has the idea of cultural sensitivity to hold on to, the risk is that, in his/her resolution to respect otherness, he/she would be desperately careful not to offend, which might result in a kind of passivity—a not-knowing what to think or say—in which the therapist as a person disappears. The therapist is then absent, rather than respectful.

This is what this book does: to reflect deeper on culture in family therapy practice, and especially on ways to deal through reflexivity with difference and sameness in the construction of intercultural therapeutic relationships (Malik & Krause, 2005). Writing about family therapy and culture is a challenge these days, in at least two respects. First of all, because the field of family therapy seems to be leaving behind the old theoretical paradigm that has inspired practitioners in our field for many years, while it is not yet clear what will be the new paradigm. Second, it is also a challenge because writers writing about culture have to avoid some important pitfalls. One of these pitfalls, for instance, is cultural stereotyping, in which a person is seen only as a representative of a cultural group, rather than as an individual. This also means that it is important to try to explore the complexity of dealing with culture beyond the obvious issues of racism, discrimination, and colonialism that, in a certain sense, can be considered stereotypes in their own right.

Let me first consider the present state of the field of family therapy. Family therapy is a practice in search of a theory (Andersen, 1991). The history of family therapy can be told as a history of practitioners exploring the usefulness of concepts, models, and theories in order to talk and think about their practices. In general, there is a paradigmatic evolution in the field from cybernetics to a narrative/postmodernist paradigm. It is important to note that the narrative/postmodernist paradigm implies an anti-essentialist perspective that highlights the importance of cultural differences. While such a perspective sounds promising for a book on culture, today a vague unease with social constructionism as a theoretical foundation for family therapy is building up, especially because of its radical anti-realist stance and its strong emphasis on the local and the particular. Because the narrative paradigm has become the dominant discourse in the field, and the postmodernist perspective is often presented as the one and only right perspective from which to look at family therapy practice, in the field, voices can be heard that suggest that it might be time for something new.

But, if the narrative/postmodernist paradigm has run its course, then what now? What comes next? This is not at all clear, and here lies the challenge. Family therapy writers in these times have to have the courage to let go of some of the old certainties, and explore what lies beyond the simplistic division modernist/postmodernist. In this book, the concept of reflexivity is central in trying to get beyond this division. While, in myriad ways connected with the history of family therapy, the use of this concept can be a big step in shaping the future of the field of family therapy, it stresses the importance of using ourselves to learn about how to position us towards others, and, in that sense, it is an significant move away from the postmodernist idea of "not-knowing". In fact, such a step might possibly reconnect us with the rich psychodynamic tradition in which the therapist's reflections have been subject to exploration and thought for decades. This also opens space for reflection on what is present in the therapist but out of his/her immediate awareness; what is expressed in his/her fantasies, in his/her body, in his/her emotions, and in his/her breathing while he/she is present in the moment.

There is also a second challenge in writing a book on culture and family therapy practice, and this has to do with the concept of culture itself. How can we talk about culture when we are culturally situated ourselves? To deal with this, in our talking we often qualify our words, saying something like, "whatever I say/think is not the truth, but has to be situated in cultural and historical context". In that way, we immediately distance ourselves from what we say/think. We apologize for our thoughts and we do not take full responsibility for the position we occupy in the world. How does one write about culture and go beyond the apology for one's cultural situatedness? This is probably the biggest challenge, as it is connected to our Western history as colonizers and our historic debt to the less privileged. However, moving on in to the future and trying to give shape to our future society, we will have to come up with new ideas about ways for all of us (whatever our colour) to be culturally situated without being pinned down as frozen images of our cultural labels and stereotypes, such as "Muslim", "African", "racist", "colonizer", and so on. How can we avoid this kind of cultural stereotyping? How can we find a way to be who we are and to be who we are *together*, without fear, without reservation, and without apology? This is a central question addressed in this book and, although the answers offered by the different authors are quite diverse, their contributions paint a picture of creating an intercultural therapeutic relationship as more than just a question of good intentions and cultural openness. Intercultural therapy involves dealing with the constant tension between sameness and difference in new ways each time. It often necessitates leaving our own comfort zone and venturing into unexplored territories, not only of the family's strange culture, but also of our selves, as well as of our own culture. In this process, the therapist's reflexivity is central as a kind of turning to ourselves in an attempt to get an orientation towards others. The aim of this reflexivity is not to maximize sameness through the toning down of our own culture; being "other" is our contribution to the mutual process *with the family* of trying to find a way in the complexity of cultural differences, of historical debts, and also of a sense of shared humanity. This idea of a sense of shared humanity is at odds with the narrative/postmodernist paradigm that adopts an anti-essentialist perspective, stressing the importance of cultural differences. A postmodernist perspective highlights the local and particular, being suspicious of universality. However, while cultural differences are indeed not to be neglected, it is important to realize that particularity can mask universality (Žižek, 2008a). Besides cultural differences, there is also a shared humanity that can rise out of the particular moment, especially in our therapeutic work with stressed or despairing families. Here we can refer to Buck-Morss's (2009) definition of the universal as that which emerges at the point of rupture:

> It is in the discontinuities of history that people whose culture has been strained to the breaking point give expression to a humanity that goes beyond cultural limits. And it is in our empathic identification with this raw, free, and vulnerable state, that we have a chance of understanding what they say. Common humanity exists in spite of culture and its differences. [Buck-Morss, 2009, p. 133]

In a previous publication, I and a colleague articulated this sense of shared humanity as being in contact with our mortality (Rober & Seltzer, 2010). Mortality is something we share with all human beings, whatever their culture. However, whenever we try to talk about this shared universal, the particulars move in and fill in the universal in contingent ways that always, necessarily, fail to really capture the universal. The universal can never be observed except through the veil of cultural differences. In that way, there is an insoluble tension between the universal (that is always there) and the particular.

The importance of the dialectic between the universal and the particular can be captured in the metaphor of a bridge. Differences can only be bridged if the bridge can rest on two strong foundations, one on each riverbank. The wider the river, the stronger the foundations have to be.

References

Abu Baker, K. (1999). The importance of cultural sensitivity and therapist self-awareness when working with mandatory clients. *Family Process*, 38: 55–67.

Andersen, T. (1991). *The Reflecting Team: Dialogues and Dialogues About Dialogues*. New York: Norton.

Bean, R. A., Perry, B. J., & Bedell, T. M. (2002). Developing culturally competent marriage and family therapists: treatment guidelines for non-African American therapists working with African-American families. *Journal of Marital and Family Therapy*, 28: 153–164.

Brown, W. (2006). *Regulating Aversion: Tolerance in the Age of Identity and Empire*. Princeton, NJ: Princeton University Press.

Buck-Morss, S. (2009). *Hegel, Haiti and Universal History*. Pittsburgh, PA: University of Pittsburgh Press.

Di Nicola, V. (1997). *A Stranger in the Family. Culture, Families and Therapy*. New York: W. W. Norton.

Falicov, C. (1995). Training to think culturally: a multidimensional comparative framework. *Family Process, 34*: 389–399.

Hansson, A. (2007). The concept of tolerance. *Theoria, 73*: 284–303.

Malik, R., & Krause, B. (2005). Before and beyond words: embodiment and intercultural therapeutic relationships in family therapy. In: C. Flaskas, B. Mason, & A. Perlesz (Eds.), *The Space Between: Experience, Context and Process in the Therapeutic Relationship* (pp. 95–110). London: Karnac.

McGoldrick, M. (Ed.) (1998). *Re-Visioning Family Therapy. Race, Culture, and Gender in Clinical Practice*. New York: Guilford Press.

Mouffe, C. (2005). *On The Political*. London: Routledge (Thinking in Action).

Nehushtan, Y. (2007). The limits of tolerance: a substantive-liberal perspective. *Ratio Juris, 20*: 230–257.

Phillips, A. (2007). *Multiculturalism Without Culture*. Princeton, NJ: Princeton University Press.

Rober, P., & Seltzer, M. (2010). Avoiding colonizer positions in the therapy room: some ideas about the challenges of dealing with the dialectic of misery and resources in families. *Family Process, 49*: 123–137.

Weisman, A., Duarte, E., Konery, V., & Wasserman, S. (2006). The development of a culturally informed, family-focused treatment for schizophrenia. *Family Process, 45*: 171–186.

Žižek, S. (2008a). Tolerance as an ideological category. *Critical Inquiry, 34*: 660–682.

Žižek, S. (2008b). *Violence*. London: Profile Books.

Introduction

Along with other traditions of Western thinking about how to find order in the world, systemic psychotherapy has been preoccupied with reflexivity. That is to say, assumptions about how I, the subject, am able to access the world of things and other persons, or assumptions about the connections between persons, their behaviour, and communications have, in one way or another, been fundamental to the discipline. Existentially, such assumptions are, of course, fundamental in all cultures, and in systemic psychotherapy they have tended to be articulated in practical techniques and in theories about practical techniques, rather than as clearly articulated theories about what we take "humanity", "culture", "persons", or "the subject" to mean. The position that the systemic psychotherapist consciously takes or unconsciously occupies thus tends to be expressed in and through practice, and, for some at least, theory has tended to come "after" practice (Andersen, 1991, p. 167). So, for example, one significant paradigmatic shift in systemic psychotherapy since its beginning has been articulated in terms of the position (sometimes literally) of the therapist/observer *vis-à-vis* the family or clients and her/his possible move from the outside to the inside of the therapeutic system. This move affected the way therapists thought about reflexivity and was in turn affected by it. One way or another, reflexivity has featured as fundamental to a systemic understanding through the entire life of the discipline, and has been expressed in different concepts, each time recognized as a significant development: schismogenesis (Bateson, 1936), feed-back (Bateson, 1972), ecology (Auerswald, 1968), joining (Minuchin, 1974), curiosity (Cecchin, 1987), circular questions (Selvini Palazzoli, Boscolo, Cecchin, & Prata, 1980), prejudice (Cecchin, Lane, & Ray, 1994), observing systems (von Foerster, 1982), not-knowing (Anderson & Goolishian, 1992), reflexive questioning (Tomm, 1987, 1988), reflecting teams (Andersen, 1987, 1991), safe uncertainty (Mason, 1993), taking it back—practice (White, 1997), the self of the therapist (Real, 1990), relational reflexivity (Burnham, 2005), inner conversations (Rober, 1999), and dialogue (Bertrando, 2007; Rober, 2005; Seikkula, 2003; Seikkula, Arnkil, & Eriksson, 2003). These are all ways in which systemic psychotherapists have captured the notion that differences which make up a thought, a feeling, a meaning, an action, a relationship, a dialogue, a communication, a pattern, or a process, are turned back or turn back on the subject or subjects in such a way that the relationship, dialogue, communication, thought, action, etc. is maintained or changed.

This book is a journey through this territory with the widest possible frame: culture. It starts with culture and strives to consider everything else through a cultural lens. It seeks to explore the way in which it would make a difference to the worlds we systemic psychotherapists know to acknowledge our own as well as other cultural perspectives. This means that cultural dimensions will weave in and out of human and ontological concerns, and it includes politics because race and culture are contiguous in so far as they might both function as markers upon which discrimination can be, and frequently is, justified. The travellers are systemic psychotherapists and, as is the way with travellers, they feel and experience the impact of embodied, linguistic, cognitive, semantic, spiritual, economic, and political differences through their selves and on their selves and must find a way of accommodating, existing, and moving on. It is this process that they write about.

The book aims to contribute to two significant shifts in family therapy practice and theory. First, a shift from a position where race and culture appear salient only to those who are different and in minority to a position where the culture and race of the therapist, whatever his or her background, are part of, and integrated with, the discourse and process in therapy (Hardy, 1996). Second, a shift away from a position in which race and culture are approached solely within an ethnic focused frame of reference (McGoldrick, Pearce, & Giordano, 1982) in which cultural populations are seen as homogenous and stable with well-defined boundaries and where information about cultural patterns tend to be given in separate culture-focused lectures and seminars. Most systemic psychotherapists know how to criticize such an approach (Falicov, 1995), but it still provides the frame for much training within the discipline and it is not easy for either trainees or trainers to transfer this approach reflexively and recursively into the clinical setting. The second shift is, therefore, towards more integration of cultural aspects of experience with all other experiences that therapists observe, think about, feel, act, communicate, and work with in the consulting room. This means that culture and discrimination might be located where we least expect it.

Placing culture at the centre also highlights what might be unconscious and outside awareness. That is to say, there is more of ourselves, of our relationships, of our experiences and our feelings which are culturally constructed than we know or realize. This is a result of social, economic, and political patterns and the "imprints" these leave on our bodies, minds, our capacities for language, for relating and experiencing (Bourdieu, 1977). This influence takes place through our earliest relationships and developments, throughout our lives in our relationships, and through ideological and physical structures, which constrain as well as facilitate our social contexts. We do not see, comprehend, or experience these patterns as a whole, even though our actions might be based on a presumption that we do (Hastrup, 2007),[1] much in the way our clients in families might not see the full extent of the patterns in which they participate. But we also do not see, comprehend, or experience the extent to which our own motivations, inclinations, and aversions are culturally and, indeed, politically constructed (Fanon, 1952). What is obscured in ordinary every-day life is the full extent to which our existence is relational. From this point of view, of a relational understanding (Flaskas, 2002) of the cultural and social content of the unconscious, systemic psychotherapy could have an important contribution to make to psychotherapy generally.

An emphasis on practice is admirable as well as necessary in a therapeutic discipline. After all, application poses one of the most difficult challenges to ideology and thought. However, an emphasis on practice also runs the risk of missing those aspects of life and experience which are not obvious, but which, nevertheless, constitute the background for, and sometimes the very nub of, what a person or persons might want or need to communicate. In other words, what happens in the therapy room is contingent, and although this in itself is not news to systemic psychotherapists, the full extent of this contingency might be. This is where a de-emphasis on concepts, ideas, or theory might be unhelpful. Although I agree that we must check our theories in practice, I also believe that too little emphasis on theory indicates an absence of thinking and reflection in the discipline and that this shows up particularly where race and culture is concerned. In this spirit, the contributors to this volume aim to make theory–practice links central to their thinking and their writing.

Together, the chapters combine theoretical explorations with personal reflections and clinical accounts and can be read singly or together as so many examples of how we might think about, use, and practise reflexivity if we truly aim to place culture, race, and politics at the centre of it. Most of the chapters are written by systemic psychotherapists from majority white backgrounds. Persons from white majority backgrounds, including psychotherapists, tend to have less practice in confronting the cultural, race, and ethnic aspects of their own subject positions than do those from minority backgrounds. As a consequence, this is also the category of persons who need the most practice in thinking about themselves in relation to these issues (Dempster, 2000; Frankenberg, 1993; Krause, 1998, Steyn & Conway, 2010). The choice of contributors was made with this in mind. In addition, several of these authors are well known for having made important contributions to the field, but had not addressed the issues of race and culture in their writings directly before. Again, this was a deliberate choice made in order to highlight, first, that theories in systemic psychotherapy have reflected the identity of their authors, and second, that, as a consequence, culture and race have been neglected in generic approaches as if these aspects of identity and social relations do not in themselves make a difference to the way theories are conceived, developed, extended, and put into practice. Thus, the important message of the book as a whole is that theories and practices (however generic these might seem to be) always require questions to be asked about the role of culture and race in their origin, development, and contemporary use.

The volume comprises an introductory chapter, followed by three parts, and ends with a postscript. In the introductory chapter, I argue for the development of a comprehensive reflexivity, one which encompasses recursiveness between the different aspects of meaning, interpretation, and experience held or expressed by persons (either clients or therapists), *as well as* the self-reflexivity of both the therapist and clients *vis-à-vis* their own history, development, and background and the contexts in which they participate. I discuss the kind of assumptions implicit in ideas about the "subject", or the "person", in systemic psychotherapy and explore what we might mean by culture in the contemporary context. I argue that placing culture at the centre of contemporary approaches means paying attention to patterns and continuity as well as agency and social construction in the lives of both therapists and clients. The implication of this is that recognition must be given to aspects of subjectivity and personhood (of ourselves and our clients), which, on the one hand, are unconscious and outside awareness and, on the other, historically, politically, socially, and culturally generated, behind which lie ideas and points of view that might be difficult for us to comprehend, but that, nevertheless, reflect the premises or the background understandings against which we all live our lives. I attempt to capture this complexity with the notions of "perspective" and "the contemporary".

Part I contains three papers, which address the role of culture and race in the "intersubjective space". Campbell writes about the use of positioning in cross-cultural supervision. More generally, he notes the need to persevere with conversation despite being faced with conflict and difficulties arising from social and political contexts. To "keep on talking", to never let the conversation cease, is a matter of survival, and alerts us to the need for commitment; for the authors of the chapters and the readers of this book, it is poignant to be reminded about this by Campbell, who himself did not survive to see the publication of this volume. Flaskas (Chapter Three) begins with her own lived experience: contemporary Australia, consisting of a white population and a history of migration from many different European countries (this also applies to herself) and an Aboriginal population with a history of subjugation and denial of belonging and ownership. In this setting, she explores the limits of what she can and cannot know and understand in relation to her own imagining about the similarities and differences between herself and her clients. She refers to this as an "interactional slide", which interferes with our practices of curiosity, and her own example encourages us to hold on to, even to nurture, humility. Building on previous work, Flaskas highlights the realness of the specific historical and social contexts which form the background to, and influence, what we know and imagine in our (cross-cultural) psychotherapeutic practice. In Chapter Four, Pocock picks up the dynamic of differences and similarities in intersubjective processes, arguing that cultural essentialism implicates the extreme pole of "objectification of the other". He advocates a fluid continuum of intersubjective processes in which he suggests that we think of "relationship" as a small intersubjective domain and "culture" as a bigger one. In both areas, it is required that conscious and non-conscious assumptions break down, and, with his case examples, Pocock shows that it is by no means predictable how this process is going to be played out in the therapy process.

Part II also contains three papers. In these, the authors expand on previous thinking about reflexivity in systemic psychotherapy. Their writing shows how thinking about "culture" and "race" necessitates an expansion into other aspects of psychotherapeutic work, which either have not received much recognition or might be seen to stand in an awkward relationship to these issues and, therefore, have not inspired the development of coherent theories or frameworks for practice. Daniel (Chapter Five) highlights the difficulties of how to reconcile "gender" and "culture", but also points out that both these themes of difference share the central issue of how to engage with processes of "othering". She draws on feminist writers in order to help us to develop this thinking in relation to culture, race, and power. She wonders how majority therapists can engage with ideas about "otherness" in ways which facilitate a view of themselves from the vantage point of (minority) others in such a way that they do not lose their own subject positions, without which reflexivity cannot emerge. Daniel urges a commitment to "cultural reflexivity" and to the fostering of a deep awareness of "othering", of what Levinas (1969) refers to as "ethics". Minority therapists are better at engaging with these processes than are therapists from the majority, and the specifics of these processes are also influenced by their historical, contemporary, and local contexts, as Daniel shows in her case examples. Bertrando (Chapter Six) takes inspiration from Gregory Bateson and from anthropology and makes a case for the role of emotions in the process of reflexivity. This is because emotional communication is the most immediate and least intentional form of communication. Bertrando summarizes the anthropological literature on the social construction of emotions and draws a parallel between the anthropologist and the systemic psychotherapist. He explores, in several case examples, the usefulness of being "other", or "different", to clients in order to provide different points of view and the way this challenges much writing about cross-cultural therapy. For Bertrando, this "other" is someone who takes seriously the idea of deep prejudices, which, like "premises", as Boscolo told him, "are like the soles of your feet: you cannot see them, because you are standing on them", and whose "otherness" is a condition both for dialogue and communication and for inexhaustible variation. The ability to feel emotions as a consequence of communication with others constitutes the bedrock for specific therapeutic communications and, at the same time, offers the therapist an opportunity to be wary of them. In the final chapter of this part of the book, Burnham develops his thinking about the Social GRRRAAACCEEESSS by including visible, invisible, voiced, and unvoiced aspects of these in his, by now, well-known paradigm. Burnham traces the history of the "graces" and their place on the continuum between rigour and imagination in systemic approaches inspired by Bateson. He discusses the challenge of keeping these aspects of our lives in mind while, at the same time, not essentializing them and taking them for granted. Using clinical examples, Burnham explores the dimensions of voice–unvoiced and visible–invisible. He notes the specific challenge of the unvoiced–invisible dimension and how this alerts us to the limits of curiosity because of the very premise (Bertrando, this volume; Krause, this volume) that this curiosity might take for granted. He advocates relational curiosity, a curiosity about our own curiosity, and relational hypothesizing, hypothesizing about our own hypotheses.

In the final part of the book, Part III, the three chapters explore therapy and healing as a social relationship. In Chapter Eight, Mason explores different influences, deriving from his childhood in northern England, on his own values and the way he explores and makes use of these in the therapeutic process. He traces these influences both from general ideological outlooks in the context of his childhood: class, religious orientation, and gender, and from specific family relationships and events. Building on his ideas about "safe uncertainty",

Mason shows how he makes use of these values in the relationships which emerge between himself and his clients and emphasizes the need to feel both sceptical about and grounded in these values in such a way that reflexivity is facilitated and extended. Mason also highlights the need to keep this focus at different levels of relational reflexivity in the therapeutic process, including the relationships of the clients, the therapeutic relationship, and the supervisory relationship. In particular, he argues for the need to develop this process within the context of group supervision. Smith (Chapter Nine), who is a family therapist and a pastor, widens the idea of therapy to healing within the reading and interpretation of Christian scripture. He describes a presentation given to an audience of Korean Christians. The audience and the event were characterized by an atmosphere of suffering, depression, and bewilderment about suicide. Drawing inspiration from a famous speech by Martin Luther King, Smith interprets Psalm 42, from the *New Living Translation* of the Bible, in order to generate hope in the congregation. He takes us slowly through the verses of the psalm to its conclusion in a manner reminiscent of the seminal paper, "The effectiveness of symbols" (Levi-Strauss, 1963) in which Levi-Strauss analysed a Cuna Indian song, the purpose of which was to facilitate a difficult childbirth. Like the song, Psalm 42 expresses a quest and the reading of it takes the listener on a symbolic journey, culminating in the realization that the sufferer is part of a community and, therefore of the restoration of hope. This is relational reflexivity grounded in a spiritual sense of togetherness. The polyvalence of the symbols of the psalm serve to highlight both individuality and communality and help the listeners reflect on both, and Smith argues that this process generates "communitas" (Turner, 1969), an "undifferentiated experience of communion, equality, and openness to the other". In the final chapter, Malik and Mandin pick up this and show how, in a process of careful cross-cultural engagement, therapists can foster a sense of "communitas" in the therapeutic process, even when this process begins with conflict and mistrust, as is so common in court work. They trace their own histories as points for self-reflection, and this parallel process allows us a glimpse into the stages and processes of co-work, as well as the engagement with the clients. Malik and Mandin refer to Bion's (1988) notion of "without knowledge and desire" and to Kakar's (2006) idea of "ethical relativism" in their discussion of how to move from polarizing objectifying processes to processes of awareness of reciprocal subjectification and mutual "othering". They do not lose sight of the way processes in cross-cultural therapy resonate with wider social systems and colonial histories. The polarization in the system in their case was exacerbated by this history, and it was by showing commitment, taking time, and demonstrating appreciation of the meaning of relationships and the premise behind expectations of persons in these relationships that Malik and Mandin were able to build up the trust without which their own self-reflection could not have facilitated the reflexivity of the therapy process for the family.

Together, the chapters convincingly demonstrate the case for accepting issues of race and culture as central preoccupations without which no activity in systemic psychotherapy, theoretical or practical, ought to take place. They also show how it is possible to take this agenda forward in different ways and directions. In the Epilogue, I draw together a few general themes from the chapters, in this way suggesting possibilities and directions for this task. However, the chapters also show how important it is to pay attention to personal outlooks, contexts, and contemporary circumstances, and, as a final point here, I want to note that many of the contributors to this volume reported that these chapters were difficult to write. I want to thank them for taking the risk.

Note

1. Culture is constantly being reproduced and changed in interactions and communications. No action makes sense without shared and ongoing expectations about the social space in which persons participate. In this view, culture refers to the sustained expectations of, and ideas about, specific social spaces and communications in which persons participate.

References

Andersen, T. (1987). The reflecting team: dialogue and meta-dialogue in clinical work. *Family Process*, 26: 415–428.
Andersen, T. (1991). *The Reflecting Team. Dialogues and Dialogues About Dialogues*. New York: W. W. Norton.

Anderson, H., & Goolishan, H. (1992). The client is the expert: a not-knowing approach to therapy. In: S. McNamee & K. J. Gergen (Eds.), *Therapy as Social Construction* (pp. 25–39). London: Sage.

Auerswald, E. H. (1968). Interdisciplinary versus ecological approach. *Family Process*, 7: 202–215.

Bateson, G. (1936). *Naven. The Culture of the Iatmul People of New Guinea as Revealed Through a Study of the "Naven" Ceremonial*. London: Wildwood House, 1958.

Bateson, G. (1972). *Steps to an Ecology of Mind. Collected Essays in Anthropology, Psychiatry, Evolution and Epistemology* (pp. 128–152). London: Jason Aronson.

Bertrando, P. (2007). *The Dialogical Therapist*. London: Karnac.

Bion, W. R. (1988). Notes on memory and desire. In: E. B. Spillus (Ed.), *Melanie Klein Today — Volume 2: Mainly Practice* (pp. 15–18). London: Routledge.

Bourdieu, P. (1977). *Outline of a Theory of Practice*. Cambridge: Cambridge University Press.

Burnham, J. (2005). Relational reflexivity: a tool for socially constructing therapeutic relationships. In: C. Flaskas, B. Mason, & A. Perlesz (Eds.), *The Space Between. Experience, Context, and Process in the Therapeutic Relationship* (pp. 1–18). London: Karnac.

Cecchin. G. (1987). Hypothesizing, circularity, and neutrality revisited: an invitation to curiosity. *Family Process*, 26: 405–413.

Cecchin, G., Lane, G., & Ray, W. (1994). *The Cybernetic of Prejudices in the Practice of Psychotherapy*. London: Karnac.

Dempster, C. (2000). *Being and Doing Whiteness*, unpublished Masters Dissertation. University of London.

Falicov, C. (1995). Training to think culturally: a multidimensional comparative framework. *Family Process*, 34: 389–399.

Fanon, F. (1952). *Black Skin, White Masks*. London: Pluto Press, 1986.

Flaskas, C. (2002). *Family Therapy Beyond Postmodernism. Practice, Challenges, Theory*. Hove: Brunner-Routledge.

Frankenberg, R. (1993). *White Women, Race Matters. The Social Construction of Whiteness*. London: Routledge.

Hardy, K. (1996). The ethics of participation: bringing culture into the room. A narrative approach (reflections). Paper presented at the annual meeting of the American Family Therapy Academy.

Hastrup, K. (2007). Performing the world: agency, anticipation and creativity. In: E. Hallam & T. Ingold (Eds.), *Creativity and Cultural Improvisation* (pp. 193–206). Oxford: Berg.

Kakar, S. (2006). Culture and psychoanalysis. a personal journey. *Social Analysis*, *50*(2): 25–44.
Krause, I.-B. (1998). *Therapy Across Culture*. London: Sage.
Levinas, E. (1969). *Totality and Infinity*. Pittsburg, PA: Duquesne University Press.
Levi-Strauss, C. (1963). The effectiveness of symbols. In: C. Levi-Strauss, *Structural Anthropology* (pp. 186–205). Harmondsworth: Penguin.
Mason, B. (1993). Towards positions of safe uncertainty. *Human Systems: The Journal of Systemic Consultation & Management*, *4*: 189–200.
McGoldrick, M., Pearce, J., & Giordano, J. (Eds.) (1982). *Ethnicity and Family Therapy*. New York: Guilford Press.
Minuchin, S. (1974). *Families and Family Therapy*. London: Tavistock.
Real, T. (1990). The therapeutic use of self in constructionist systemic therapy. *Family Process*, *29*: 255–272.
Rober, P. (1999). The therapist's inner conversation in family therapy practice: some ideas about the self of the therapist, therapeutic impasse and the process of reflection. *Family Process*, *38*: 209–228.
Rober, P. (2005). The therapist's self in a dialogical family therapy: some ideas about not-knowing and the therapist's inner conversation. *Family Process*, *44*: 477–495.
Seikkula, J. (2003). Dialogue is the change: understanding psychotherapy as a semiotic process of Bakhtin, Voloshinov and Vygotsky. *Human Systems: The Journal of Systemic Consultation & Management*, *14*: 83–94.
Seikkula, J., Arnkil, T., & Eriksson, E. (2003). Postmodern society and social networks: open and anticipation dialogues in network meetings. *Family Process*, *42*: 185–203.
Selvini Palazzoli, M., Boscolo, L., Cecchin, G., & Prata, G. (1980). Hypothesizing–circularity–neutrality: three guidelines for the conductor of the session. *Family Process*, *19*: 3–12.
Steyn, M., & Conway, D. (2010). Introduction: intersecting whiteness. Interdisciplinary debates. *Ethnicities*, *10*: 283–291.
Tomm, K. (1987). Interventive interviewing: Part II. Reflexive questioning as a means to enable self-healing. *Family Process*, *26*: 167–183.
Tomm, K. (1988). Interventive interviewing: Part III. Intending to ask lineal, circular, strategic or reflexive questions? *Family Process*, *27*: 1–15.
Turner, V. (1969). *The Ritual Process: Structure and Anti-Structure*. London: Aldine Transaction.
Von Foerster, H. (1982). *Observing Systems*. Seaside, CA: Intersystems.
White, M. (1997). *Narratives of Therapists' Lives*. Adelaide: Dulwich Centre.

CHAPTER ONE

Culture and the reflexive subject in systemic psychotherapy

Any history or genealogy must remain incomplete, because it depends on the starting point of the author and how much context he or she includes. History and genealogy are themselves contingent, and I do not pretend to be able to offer a comprehensive account of the life of reflexivity in systemic psychotherapy. I do offer punctuations, which I hope will give food for thought. Much hinges on what we consider a system to be. Do we consider a system to be like a mechanical or a physical body, or a language structure with attributes, which wholly or partially exists outside the consciousness of the persons who engage in it? Or do we consider a system to be a series of transactions with attributes which are wholly accessible and transparent to those who consciously are engaged or choose to be engaged in it? Or a bit of both? And what are the implications for reflexivity of these two positions?[1]

An incomplete history of reflexivity in systemic psychotherapy

A historical account of reflexivity in relation to cultural differences in systemic psychotherapy must begin with Bateson and particularly with his two postscripts (1936 and 1958) to his ethnographic study *Naven* (Bateson, 1958; Krause, 2007). This starting point also allows us to draw parallels between systemic psychotherapy and anthropology. I think that we want to do so not only because Bateson was an anthropologist, but also because there are similarities in what systemic psychotherapists and ethnographers do. For me this also articulates two feelings of bewilderment. The first relates to my discovery (as an anthropologist) that Bateson's ethnographic work among the Iatmul people, despite yielding extraordinary insights (Bateson, 1972a; Berger, 1978; Nuckolls, 1996; Strathern, 1988; Wilder-Mott & Weakland, 1981), held no interest for trainers and teachers of systemic psychotherapy during my own training twenty years ago. The second relates to the more recent disappearance of the concept or the idea of a "system" from much teaching and writing in systemic psychotherapy. This is a subversion, because one way or another, and whichever particular school of systemic psychotherapy one follows, the notion of "system" is still a central assumption, theory, or concept in the discipline. It is what distinguishes us from other psychotherapies.

"Schismogenesis" has also virtually disappeared from our vocabulary and our training. It is Bateson's term and it appeared first as a description of gendered processes of interaction in New Guinean Iatmul society generally and in one Iatmul ritual in particular. In 1936, Bateson described schismogenesis as "a process of differentiation in the norms of individual behaviour resulting from cumulative interaction between individuals" (Bateson, 1958, p.175). I have discussed the details of how Bateson arrived at this description elsewhere (Krause, 2007). Here, I want to reiterate the difference between this early description of schismogenesis and a later one. This later description defined schismogenesis in a new language as

> An implicit recognition that the system contains an extra order of complexity due to the combination of learning with the interactions of persons. The schismogenic unit is a two person subsystem. This subsystem contains the potentialities of a cybernetic circuit which might go into progressive change; it cannot therefore be conceptually ignored and must be described in a language of a higher type than any language used to describe individual behaviour. [Bateson, 1958, p. 297]

This second definition moved the description of relational dynamics from a level of synchrony, as a kind of "snapshot" of the relationship between relationships, to one of a short-term process in which change could be captured through the notion of feedback, learning and learning how to learn, and where the explanation of any given behaviour or communication could be explained by the context in which it is taking place (Bateson, 1958, p. 200; Krause, 2007, p. 122). There is, however, another difference between the two ideas of schismogenesis, which speaks more clearly to our present concern with reflexivity. In 1936, and in his ethnographic fieldwork, Bateson had been preoccupied with the thought that how he interpreted his fieldwork data might not be how the Iatmul themselves would interpret it. The question was, how could he be sure that his own interpretation was correct, or even relevant? He concluded that he could not be sure and that, in fact, no one can be sure because the way anyone explains any bit of culture depends on one's own point of view. This is Whitehead's idea of the "fallacy of misplaced concreteness", referring to observations being presented as if they are "hard" or objective data, instead of points of view (Whitehead, 1925).

This dilemma did not mean that Bateson gave up on contributing to a framework for the understanding of human nature. He continued to think about his own position *vis-à-vis* that which he was observing (Bateson, 1972a,b,c,d, 1979; Bateson & Bateson, 1987), but his immediate legacy to systemic or family therapy became the idea of recursiveness as a generic ingredient of human relationships and systems. In systemic psychotherapy, this cybernetic understanding led to a language of meta-orders, meta-systems, and abstractions, rather than an interest in how local details might contribute to this process and be understood as part of it (Dell, cited in Hoffman, 1981, p. 343). The role and influence of the observer–therapist became akin to that of a controller or assessor looking in, interpreting, perturbing, or strategizing from the outside. This was in keeping with Bateson's observation from 1958 that the categories he used to describe Iatmul society were unequivocally processes of knowing adopted by social scientists. It was also in keeping with the prevailing structural–functionalist approach in British social anthropology at the time, in which societies and social systems were considered to be, if not steam engines, like organisms with patterns and processes, which are not, at least not entirely, transparent to those who participate in them.

However, neither anthropologist nor therapist can work without the acknowledgement of contact with their interlocutors, and in anthropology this tension between theory and practice was most clearly articulated in the ethnographic research method of "participant observation". In this method, the ethnographer lives with, and learns the language of, people she is studying and takes part in daily tasks and rituals, talks to people about what they are doing, observes activities and communications, takes notes about it all, and keeps a personal diary. The complexity of this method and the similarity with systemic psychotherapy were not lost on therapists (Andersen, 1991; Anderson & Goolishian, 1988; Bertrando, this volume; Hoffman, 1981; Tomm, 1984). At one stage, the Milan team divided their trainees into two groups, the supervision "S" group and the observation "O" group (Hoffman, 1981; Tomm, 1984), articulating and perhaps anticipating the debates and the developments that were to come. The method of participant observation does not, of course, in itself exclude the therapist or the ethnographer considering herself outside the system. Anthropology had matured under colonialism and, therefore, had been under the protection of administrators and tax collectors, who often made use of ethnographic data. Similarly, the therapist's recognition of a need to "join" a system (Minuchin & Fishman, 1981) is not necessarily coterminous with the therapist understanding what goes on in this system or being able to see the world from her client's point of view. Indeed, an acknowledgement that the communication patterns in a family affect and even draw in the therapist was considered to be an advantage for the therapist in aiming to beat (or cure) the family at its own game (Selvini Palazzoli, Boscolo, Cecchin, & Prata, 1978; Selvini Palazzoli, Cirillo, Selvini, & Sorrentino, 1989).

The continuum of positions, from being outside the observed system to becoming a member of it, captured the struggles and the dilemmas in the development of, and thinking about, reflexivity during the 1980s and early 1990s. It was realized fairly early that the analogy of the homeostatic steam engine for social systems was unsatisfactory (Dell, 1982; Dell & Goolishian, 1981; Hoffman, 1981) and that if a family system is seen as evolving and only to *appear* to be stable, then the therapist, whether she is inside or outside the system, will not know the future course of it and, therefore, her task is one of facilitation rather than direction (Tomm, 1984). The three guidelines of hypothesizing, circularity, and neutrality described by the Milan team conveyed this much less directive activity of the therapist (Selvini Palazzoli, Boscolo, Cecchin, & Prata, 1980) and the idea of evolution of social systems also challenged the structural–functionalist notion of a system and a society as a tightly integrated whole. This did not mean, *pace* Bateson, that aspects or levels of a system could not be recursively related in either coherence or in contradiction, as in double bind theory (Bateson, 1972e), and this recursiveness in the interaction between different parts of the system as experienced by persons in it, continued to be articulated, for example, in the way the Milan team thought about and developed circularity. In this vein, Tomm, embracing Cecchin's emphasis on curiosity (Cecchin, 1987) used the term "reflexivity" to refer to a type of question:

> Reflexive questions are questions asked with the intent to facilitate self-healing in an individual or family by activating the reflexivity among meanings within pre-existing belief systems that enable family members to generate or generalize constructive patterns of cognition and behavior. [Tomm, 1987b, p. 172]

From the client's point of view, such a question might help to consolidate a new choice by orientating a person towards perceptions held by other persons or in other parts of the system, which might help support this new choice. The perceptions and meanings expressed by individual persons are contingent upon, but are not seen to be determined by, the system. From the point of view of the therapist, a reflexive question is a type of question which can be used along with other types of questions (Tomm, 1988) and although such a question might guide the therapist herself to become more creative and in this way more facilitative, it is considered to be a strategy. The therapist can see things that the clients cannot see, and she knows, if not about what change should look like, about how to ask. She has a choice about which intervention to use, as Tomm extensively described (Tomm, 1987a,b, 1988), but an examination of the circumstances of her own perception and meanings, although of interest (Tomm, 1988, p. 14), was kept at arm's length. The reflexivity, or recursiveness, can be mobilized by the therapist because it is in the family system.

Cecchin pointed out that "curiosity" was not a technique or a strategy, but an attitude or a position of the therapist: a stance (Cecchin, 1987, p. 411). This notion of "stance" signalled a new departure as far as the therapist was concerned. Both Hoffman and Real used it to convey a less directive and more personal disposition of the therapist

(Hoffman, 1985; Real, 1990). Now the cybernetic analogy also became somewhat strained. There was a move to introduce a biological one in order to capture the self-generating properties of systems (Maturana & Verala, 1980), and with an increasing acknowledgement of ideology, beliefs (Pearce & Cronen, 1980), and power differentials between men and women (Goldner, 1988; Goldner, Penn, Sheinberg, & Walker, 1990; McKinnon & Miller, 1987), the discipline settled down to accept systems as social systems (Andersen, 1991; Anderson, 1997; Bertrando, 2007; Krause, 2002) even if there was no clear agreement about what this meant. Anderson and Goolishian considered that systems create and reproduce themselves, perhaps around problems in an ecological type of way, with adaptation and articulation of fit held together by indirect communication rather than by design, planning, or predictability. The therapist was considered to be a member, along with other participants, and participated or facilitated (Real, 1990) rather than controlled (Anderson & Goolishian, 1990; Atkinson & Heath, 1990; Hoffman, 1985). In practice, reflexivity and recursiveness was also redefined:

> The new format became known as the reflecting team. We thought of the French meaning of the word, not of the English one, which in our understanding comes close to replication. The French *'réflexion'*, having the same meaning as the Norwegian *'refleksjon'*, means: something heard is taken in and thought about before a response is given. . . . Our understanding of the beforehand-information about a system would inevitably be within our context. In other words, our own context was the background for the information. Therefore, the hypotheses were at least to some extent close to where we were. And we started to wonder how close we were to those with whom we met. [Andersen, 1991, pp. 12–13]

Here, reflexivity is a process between the therapist and her clients with an acknowledgement of the baggage or "prejudices" (Cecchin, Lane, & Ray, 1994) that the therapist brings to the therapeutic encounter. The therapist was in the system, but this did not ensure that she could access her client's points of view. The system was now conceptualized as a particular aspect of a meaning generating process. Anderson and Goolishian explicitly distanced themselves from the meaning, which persons acquire as part of their development, learning, and general participation in social patterns, and instead privileged the personal meanings that individuals themselves construct as they engage in these social processes (Anderson & Goolishian, 1988, p. 375). In therapy, as in life, this second aspect of meaning tends to be communicated through language, and accordingly systems, including those in which therapist and clients take part, were, first and foremost, considered to be linguistic systems. Therapy now came to be seen as an open conversational domain (Hoffman, 1985), in which therapist and clients are constructing meaning through language collaboratively. This is social constructionism in systemic psychotherapy. Reality and experience are seen to be socially constructed, but the focus is on the individual and his or her relationship to the wider social context and ideology and not on relationships, defined as two or more intimately related persons sharing a history. The focus, thus, moves away from privileging one level of a system, for example the family, over another (Anderson, 1997, p. 28). The therapeutic conversation could now be redefined, away from the constraint of the family as an institution, and therapists became preoccupied with how to develop techniques, such as the reflecting team, aimed at promoting and generating an atmosphere of equality (Andersen, 1991; Anderson, 1997; White, 1997). With echoes of a first-order position, the therapist became a different sort of expert, an expert in bringing forth new meanings, a master conversationalist (Anderson & Goolishian, 1988, p. 372). Therapy sessions now emphasized the narratives that individual persons and clients tell about themselves and therapists continued to develop frameworks and models for how to ask (Epston & White, 1992; Freedman & Combs, 1996; Morgan, 2000) in such a way that new meanings, narratives, and stories can be generated. Both in theory and in practice, this approach emphasized individuals and how individuals with the therapist, sometimes serially, co-author and co-construct new experiences (Anderson & Goolishian, 1990, 1992; Freedman & Combs, 1996; Tomm, 1988). The other aspects of meaning generation, referring to those processes which implicate continuity, development, family relationships, history, patterns, and, as we shall see, power, were deliberately put out of view (Hoffman-Hennessy & Davis, 1993). Some systemic thinkers were, however, wondering whether the understanding of each by the other was quite so straightforward (Fine & Turner, 1991; Golann, 1987; Real, 1990).

It seems, then, that in earlier approaches in systemic psychotherapy, persons were considered to exist in the grip of fairly tightly connected systems of relationships of which they were not wholly aware, while in contemporary social constructionist approaches we have swung the other way, to consider individual persons to be relatively unfettered by their relationships and their social contexts and language to be a privileged, if not exclusive, vehicle for the expression of experience and identity. In either version, the therapist is some kind of expert. Either she knows how life should unfold or she knows how to ask questions to help life unfold. The move from certainty to caution about how things should be has been a welcome aspect of social constructionism. However, there has been unease about what the reflexive therapist actually should do. Thus, Anderson and Goolishian's "not-knowing" (1988) and, although from a different position, Mason's "safe-uncertainty" (1993) refer to stances with which the therapist can position herself in order to get "alongside or slightly behind the client" (Mason, 1993, p. 195), using markers of uncertainty, such as conversational questions, non-intrusive curiosity, and speaking from within the conversation (Anderson, 1997). Rober has pointed out that, paradoxically, these strategies focus on the receptivity of clients rather than on reflexivity of the therapist. Referring to Bakhtin's (1935) notions of "voice" and "dialogue", Rober suggested that the therapist might use inner conversations between her experiencing self and her professional self in order to create a space for her own reflections (Rober, 1999). This acknowledges reflection as a more complex process for the therapist and, as we shall see below, also provides a position from which the approach to the generation of meaning espoused by conversationalist therapists can be critiqued.

With emerging postmodern and late capitalist views of individuality, practitioners in all social sciences and psychotherapies have had to address reflexivity anew and there has been a tendency to similar solutions. Donovan (2009) describes the similarity between Tomm's notion of reflexivity and reflective functioning and mentalization in psychoanalysis (Fonagy & Target, 2003), and states that both aim to help clients develop a capacity to interpret the feelings, thoughts, actions, etc., of other persons. Donovan does not mention how mentalization engages therapists, but notes that it is doubtful that mentalization can be described as psychoanalysis (p. 159). Social anthropologists have turned to psychotherapy for a promise of solutions to the difficult methodological problems presented both by theory (Moore, 2007) and participant observation (Mimica, 2007). Here, for some of the most well-known anthropologists, self-reflexivity has shifted the emphasis from the anthropologist as ethnographer to the anthropologist as author (Clifford & Marcus, 1986; Geertz, 1988), while others have sought to be explicit about the way their scholarly work expresses their own political orientations (Graeber, 2007; Rabinow & Marcus, 2008).

It is clear that using our own selves to learn about others and the world presents difficult and thorny problems. How might we then set about developing a *comprehensive reflexivity*? That is to say, reflexivity which encompasses recursiveness between the different aspects of meaning, interpretation, and experience held or expressed by persons (either clients or therapists) *as well as* the self-reflexivity of both the therapist and clients *vis-à-vis* their own history, development, and background and the contexts in which they participate. Can we open up meanings and possibilities for clients, that is to say, produce new knowledge *and* broaden the enquiry to include the social production of therapy knowledge and techniques and of the power embedded in these? Can systemic psychotherapists both participate and observe?[2] Bourdieu has suggested the concept of "participant objectivation" for social anthropologists. He wrote,

> What needs to be objectivised . . . is not the social anthropologist performing the anthropological analysis of a foreign world, but the social world that has made both the anthropologist and the conscious and unconscious anthropology that she (or he) engages in her anthropological practice—not only her social origins, her position, her trajectory in social space, her social and religious membership and beliefs, gender, age, nationality, etc., but also, and most importantly, her particular position within the microcosm of anthropologists. [Bourdieu, 2003, p. 283]

We might not go along with Bourdieu in dismissing what the therapist does in the therapy room, but we can incorporate his idea of "classifying the classifiers", or "observing the observers observing" (Rabinow, 2008, p. 57) into our thinking and practice. Indeed, some systemic thinkers have made suggestions along these lines. Thus, White's idea of "taking it back" advocates that the therapist reflects on her own position to the client (White, 1997), which might or might not include a recognition of the institutional and historical embeddedness of her and her work. Rober and Seltzer (2010) consider how details of therapeutic practices of which the therapist is unaware could colonize clients and handicap their self-determination. Burnham (2005) describes asking questions about questions about the therapeutic relationship, and Guilfoyle (2003) points out that conversational or dialogical therapies both reflect and conceal power, because, following Foucault, power is already there in the social, cultural, and institutional context outside the therapy room and, therefore, firmly embedded in the lives of the people in it. I think that we can discern that we are beginning to come full circle. By interrogating what the therapist actually does in the therapy room, how she thinks and what she says, we begin to be drawn to *her* context, development, and history, and in this way to glimpse earlier systemic preoccupations with patterns and continuity. We can find a similar tendency in how systemic psychotherapists have thought about "the subject", "the person", and "the individual", to which I now turn.

The subject in systemic psychotherapy

Take a look through the index of prominent texts in systemic psychotherapy and you will find virtually no references to "individual", "person", or "subject". This probably reflects the reaction to psychoanalysis at the beginning of the life of the discipline and, indeed, where we do find systemic psychotherapists referring to "subjects", they also tend to be those writers who are interested in psychoanalytic ideas (Flaskas, 1996, 1997, 2002, 2005, 2009; Frosh, 2009; Larner, 2000; Pocock, 1997, 2005, 2006, 2009). As systemic psychotherapists, we have no explicit theory of subjectivity and we do not say what we think constitutes "a person", "an individual", or "a subject". Are the clients and families we see similar to or different from ourselves? In what way? To what extent? Unless of explicit interest, few systemic psychotherapists, including most of those referred to in this chapter, mention the cultural background, race, or ethnicity of either themselves or the clients they describe.[3] Our ideas about social construction relate to what goes on between family members and clients or between ourselves and clients, and not to the extent to which personhood, individuality, and subjectivity itself might be socially or culturally constructed.

It has not helped that we have not been interested in the limits of these processes of social construction. Our attention has been on diversity and difference, and yet our understanding of differences and diversity implies that something must be universal, but we do not say what we think this might be (Krause, 2009). I suggest that terms such as "the individual" and "the person" have articulated this universality obliquely in such a way that it has become an assumption, which we do not interrogate. Perhaps we assume that "individual" and "person" are empty or abstract entities, which only come to life in relationships? Or do we assume that all individuals and persons are more or less like us and live in families like ours, that is to say, in late capitalist families with Euro-American ideas of family life and kinship relations? Some of us (including myself) have ideas about our own families in which kinship tends to be seen ". . . to be concerned with what people do [did] everywhere with the facts of nature" (Strathern, 1992, p. 46). So, the symbols we use in genograms derive from genetics and we start with an egocentric view, following lateral relationships, excluding collateral ones, and tracing relationships bilaterally (Krause, 1998). Our assumptions about what constitutes individuals, persons, and subjects have, thus, functioned as constraints on diversity in two ways. First, because this domain was not theorized, but assumed to be more or less homogeneous, and second, because the cultural model on which it was based was seen to be nature itself. In this, we exclude other points of view, such as those in which the maternal or paternal relations might be considered more important for identity and personhood or those in which kinship relationships come before rather than after individuality (Strathern, 1988). And yet this dominant view is being challenged in several ways by the demands of clinical practice in our own contemporary societies. Thus, crosscultural psychotherapy, gay and lesbian relationships, the reconstitution of families, fostering and adoption, and the increasing incidence of IVF and surrogacy all challenge orthodox assumptions about relatedness and about the generation and constitution of personhood and individuality (Carstens, 2004).

This notion of "the individual" and "the person" was carried into second order approaches in the form of an overtly stated discontinuity between political, cultural, and social processes on the one hand, and what Anderson and Goolishian called active communication, on the other (Anderson & Goolishian, 1986, p. 6). They saw meaning as being generated in language through conversations intersubjectively constructed, placing emphasis on the agreement between persons about understanding that they are experiencing the same event in the same way (Anderson & Goolishian, 1988, p. 372). As we have seen earlier, in this view, social and cultural ideologies have little hold on individuals, who together are seen to create shared meanings by talking to each other, by having a dialogue. "Social organisation is the product of social communication, rather than social communication being a product of social organisation" (Anderson & Goolishian, 1988, p. 278). Thus, the emphasis on language becomes intelligible. But which language? Why did the existence of different languages and the different cultural meanings and traditions they reflect not pose both a theoretical and a clinical problem for this model of human relationships? Of course, the learning and use of language is a human capability, but, as we all know in practice, this does not mean that communicating in and across different languages is straightforward. By focusing on language as a formal phenomenon, this line of thinking trivializes differences in specific and local experiences and understandings (Burck, 2005) and is in danger of obscuring potential conflict between therapists and clients. No wonder that the generation of equality in the therapy room was seen to be more or less straightforwardly achievable through technique.

Anderson and Goolishian (1988) wrote that "meaning and understanding do not exist prior to the utterances in language" (p. 378), but the emphasis on linguistic aspects of semiotics is a problem. Semiotics is the study of meaning as signs and symbols and is closely implicated in what we generally understand to be culture. However, not all individuals who consider themselves to belong to the same culture share all meanings, and individuals also participate in cultural meanings of which they are not aware (Krause, 2002). Thus, meaning is not coterminous with language and, indeed, might not be expressed adequately in words. The idea that meaning is developed and generated through representations in conversation or dialogue in the therapy rooms is, therefore, only one half of the story. The other half is that meaning is generated in the relationship between those representations and knowledge that already exists (Milton, 2002). Persons have knowledge about the world, which they have acquired through past relationships with others who have occupied particular positions and had particular relationships to them, and this knowledge is modified, influenced, and changed according to a person's own interactions and communications with others and their experiences as their lives unfold. The dialogue and the conversation in the therapy room is a process which creates new meanings, but there is much knowledge before and behind these new meanings (Malik & Krause, 2005) and therapists and clients themselves might have much less access to this and be less aware of it. To be sure, persons and individuals are subjects of their actions, their communications, and their words, but there are other aspects to subjectivity, many of them more obscure.

This is why conversations, narratives, and dialogues, and particularly cross-cultural ones, are so much more problematic than is often made out. It is one thing to acknowledge one's own position as a white, middle-class therapist, but quite another to become aware of the extent to which one's own ideas, attitudes, and knowledge about the world, about relationships, about bodies, about personhood and subjectivity are culturally constructed. These aspects of experience and meaning might facilitate or constrain and they might not be visible or available to be voiced. This presents a dilemma for interpretation and understanding. The psychotherapist, like the ethnographer, is a little like Hermes, the messenger for the Greek gods. In her interpretations, she must communicate the very foreignness that her interpretations deny in their claim to universality (Crapanzano, 1992, p. 44). This dilemma cannot be solved, and we might say that the process of therapy is to be found in the very dynamic of it.[4]

To an extent, this dilemma is captured in what is referred to currently as dialogical approaches in systemic psychotherapy. Indeed, dialogical approaches could be considered a contemporary attempt to develop and incorporate a theory of "the subject" in the discipline. The inspiration derives from Bakhtin's idea of the dialogical self (Bakhtin, 1935). I shall give a brief summary, and I refer readers to Holquist (1990) and Hermans and Kempen (1993), as well as to the authors discussed below. In brief, the dialogical self can be described as a multiplicity of "I"-positions in the mind of a person intertwined with the minds of other people. The "I" is always open and unformed, as opposed to another part of the self, which is finalized in language. We represent ourselves to ourselves as well as to others in this finalized, more categorical way in the form of words. The dialogical self refers to this dialogical process in the meaning that we make of ourselves, and Bakhtin calls this "the authoring of the self" (Holquist, 1990, p. 84). Existence is experienced as a mass of stimuli from the natural environment, individual organisms, and other persons. This is "heteroglossia", from which meaning in the world is authored. But the "I" is not a free agent. Rather, the "I" puts words to the world, drawing upon the languages, the dialects, and the words of others, to which a person has been exposed. Understanding, then, is a creative dialogical process in which meanings of different parties come into contact and new meanings are created. The self is, thus, a relational phenomenon, which transcends the boundaries between inside and outside, between the self and others.

It is not difficult to see the attraction of these ideas to systemic psychotherapists. The relational domain, which we have been so used to locate between individual persons, can now be seen to be internal to them in the processes of identity formation. The model also allows us to understand personhood, identity, and selfhood as changing and contested according to individual circumstances, rather than as so many identical copies. As therapists, we must welcome this, while at the same time not ignore the myriad cultural meanings that enter the events, languages, and utterances in local lives. For example, we have to accommodate the experiences of persons such as one of my clients, who chooses to remain a single mother despite the protestations of her Bangladeshi family and, at the same time, insists on taking preventative actions to counter black magic. We also have to acknowledge that we cannot predict, or sometimes even identify, the combinations of events and meanings in the lives of our clients. The model of the dialogical self allows for this complexity, but this has not been acknowledged by all its advocates.

Although the question of whether therapy constitutes a special kind of conversation is a legitimate one (Bertrando, 2007; Guilfoyle, 2002), here. I am interested in the way different systemic psychotherapists have used Bakhtin's ideas and the implications for assumptions about "the person" or "the subject". Seikkula, Arnkil, and Eriksson suggest that dialogism is less a theory about human beings everywhere than a "professional expertise called for by post-modern development" (2003, p. 186). In this, they seem to suggest that open dialogue is a technique, which aims to encourage individual subjectivity, encourage reciprocal dialogue, create polyphony, and tolerate uncertainty. This is based on the idea that "in every social situation the reality is constructed entirely in the specific connection taking place in this particular situation" (Seikkula, 2003, p. 84). I think that there are problems with this interpretation. If open dialogue is a technique, then perhaps, as Bertrando has pointed out (2007, pp. 152–153), the therapeutic dialogue is not a real dialogue after all. With the focus on the social construction of reality in the therapeutic conversation, Seikkula and his colleagues ignore Bakhtin's other process of self-authoring: that which draws upon the events to which a person has been exposed throughout her life, or what Holland and Lave (2001, pp. 3–33) have referred to as "history in person". This refers to bundles of discourses, some from the past, some from the present, some in fantasy, some from rituals and myths, and some from dreams. These processes are "languages of heteroglossia", from which we make choices in the authoring of ourselves, but we might not always be conscious that this is what we are doing. By referring to dialogue as a technique rather than as a theory of subjectivity, Seikkula and other advocates of dialogical therapies obscure the full extent of the authoring of their selves from themselves. In doing so, they produce an imbalance in which they implicitly make use of the full complexity of their own subjectivity (because how could they do otherwise?), while simplifying these processes for their clients.

I agree with Bertrando that Bakhtin's ideas require more robustness from the therapist, because only in this way can dialogical understanding unfold. Thus, Bertrando argues that, as a therapist, he must express an opinion, because it is only when his ideas are put into play with the ideas of his clients that true dialogue can take place (Bertrando, 2007, p. 153). With the therapist expressing opinions, the therapeutic dialogue is closer to all dialogues and the theory of the subject applied to all parties. This is a less colonizing starting point for the therapist. However, Bertrando also tells a story of a sexologist therapist and his work with a woman client, who, in her sessions, told her story, while the therapist listened. One day, this client surprised the therapist by suing him for trying to seduce her. Bertrando explains that in this case the dialogue between the therapist and the client was not a true dialogue. "To him they were sharing a narrative, to her, they were distant and he was threatening" (p. 152). I can think of many cross-cultural and cross-race scenarios in therapy, particularly involving gender, where the dialogue has unfolded or has been in danger of unfolding in just this way. Dialogue in therapy is not free of conflict, particularly not when the social context is laden with it in the form of racism, sexism, class differences, and other types of discrimination. This is acknowledged by Rober, who emphasizes the polyphony of voices in which persons might speak (2005), and in particular the potential of our own voices, empowered by our own dominant culture, to colonize (Rober & Seltzer, 2010). How could power, authority, and conflict be eradicated from the therapy room, when these processes exist in the wider social institutions that provide the context for therapy?

In anthropology, Bakhtin's ideas have been attractive precisely because they have offered a theory of the "subject" which acknowledges the social aspects of expression and social life and an alternative to a psychoanalytic framework. As we have seen in systemic psychotherapy, the "behavioural subject" was replaced by "the cognitive subject" and, although a promising framework, if considered in its totality, approaches inspired by Bakhtin remain within a cognitive theory of subjectivity. However, neither the "behavioural subject" nor "the cognitive subject" captures comprehensively what it is like to be a person. In particular, they leave out emotions and feelings. This is not to say that emotions and feelings have been ignored in practice. It is difficult to conceive of any therapy without emotions, and emotional bondedness has been assumed to be the basis for all relationships (Bowen, 1978) and the foundation for all human systems (Bertrando, 2007). Emotions have also recently been the subject of several publications (Bertrando, 2002, 2006, 2007, 2010; Bertrando & Arcelloni, 2009; Fredman, 2004; Krause, 1993, 2007, 2009, 2010a,b; Pocock, 2009, 2010a,b). It was, in fact, the emotional outlook of the Iatmul men and women, and the inversion of this in the *naven* ritual, which first alerted Bateson to the dynamic of these relationships and to schismogenesis.

The *naven* ritual was a ritual of initiation for a young man, marking his entry into adulthood. In everyday life, Iatmul women were expected to be co-operative and self-effacing, whereas men were expected to be fiercely competitive and flamboyant. In *naven*, this was reversed, so that men who were mother's brothers to the young man dressed in dirty women's clothes, smeared themselves with ashes, and carried symbols of femininity and motherhood, while women strutted around dressed like men with feathers, headdresses, and ornaments made from the bones and teeth of enemies killed in warfare. The whole thing was embarrassing for the young man, but it also took place with much hilarity and mockery. By providing opportunities for both men and women to experience emotions that were not normally an aspect of their own gendered social personhood, the *naven* ritual,

Bateson argued, contributed to psychological integration. But emotions also expressed two other aspects. One was a convergence of subjective and cultural outlooks. Bateson argued that it is not possible to interpret a particular emotion expressed by an individual without first knowing something about the general emotional outlook of a culture, a system, or a relationship (1958). The other referred to a more general capacity of humans to experience and express emotions. Bateson described how it was not until he realized and experienced the fun and hilarity in the *naven* ritual himself that he could get an idea about what the ritual was about (Bateson, 1958, p. 259). So, while emotions articulate subjective and cultural experiences and outlooks, they might also provide an anchor for cross-cultural experience even if this by itself is not enough for understanding. In this sense, as I have argued elsewhere, emotions might call the context and this context, as well as referring to past experiences of clients and therapist, is also a place (the therapy room at a specific time) where our education about our clients begins (Crapanzano, 1992; Krause, 2010b). Such a framework opens up a consideration of processes which are less accessible, perhaps outside awareness and unconscious, such as, for example, fantasies (Pocock, 2010b), dreams (Luepnitz, 2009) and embodiment (Csordas, 2002; Malik & Krause, 2005; Wilson, 2007).

Emphasizing relationships has meant that it never was straightforward to develop a theory of the "the subject" or "the person" in systemic psychotherapy. As an assumption, the "behavioural subject" emerged alongside the cybernetic metaphor for relationships. But this itself was a development from an earlier structural functionalist notion of social systems as organisms, in which different aspects of the system were seen to be tightly interrelated. Bateson's brilliance consisted in realizing early in the history of anthropology that such a view of a social system must be accompanied by the meaning attributed to the different social, cognitive, and emotional processes by persons who are engaged in them. But, with an emphasis on cybernetics, the role of culture in systems and relationships was lost (Harries-Jones, 1995) and emotions and feelings tended to be conceptualized as being generated inside individual bodies (Krause, 2007).

With the linguistic turn, the individual person's or client's relationship to the wider social context came into view, but the full range of possibilities of variations in language/meaning could not be accessed because language and cognition defined the system rather than being an aspect of it. The "cognitive self" entailed a formal view of language and linguistics and meant that different languages and different, sometimes unconscious, meanings were not within view. Within this framework, it has been difficult to develop a nuanced theory of the subject and to link individuals to social systems or to systems of relationships in anything but a simplistic manner. In turn, the role of individuals and persons have been conceptualized in terms of biological or social reductionism, neither of which can do justice to the complexity of diversity. Bakhtin's ideas about the "dialogical self" have helped to straddle external and internal worlds and provided a possibility for developing a space in the discipline with room for the unfolding of the dynamic of the behavioural, cognitive, emotional, social, co-temporal, and historical processes in real life. I now consider what this implies for how we think about culture.

Culture

Those therapists who have continued to emphasize patterns, past and present contexts, history, often colonial history, and systems have also been those who have addressed issues of culture and race as central issues in their writings and many of them are from minority backgrounds themselves (Boyd-Franklin, 1989, DiNicola, 1997; Falicov, 1988, 1995, 1998a,b, 2005; Fisek, 1991; Hardy & Laszloffy, 1995, 1998; Krause, 2002; McGoldrick, 1998; Watts-Jones, 1997, 2002). Early on, some of these approaches iterated the strong grip that systems were seen to have on individual persons and, therefore, tended to promote essentialized notions of culture, race, and ethnicity (McGoldrick, Pearce, & Giordano, 1982). However, later approaches have paid attention to cultural and ethnic dimensions while at the same time exploring the kinds of structures that might help us to think about these. Thus, Falicov has advocated thinking about cultural context, migration–culturation, family life cycles, and family organization in order to provide a focus for a comparison and an exploration of the similarities and differences between therapists and their clients (Falicov, 1995, 1998b, 2005). Boyd-Franklin focused on the empowerment of black families and emphasized the need for therapists to draw on different systemic models. The inter-institutional perspective (Montalvo & Gutierrez, 1988), the ecological systems approach

(Auerswald, 1968), and the eco-systemic approach (Falicov, 1998a) are further examples of approaches that have highlighted the connections between social ideology and institutions and individual and family experiences. Why does attention to race, culture, and ethnicity make it more likely that both individual dimensions and social dimensions of meaning and experience are kept in view? I have argued elsewhere that this is because culture has system-like properties, that is to say, over time there is some continuity in cultural patterns. This is not total and predictable, but it is enough for persons to have expectations as if such continuity exists (Hastrup, 2007; Krause, 2002, p. 24). This does not mean that persons cannot construct something new, only that whatever is new is always brought forth against the background of something that was there before. A similar continuity, but more fixed, exists in racial and ethnic categories. These categories reflect the construction, negotiation, and maintenance of social and political boundaries as expressed in individual identities (Jenkins, 1997), and they, too, articulate patterns and have a history, and often a colonizing one, even if this might not be reflected in the conscious experience of the majority of professionals.

Accepting this also means accepting that the complexity is not always within the awareness of persons, either therapists or clients. Thus, persons are not fully aware of Bakhtin's heteroglossia and internal dialogues are not necessarily explicit in conversation, but depend on the position and receptivity of the interlocutor. Despite the challenges posed by communicating across different languages, language can be made accessible. We can identify a glossary, a dictionary, or a native speaker, and, in this way, make progress towards finding translations, either with interpreters or by our own trial and error. Or we can rely on signs and physical connections. Other, more implicit, aspects of the conversation, such as past experiences of discrimination or assumptions about what kind of reciprocity or what kind of connections make a relationship, might be more tricky. Thus, we might not be aware ourselves that our notions of kinship and family are built upon particular assumptions about the way nature and culture intersect, or that persons from other cultural traditions might build relationships on different premises (Carstens, 2004; Strathern, 1992, 1999). We have begun to take some of this to heart, such as in a recognition of the different emphasis between sociocentric and egocentric outlooks in kinship relationships (Fisek, 1991; Krause, 1998; Malik &

Mandin, this volume; Singh & Clarke, 2006; Tamura & Lau, 1992), but other aspects of persons, such as the body, the self, perception, emotion, and the notion of a relationship in itself might also articulate different orientations. Strathern comments, on the limits of Euro-American perspectives,

> what might interpretation look like in a society that does *not*, as here, imagine perspectives as self-referential, 'unique' contexts for action and hence with the potential to coexist with, and overlap with, limitless numbers of 'unique' others? . . . One must simply be prepared for the unpredictable, including different distributions of what people take as finite and what they take as infinite about their circumstances. [Strathern, 1999, p. 249]

Of course, one perspective can provide a perspective on another perspective.[5] The client's perspective can provide a perspective on the therapist's perspective. But this does not necessarily yield a reciprocal or a mutually defined relation or understanding. Neither may be defined in the terms of which the other is not. On the contrary, each perspective might be connected to a unique range of phenomena and refer to quite different contexts for action. Inger and Inger (1994) suggest that ethics is the ability of holding two or more points of view simultaneously. I prefer to say that the process in ethical practice, reflexivity, is assessing your own perspective while, at the same time, developing the perspective which the other comes to have of your perspective against the background of their own perspective. This means that we are always representing our relations to others and we cannot do so independently of perspective (for perspective, read assumptions, history, theory, or epistemology).

We may take "othering" to exemplify one such perspective in current social science and psychotherapy (Benjamin, 1998; Clifford & Marcus, 1986; Das, 2007; Dalal, 2002; Fanon, 1952; Kitzinger & Wilkinson, 1996; Klein, 1946; Said, 1978; Segal, 1994; Winnicott, 1971). This is a complex area, and here I wish to provide a very summary statement of two main positions, as I see these. One is the psychoanalytic view. In this, subjectivity develops as a result of the introduction of a third party to the dyadic relationship between infant and primary carer. This triangle helps the infant tolerate frustration and discomfort. If the blissful, idealized state of one-ness is unmediated, this generates states of mind in the baby in which the baby feels attacked, as in an earlier stage of development, and reacts without being able to think and reflect (Klein, 1946). Because these states and functions are the primitive building blocks of persons in relationships throughout our lives, they are also considered to be states of mind into which mature persons might fall again and again. Winnicott (1971) suggested that these processes involve transitional phenomena in the form of symbols and play in such a way that when a baby develops the capacity to use a symbol of union (and this depends on the building of trust between baby and care-taker), he or she comes to benefit developmentally from separation. This is where Winnicott locates cultural experience:

> I have used the term "cultural experience" as an extension of the idea of transitional phenomena and of play without being certain that I can define the word "culture". The accent indeed is on experience. In using the word "culture" I am thinking of the inherited tradition. I am thinking of something that is in the common pool of humanity, into which individuals and groups of people may contribute, and from which we may all draw if *we have somewhere to put what we find*. [Winnicott, 2006[1971], p. 133, original italics]

and

> The interplay between originality and the acceptance of tradition as a basis for inventiveness seems to me to be just one more example, and a very exciting one, of the interplay between separateness and union. [Winnicott, 2006[1971], p. 134]

I think that Winnicott's thoughts on "the location of cultural experience" help us to understand something fundamental about cultural processes, which is that these are processes that are experienced emotionally, on the body and in the mind, from the very beginning of life. However, even though as Winnicott's ideas suggest, "the other" is outside, possibly bent on omnipotence and destructiveness, just as we ourselves might be, we cannot simply scale up this view to encompass and account for whole societies and their alliances and conflicts. Benjamin has pointed to the correspondence between the psychoanalytical problem of overcoming omnipotence and the political problem of non-violence,

> The question—Can a subject relate to the other without assimilating the other to the self through identification?—corresponds to the political question, Can a community admit the Other without her/him having to already be or become the same? [Benjamin, 1998, p. 94]

While this correspondence is clear, it does not attend to the myriad different ways, inside and outside of awareness, alterity might be experienced and (mis)understood in the communication between persons of different cultural and racial backgrounds in actual communities and social contexts.

For this, we have to turn to the second position, that of social science. In this, our epistemologies and our descriptions of other societies and cultures reflect particular dominant economic, political, historical, and colonizing interests in our own societies (Khanna, 2003; Said, 1978). These are also reflected in the terms employed by states and bureaucracies to categorize populations and to bestow rights and duties, privileges and penalties, and in the rhetoric through which this is communicated. They are also tacit in the expression and experience of identities and relationships (Baldacchino, 2011; Clifford & Marcus, 1986; Collini, 2010; Ewing 1997, 2008; Foucault, 1978; Hall, 1996; Žižek,1989). While, in general, the constraints and influences of these social processes upon persons and populations take place in any society or social organization, the categories in which they find expression are cultural ones, that is to say, they are imbued with specific meaning, conscious and unconscious, and contextually and historically constructed. In one way or another, these meanings, in turn, enter the processes of unity and separateness in the dynamic between carers and children referred to by Winnicott.

As I see this, these two views underpin each other. In everyday practice in systemic psychotherapy, differences, and especially those which are conceptualized in terms of race, culture, and ethnicity, evoke primitive states and "othering" processes in therapists no less than in other persons. I think that this explains the persistent practice in systemic psychotherapy of not mentioning cultural, racial, or ethnic background or context in clinical discussions or in case examples and scenarios in written papers about generic theoretical issues, such as reflexivity. I also think that this explains the difficulties and imbalances in applying dialogical theories comprehensively. In Bhaktin's notion of the dialogical self, a person is both subject and object to herself. However, in the actual lives of persons, subject and object easily slide into a distinction between the self and other and between a complex and reified view of subjectivity. Intuitively, we know that, despite our embodied selves, we are not objects, but when it comes to other bodies and persons and, in particular, other bodies that are very different from ourselves, we run the risk of objectifying them. Power, stereotyping, discrimination, and racism are processes of objectification in which one party relates to the other as subject to object and mutuality in perspectives has been lost.

Concluding thoughts

Is relating to others in this way inevitable? I do not think so, at least not for all of the time. In this chapter, we have seen that even with the development of social constructionism and second order approaches, which have encouraged therapists to take more responsibility for their practice, systemic psychotherapy has continued to promote certain blind spots. The most glaring of these have been the failure to think about or define "the subject", "the person", or even "the individual". Because we have not paid attention to our own assumptions about what constitutes a person and what it is about subjectivity or personhood that we assume to be universally applicable, we have also remained unclear about what it is that makes possible what we do know about ourselves and our clients. This lack has come under pressure from the increasing interest in the discipline in "reflection" and "reflexivity" and in "culture" and "power/race", but it seems to have taken a long time for the discipline to be able to connect these areas of theory and practice within a systemic framework of theoretical practice, and there is still a tendency to ascribe more complexity to ourselves than to our clients. In this chapter, I have argued that we need to move away from implicitly promoting a view of subjectivity as either "empty" or "just like us", or as repeatedly socially constructed and reconstructed in interaction with us. I have suggested that the emphasis on language and texts has not been helpful, not only because the privileging of language itself is a cultural assumption, but also because this emphasis has tended to exclude embodied, emotional, and experiential dimensions of "the subject" and "the self". These dimensions implicate cultural meaning, expectations, and history, and an emphasis on culture, race, and power, therefore, raises questions about continuity as well as patterns of meaning which may be historically and socially implicit and outside consciousness altogether. I believe that, while this all complicates the picture for us as psychotherapists, this complexity also offers us an opportunity to take proper account of it and, in doing so, to move forward. I also believe that here systemic psychotherapy might have a contribution to make to psychotherapy and mental health practice generally in the twenty-first century. So, how do we begin to develop a comprehensive reflexivity, that is to say, a reflexivity which acknowledges recursiveness between different aspects of meaning, interpretation, and experience, as well as a self-reflexivity *vis-à-vis* our own history, development, and background? Perhaps we might reframe our stance in the following way.

Mattingly comments that cross-cultural or cross-race narratives are remarkable, not so much for what they convey as for what they leave out (Mattingly, 2008). She refers to such discourses as "the border zone" (p. 139), because, although in cross-cultural systemic psychotherapy therapists and clients cannot be said to belong to a single shared culture even when they have been members of the same society for a long time, it is also misleading to consider that they operate in discontinuous worlds. In the therapy room therapist and clients are exemplifying moments of cultural differentiation (Bhabha, 1994), while, at the same time, they must have been brought together there by some coterminous process. This idea of "borders" has been described and debated by many others, including systemic psychotherapists interested in these issues (Daniel, this volume; DiNicola, 1997; Falicov, 1995, 2009; Henderson, 1995; Turner, 1969; Werbner & Modood, 1997), but I want to highlight the reference to time and context in the idea. To me, "border zone" refers to a contemporary site where the therapist and clients come together. This site is characterized by being in a specific context and historical time with a specific task (the clinical encounter). "The contemporary" refers to what goes on in this site, in the moment of the session, in the dialogue, and in the interactions, in the present. However, the reference to time also reminds us that in this domain old and new elements coexist in multiple configurations and variation and that we cannot assume that what is new, what happens in the present, in the conversation or in the dialogue between the therapist and the clients, always is dominant and that what is old is always residual (Rabinow, 2008, p. 2). The idea of the contemporary alerts us to the need to acknowledge that what happens in the conversation in the therapy office always incorporates and is set against the background of the past, as well as the possibilities for the future (see also Boscolo & Bertando, 1992, for an early expression of this). We need to bear this in mind with all the force of comprehensive reflexivity we can muster. Bateson's idea of premise (see also Bertrando, 2007, and this volume) might assist us here. Bateson defined a premise as "a generalised statement of a particular assumption or implication recognisable in a number of details of cultural behaviour" (Bateson, 1958, p. 24). Batson's idea was shaped by dominant ideas in anthropology at the time, which undoubtedly underemphasized change and individual agency. Placing premise in our current context, we might say that a premise is a perspective. It is like a thread of coherence running through meaning, representations, and expectations, but that may be experienced only in a fragmentary shifting form by individual subjects. The Euro-American emphasis on unique self-referential subjects noted by Strathern, above, is an example of a perspective.[6] A perspective is, thus, a result of cultural, social, historical, and relational contexts and individual persons' experiences of these, and refers to the relationship between the past, the present, and the expectations for the future from a particular point of view. A perspective is what persons (therapists and clients) consciously or unconsciously bring to the contemporary site of psychotherapy. "Perspective" and "the contemporary" alerts us to the temporality in "voice" and "dialogue" as well as to the existence of some kind of pattern in the lives of ourselves and our clients. At the same time, they also ought to alert us to how uncertain and downright wrong we might be in guessing about them.

With the therapist moving inside the system in systemic psychotherapy and with an accompanying emphasis on formal language and on the present in the form of conversation and dialogue in the therapy room, both the present and the future have come to be seen as relatively unfettered by the past. Pattern, context, and system have been replaced by co-construction, text, and narrative. This has obscured both the continuity and containment, which culture affords to individual persons and, somewhat paradoxically, the social and political conflict, which exists in wider contemporary social processes and institutions and has, in this way, contributed to collective processes of othering and objectification in the discipline. Viewing reflexivity through culture alerts us to the similarity between ourselves and our clients, in so far as it points us to a complex mixture of fragmented conscious and unconscious cultural and political processes which constitute the conditions for our existence and our relationships. The possibility of our communication within and across cultures, races, ethnicities, and power positions is based on all of us sharing these conditions for existence. At the same time, constructive communication is only a possibility if we are able to acknowledge perspectives other than our own in both theory and practice. For this we must develop an understanding of history, memory, pattern, and continuity *as well as* of the beliefs, motivations, wishes, aims, and intentions of our clients and ourselves, and it is this that is called forth in the contemporary context of systemic psychotherapy.

Notes

1. We may describe the first as a modernist approach and the second as a postmodern one.
2. This methodological debate is ongoing in anthropology, with many different positions. Probably the position taken by most anthropologists is a pragmatic one rooted in critical realism (Borneman & Hammoudi, 2009; Davies, 1999; Graeber, 2007).
3. When the race or ethnicity of clients are included as clinical material, this also commonly tends to be problematized and racialized.
4. Anderson also refers to Hermes, Zeus's messenger, and his tasks (Anderson, 1997). However, she does not emphasize the dilemma in all translation, which Benjamin has characterized thus: "All translation . . . is only a somewhat provisional way of coming to terms with the foreignness of languages" (Benjamin, 1998, quoted in Crapanzano, 1992, p. 43).
5. Positioning may be seen as an aspect of perspectivism. See Campbell and Grøenbaek (2006), and Campbell (this volume).
6. Andersen (1991) and Taylor (1985a,b) both refer to the idea of premise using the terms "pre-understanding" and "background understanding", respectively.

References

Andersen, T. (1991). *The Reflecting Team. Dialogues and Dialogues About Dialogues*. New York: W. W. Norton.

Anderson, H. (1997). *Conversation, Language, and Possibilities. A Postmodern Approach to Therapy*. New York: Basic Books.

Anderson, H., & Goolishian, H. (1986). Problem determined systems: towards transformation in family therapy. *Journal of Strategic and Systemic Therapies, 5*: 1–13.

Anderson, H., & Goolishian, H. (1988). Human systems as linguistic systems: preliminary and evolving ideas about the implications for clinical theory. *Family Process, 27*: 371–393.

Anderson, H., & Goolishian, H. (1990). Beyond cybernetics: comments on Atkinson & Heath's 'Further thoughts on second-order family therapy'. *Family Process, 29*: 157–163.

Anderson, H., & Goolishian, H. (1992). The client is the expert: a not-knowing approach to therapy. In: S. McNamee & K. J. Gergen (Eds.), *Therapy as Social Construction* (pp. 25–39). London: Sage.

Atkinson, B., & Heath, A. (1990). Further thoughts on second-order family therapy—this time it's personal. *Family Process, 29*: 145–155.

Auerswald, E. H. (1968). Interdisciplinary versus ecological approach. *Family Process, 7*: 202–215.

Bakhtin, M. (1935). Discourse in the novel. In: M. Holquist (Ed.), *The Dialogical Imagination. Four Essays by M. M. Bakhtin* (pp. 259–422). Austin, TX: University of Texas Press, 1981.

Baldacchino, J-P. (2011). The eidetic of belonging: towards a phenomenological psychology of affect and ethno-national identity. *Ethnicities, 11*: 8–106.

Bateson, G. (1958). *Naven. The Culture of the Iatmul People of New Guinea as Revealed Through a Study of the "Naven" Ceremonial*. London: Wildwood House.

Bateson, G. (1972a). *Steps to an Ecology of Mind. Collected Essays in Anthropology, Psychiatry, Evolution, and Epistemology*. London: Jason Aronson.

Bateson, G. (1972b). Experiments in thinking about observed ethnological material. In: *Steps to an Ecology of Mind* (pp. 73–87). London: Jason Aronson.

Bateson, G. (1972c). Bali: the value system of a steady state. In: *Steps to an Ecology of Mind. Collected Essays in Anthropology, Psychiatry, Evolution and Epistemology* (pp. 107–127). London: Jason Aronson.

Bateson, G. (1972d). Style, grace and information in primitive art. In: G. Bateson, *Steps to an Ecology of Mind. Collected Essays in Anthropology, Psychiatry, Evolution and Epistemology* (pp. 128–152). London: Jason Aronson.

Bateson, G. (1972e). Double bind. In: G. Bateson, *Steps to an Ecology of Mind. Collected Essays in Anthropology, Psychiatry, Evolution and Epistemology* (pp. 271–279). London: Jason Aronson.

Bateson, G. (1979). *Mind and Nature. A Necessary Unity.* London: Fontana.

Bateson, G., & Bateson, M. C. (1987) *Angels Fear. An Investigation into the Nature And Meaning of the Sacred.* London: Rider.

Benjamin, J. (1998). *Shadow of the Other. Intersubjectivity and Gender in Psychoanalysis.* New York: Routlege.

Berger, M. (1978). *Beyond the Double Bind.* New York: Brunner/Mazel.

Bertrando, P. (2002). The presence of the third party: systemic therapy and transference analysis. *Journal of Family Therapy*, 24: 351–368.

Bertrando.P. (2006). Expressed emotion and Milan systemic intervention: a pilot study. *Journal of Family Therapy*, 28: 81–102.

Bertrando, P. (2007). *The Dialogical Therapist.* London: Karnac.

Bertrando, P. (2010). Emotional positioning and the therapeutic process. *Context*, 107: 17–19.

Bertrando, P., & Arcelloni, T. (2009). Anger and boredom: unpleasant emotions in systemic psychotherapy. In: C. Flaskas & D. Pocock (Eds.), *Systems and Psychoanalysis. Contemporary Integrations in Family Therapy* (pp. 75–92). London: Karnac.

Bhabha, H. (1994). *The Location of Culture.* London: Routledge.

Borneman, J., & Hammoudi, A. (Eds.) (2009). *Being There. The Fieldwork Encounter and the Making of Truth.* Berkeley, CA: University of California Press.

Boscolo, L., & Bertrando, P. (1992). The reflexive loop of past, present and future in systemic therapy and consultation. *Family Process*, 31: 119–130.

Bourdieu, P. (2003). Participant objectivation. *Journal of the Royal Anthropological Institute*, 9: 281–294.

Bowen, M. (1978). *Family Therapy in Clinical Practice.* Cambridge: Polity Press.

Boyd-Franklin, N. (1989). *Black Families in Therapy. A Multisystems Approach.* New York: Guilford Press.

Burck, C. (2005). *Multilingual Living. Explorations of Language and Subjectivity.* Basingstoke: Macmillan.

Burnham, J. (2005). Relational reflexivity: a tool for socially constructing therapeutic relationships. In: C. Flaskas, B. Mason, & A. Perlesz (Eds.),

The Space Between. Experience, Context, and Process in the Therapeutic Relationship (pp. 1–18). London: Karnac.

Campbell, D., & Grøenbaek, M. (2006). *Taking Positions in the Organisation.* London: Karnac.

Carstens, J. (2004). *After Kinship.* Cambridge: Cambridge University Press.

Cecchin. G. (1987). Hypothesizing, circularity, and neutrality revisited: an invitation to curiosity. *Family Process, 26:* 405–413.

Cecchin, G., Lane, G., & Ray, W. (1994). *The Cybernetic of Prejudices in the Practice of Psychotherapy.* London: Karnac.

Clifford, J., & Marcus, G. (Eds.) (1986). *Writing Culture. The Poetics and Politics of Ethnography.* Berkeley, CA: University of California Press.

Collini, S. (2010). Blahspeak. *London Review of Books,* 8 April, pp. 29–34.

Crapanzano, V. (1992). *Hermes' Dilemma & Hamlet's Desire. On the Epistemology of Interpretation.* Cambridge, MA: Harvard University Press.

Csordas, T. (2002). *Body/Meaning/Healing.* Basingstoke: Palgrave Macmillan.

Dalal, F. (2002). *Race, Colour and the Processes of Racialization. New Perspectives from Group Analysis, Psychoanalysis and Sociology.* Hove: Brunner-Routledge.

Das, V. (2007). *Life and Words. Violence and the Descent into the Ordinary.* Berkeley, CA: University of California Press.

Davies, C. A. (1999). *Reflexive Ethnography. A Guide to Researching Selves and Others.* London: Routledge.

Dell, P. (1982). Beyond homeostasis: toward a concept of coherence. *Family Process, 21:* 21–42.

Dell, P., & Goolishian, H. (1981). Order through fluctuation: an evolutionary epistemology for human systems. *Australian Journal of Family Therapy, 21:* 75–184.

DiNicola, V. (1997). *A Stranger in the Family. Culture, Families and Therapy.* New York: W. W. Norton.

Donovan, M. (2009). Reflecting processes and reflective functioning: shared concerns and challenges in systemic and psychoanalytic therapeutic practice. In: C. Flaskas & D. Pocock (Eds.), *Systems and Psychoanalysis. Contemporary Integrations in Family Therapy* (pp. 149–166). London: Karnac.

Epston, D., & White, M. (1992). *Experience, Contradiction, Narrative, & Imagination.* Adelaide: Dulwich Centre.

Ewing, K. (1997). *Arguing Sainthood. Modernity, Psychoanalysis, and Islam.* Durham, NC: Duke University Press.

Ewing, K. (2008). *Stolen Honour. Stigmatizing Muslim Men in Berlin.* Stanford, CA: Stanford University Press.

Falicov, C. (Ed.) (1988). *Family Transitions. Continuity & Change over the Life Cycle*. New York: Guilford Press.
Falicov, C. (1995). Training to think culturally: a multidimensional comparative framework. *Family Process*, 34: 389–399.
Falicov, C. (1998a). From rigid borderlines to fertile borderlands: reconfiguring family therapy. *Journal of Marital & Family Therapy*, 24: 157–163.
Falicov, C. (1998b). *Latino Families in Therapy*. New York: Guilford Press.
Falicov, C. (2005). Emotional transnationalism and family identities. *Family Process*, 44: 399–406.
Falicov, F. (2009). Commentary: on the wisdom and challenges of culturally attuned treatments for Latinos. *Family Process*, 48: 292–309.
Fanon, F. (1952). *Black Skin, White Masks*. London: Pluto Press, 1986.
Fine, M., & Turner, J. (1991). Tyranny and freedom: looking at ideas in the practice of family therapy. *Family Process*, 30: 307–320.
Fisek, G. (1991). A cross-cultural examination of proximity and hierarchy as dimensions of family structure. *Family Process*, 30: 121–133.
Flaskas, C. (1996). Understanding the therapeutic relationship: using psychoanalytic ideas in the systemic context. In: C. Flaskas & A. Perlesz (Eds.), *The Therapeutic Relationship in Systemic Therapy* (pp. 34–52). London: Karnac.
Flaskas, C. (1997). Engagement and the therapeutic relationship in systemic therapy. *Journal of Family Therapy*, 19: 263–282.
Flaskas, C. (2002). *Family Therapy Beyond Postmodernism. Practice, Challenges, Theory*. Hove: Brunner Routledge.
Flaskas, C. (2005). Sticky situations, therapy mess: on impasse and the therapist's position. In: C. Flaskas, B. Mason, & A. Perlesz (Eds.), *The Space Between. Experience, Context, and Process in the Therapeutic Relationship* (pp. 111–126). London: Karnac.
Flaskas, C. (2009). Narrative, meaning-making and the unconscious. In: C. Flaskas & D. Pocock (Eds.), *Systems and Psychoanalysis. Contemporary Integrations in Family Therapy* (pp. 3–20). London: Karnac.
Fonagy, P., & Target, M. (2003). *Psychoanalytic Theories: Perspectives from Developmental Psychology*. London: Whurr.
Foucault, M. (1978). *The History of Sexuality*. Harmondsworth: Penguin.
Fredman, G. (2004). *Transforming Emotion: Conversations in Counselling and Psychotherapy*. London: Whurr.
Freedman, J., & Combs, G. (1996). *Narrative Therapy. The Social Construction of Preferred Realities*. New York: W. W. Norton.

Frosh, S. (2009). What does the other want? In: C. Flaskas & D. Pocock (Eds.), *Systems and Psychoanalysis. Contemporary Integrations in Family Therapy* (pp. 185–202). London: Karnac.

Geertz, C. (1988). *Works and Lives. The Anthropologist as Author.* Cambridge: Polity Press.

Golann, S. (1987). On description of family therapy. *Family Process, 26*: 331–340.

Goldner, V. (1988). Generation and gender: normative and cover hierarchies. *Family Process, 27*: 17–31.

Goldner, V., Penn, P., Sheinberg, M., & Walker, G. (1990). Love and violence: gender paradoxes in volatile attachments. *Family Process, 29*: 343–364.

Graeber, D. (2007). *Possibilities. Essays on Hierarchy, Rebellion and Desire.* Oakland, CA: AK Press.

Guilfoyle, M. (2002). Power, knowledge and resistance in therapy: exploring links between discourse and materiality. *International Journal of Psychotherapy, 7*: 83–97.

Guilfoyle, M. (2003). Dialogue and power: a critical analysis of power in dialogical therapy. *Family Process, 42*: 331–343.

Hall, C. (1996). Histories, empires and the post-colonial moment. In: I. Chambers & L. Curti (Eds.), *The Post-Colonial Question* (pp. 65–77). London: Routledge.

Hardy, K., & Laszloffy, T. (1995). The cultural genogram: key to training culturally competent family therapists. *Journal of Marital and Family Therapy, 21*: 227–237.

Hardy, K., & Laszloffy, T. (1998). The dynamics of pro-racist ideology: implications for family therapists. In: M. McGoldrick (Ed.), *Revisioning Family Therapy. Race, Culture and Gender in Clinical Practice* (pp. 118–128). New York: The Guilford Press.

Harries-Jones, P. (1995). *A Recursive Vision. Ecological Understanding and Gregory Bateson.* Toronto: University of Toronto Press.

Hastrup, K. (2007). Performing the world: agency, anticipation and creativity. In: E. Hallam & T. Ingold (Eds.), *Creativity and Cultural Improvisation* (pp. 193–206). Oxford: Berg.

Henderson, M. (Ed.) (1995). *Borders, Boundaries, and Frames. Cultural Criticism and Cultural Studies.* New York: Routledge.

Hermans, H., & Kempen, H. (1993). *The Dialogical Self: Meaning as Movement.* San Diego, CA: Academic Press.

Hoffman, L. (1981). *Foundations of Family Therapy.* New York: Basic Books.

Hoffman, L. (1985). Beyond power and control: toward a "second order" family systems therapy. *Family Systems Medicine, 3*: 381–396.

Hoffman-Hennessy, L., & Davis, J. (1993). Tekka with feathers: talking about talking (about suicide). In: S. Friedman (Ed.), *The New Language of Change* (pp. 345–373). New York: Guilford Press.

Holland, D., & Lave, J. (Eds.) (2001). *History in Person. Enduring Struggles, Contentious Practice, Intimate Identities*. Santa Fe, NM: School of American Research Press.

Holquist, M. (1990). *Dialogism: Bakhtin and his World*. New York: Routledge.

Inger, I., & Inger, J. (1994). *Creating and Ethical Position in Family Therapy*. London: Karnac.

Jenkins, R. (1997). *Rethinking Ethnicity. Arguments and Explorations*. London: Sage.

Khanna, R. (2003). *Dark Continents. Psychoanalysis and Colonialism*. Durham, NC: Duke University Press.

Kitzinger, C., & Wilkinson, S. (1996). Theorizing representing the other. In: S. Wilkinson & C. Kitzinger (Eds.), *Representing the Other. A Feminism & Psychology Reader* (pp. 1–32). London: Sage.

Klein, M. (1946). Notes on some schizoid mechanisms. *International Journal of Psychoanalysis*, 27: 99–110.

Krause, I.-B. (1993). Anthropology and family therapy: a case for emotions. *Journal of Family Therapy*, 15: 35–56.

Krause, I.-B. (1998). *Therapy Across Culture*. London: Sage.

Krause, I.-B. (2002). *Culture and System in Family Therapy*. London: Karnac.

Krause, I.-B. (2007). Reading *Naven*: toward the integration of culture in systemic psychotherapy. *Human Systems: The Journal of Systemic Consultation & Management*, 18: 112–125.

Krause, I.-B. (2009). In the thick of culture: systemic and psychoanalytic ideas. In: C. Flaskas & D. Pocock (Eds.), *Systems and Psychoanalysis. Contemporary Integrations in Family Therapy* (pp. 167–184). London: Karnac.

Krause, I.-B. (2010a). "I feel therefore . . .": being there in systemic psychotherapy practice. *Context*, 107: 4–7.

Krause, I.-B. (2010b). Calling the context: towards a systemic and cross-cultural approach to emotions. *Journal of Family Therapy*, 32: 370–397.

Larner, G. (2000). Towards common ground in psychoanalysis and family therapy: on knowing not to know. *Journal of Family Therapy*, 22: 61–82.

Luepnitz, D. (2009). Interpreting dreams in psychotherapy with couples: moving between upper and lower worlds. In: C. Flaskas & D. Pocock (Eds.), *Systems and Psychoanalysis. Contemporary Integrations in Family Therapy* (pp. 57–72). London: Karnac.

Malik, R., & Krause, I.-B. (2005). Before and beyond words: embodiment and intercultural therapeutic relationships in family therapy. In: C. Flaskas, B. Mason, & A. Perlesz (Eds.), *The Space Between. Experience, Context, and Process in the Therapeutic Relationship* (pp. 95–110). London: Karnac.

Mason, B. (1993). Towards positions of safe uncertainty. *Human Systems: The Journal of Systemic Consultation & Management*, 4: 189–200.

Mattingly, C. (2008). Reading minds and telling tales in a cultural borderland. *Ethos*, 36: 136–154.

Maturana, H., & Verala, F. (1980). *Autopoiesis and Recognition*. Dordrect: Kluwer Academic.

McGoldrick, M. (Ed.) (1998). *Re-Visioning Family Therapy. Race, Culture, and Gender in Clinical Practice*. New York: Guilford Press.

McGoldrick, M., Pearce, J., & Giordano, J. (Eds.) (1982). *Ethnicity and Family Therapy*. New York: Guilford.

McKinnon, L., & Miller, D. (1987). The new epistemology and the Milan approach: feminist and socio-political consideration. *Journal of Marital and Family Therapy*, 13: 139–156.

Milton, K. (2002). *Loving Nature. Towards an Ecology of Emotion*. London: Routledge.

Mimica, J. (Ed.) (2007). *Explorations in Psychoanalytic Ethnography*. New York: Berghan.

Minuchin, S., & Fishman, H. C. (1981). *Family Therapy Techniques*. Cambridge, MA: Harvard University Press.

Moore, H. (2007). *The Subject of Anthropology. Gender, Symbolism and Psychoanalysis*. Cambridge: Polity Press.

Montalvo, B., & Gutierrez, M. (1988). The emphasis on cultural identity: a developmental–ecological constraint. In: C. Falicov (Ed), *Family Transitions. Continuity & Change over the Life Cycle* (pp. 181–210). New York: Guilford Press.

Morgan, A. (2000). *What is Narrative Therapy? An Easy-to-Read Introduction*. Adelaide: Dulwich Centre.

Nuckolls, C. (1996). *The Cultural Dialectics of Knowledge and Desire*. Madison, WI: University of Wisconsin Press.

Pearce, W. B., & Cronen, V. E. (1980). *Communication, Action and Meaning: The Creation of Social Realities*. New York: Praeger.

Pocock, D. (1997). Feeling understood in family therapy. *Journal of Family Therapy*, 19: 283–302.

Pocock, D. (2005). Systems of the heart: evoking the feeling self in family therapy. In: C. Flaskas, B. Mason, & A. Perlesz (Eds.), *The Space*

Between. Experience, Context, and Process in the Therapeutic Relationship (pp. 127–140). London: Karnac.

Pocock, D. (2006). Six things worth understanding about psychoanalytic psychotherapy. *Journal of Family Therapy, 28*: 352–369.

Pocock, D. (2009). Working with emotional systems: four new maps. In: C. Flaskas & D. Pocock (Eds.), *Systems and Psychoanalysis. Contemporary Integrations in Family Therapy* (pp. 93–110). London: Karnac.

Pocock, D. (2010a). Editorial: emotion as a systemic issue. *Context, 107*: 1–3.

Pocock, D. (2010b). Emotions as eco-systemic adaptations. *Journal of Family Therapy, 32*: 362–378.

Rabinow, P. (2008). *Marking Time. On the Anthropology of the Contemporary.* Princeton, NJ: Princeton University Press.

Rabinow, P., & Marcus, G. (2008). *Designs for an Anthropology of the Contemporary.* Durham, NC: Duke University Press.

Real, T. (1990). The therapeutic use of self in constructionist/systemic therapy. *Family Process, 29*: 255–272.

Rober, P. (1999). The therapist's inner conversation in family therapy practice: some ideas about the self of the therapist, therapeutic impasse and the process of reflection. *Family Process, 38*: 209–228.

Rober, P. (2005). The therapist's self in dialogical family therapy: some ideas about not-knowing and the therapist's inner conversation. *Family Process, 44*: 477–495.

Rober, P., & Seltzer, M. (2010). Avoiding colonizer positions in the therapy room. *Family Process, 49*: 123–137.

Said, E. (1978). *Orientalism. Western Conceptions of the Orient.* London: Penguin.

Seikkula, J. (2003). Dialogue is the change: understanding psychotherapy as a semiotic process of Bakhtin, Voloshinov and Vygotsky. *Human Systems: The Journal of Systemic Consultation & Management, 14*: 83–94.

Seikkula, J., Arnkil, T., & Eriksson, E. (2003). Postmodern society and social networks: open and anticipation dialogues in network meetings. *Family Process, 42*: 185–203.

Segal, H. (1994). *Straight Sex: The Politics of Pleasure.* London: Virago.

Selvini Palazzoli, M., Boscolo, L., Cecchin, G., & Prata, G. (1978). *Paradox and Counterparadox. A New Model in the Therapy of the Family in Schizophrenic Transaction.* New York: Jason Aronson.

Selvini Palazzoli, M., Boscolo, L., Cecchin, G., & Prata, G. (1980). Hypothesizing–circularity–neutrality: three guidelines for the conductor of the session. *Family Process, 19*: 3–12.

Selvini Palazzoli, M., Cirillo, S., Selvini, M., & Sorrentino, A. (1989). *Family Games: General Models of Psychotic Processes in the Family*. New York: W. W. Norton.

Singh, R., & Clarke, G. (2006). Power and parenting assessments: the intersecting levels of culture, race, class and gender. *Clinical Child Psychology & Psychiatry, 11*: 9–25.

Strathern, M. (1988). *The Gender of the Gift*. Berkeley, CA: University of California Press.

Strathern, M. (1992). *After Nature. English Kinship in the Late Twentieth Century*. Cambridge: Cambridge University Press.

Strathern, M. (1999). *Property, Substance & Effect. Anthropological Essays on Persons and Things*. London: Athlone Press.

Tamura, T., & Lau, A. (1992). Connectedness versus separateness: applicability of family therapy to Japanese families. *Family Process, 31*: 319–340.

Taylor, C. (1985a). *Human Agency and Language. Philosophical Papers I*. Cambridge: Cambridge University Press.

Taylor, C. (1985b). *Philosophy and the Human Sciences. Philosophical Papers II*. Cambridge: Cambridge University Press.

Tomm, K. (1984). One perspective on the Milan systemic approach. Part I. Overview of development, theory and practice. *Journal of Marital and Family Therapy, 10*: 113 125.

Tomm, K. (1987a). Interventive interviewing: Part I. Strategizing as a fourth guideline for the therapist. *Family Process, 26*: 3–13.

Tomm, K. (1987b). Interventive interviewing: Part II. Reflexive questioning as a means to enable self-healing. *Family Process, 26*: 167–183.

Tomm, K. (1988). Interventive interviewing: Part III. Intending to ask lineal, circular, strategic or reflexive questions? *Family Process, 27*: 1–15.

Turner, V. (1969). *The Ritual Process. Structure and Anti-Structure*. New Brunswick, NJ: Aldine Transactions, 2009.

Watts-Jones, D. (1997). Toward an African American Genogram. *Family Process, 36*: 375–383.

Watts-Jones, D. (2002). Healing internalized racism: the role of a within-group sanctuary among people of African descent. *Family Process, 41*: 591–601.

Werbner, P., & Modood, T. (Eds.) (1997). *Debating Cultural Hybridity. Multi-Cultural Identities and the Politics of Anti-Racism*. London: Zed Books.

White, M. (1997). *Narratives of Therapists' Lives*. Adelaide: Dulwich Centre.

Whitehead, A. (1925). *Science and the Modern World*. New York: Free Press, 1967.
Wilder-Mott, C., & Weakland, J. (Eds.) (1981). *Rigor and Imagination*. New York: Praeger.
Wilson, J. (2007). *The Performance of Practice*. London: Karnac.
Winnicott, D. W. (1971). *Playing and Reality*. London: Routledge, 2006.
Žižek, S. (1989). *The Sublime Object of Ideology*. London: Verso.

PART I
THE INTERSUBJECTIVE SPACE

Can we tolerate the relationships that race compels?

David Campbell

> "The fact remains that getting people right is not what living is all about anyway. It's getting them wrong that is living, getting them wrong and wrong and wrong and then, after careful consideration, getting them wrong again. That's how we know we're alive: we're wrong. Maybe the best thing would be to forget being right or wrong about people and just go along for the ride. But if you can do that—well, lucky you"
>
> (Roth, 1997, p. 35)

A personal statement

In the summer of 1962, I had just graduated from high school in Kansas City, and was preparing to go to university at a small men's liberal arts college in Ohio. One hot day in July, I received a letter from the college informing me that "amongst the 280 men in the incoming class were two Negroes . . ." (I will never forget the way this word, with its capital "N" stood out on the page.) The letter continued to ask if I would have any objections if one of these men were assigned to share a room with me. Partly I was shocked by this and partly I was very curious, so I wrote back saying, "on the contrary I would be very interested to share a room with one of these men" ... and so it happened.

In September, I arrived at the campus and went to the tiny room (about 10 ft × 10 ft) where Thad was unpacking his bags. He was from Detroit, and brought with him stacks of Motown records, which helped us to kick-start our relationship. As it turned out, we shared a room in the second year as well, progressing to a room that was approximately 10 ft × 15 ft!! We spent time together and also had separate circles of friends, but he became increasingly lonely in this all-white institution in the middle of Ohio. He spent more and more time at other universities where there was a larger contingent of black students ... including women ... and after this second year he left and transferred to a black college in Georgia.

Some of our best conversations took place when the lights were out before we fell asleep. In fact, we had a ritual of turning the lights out and listening to Sibelius's Finlandia as the last thing before we fell asleep, and it was during one of these bedtime sessions that I asked him, "What should I as a white person learn about what it is like to be a black person?" He thought for a few moments, and then he said, "Just don't forget that you can never know what it is like to be black."

Well, this message has stayed with me and I want to remind myself, and the reader, about its meaning as we embark on this chapter.

Introduction

For me, one of the influential ideas within the original Milan approach to family therapy was coined by Shands (1971), who advocated that we should strive to "stamp out nouns", and I think this could not be more appropriate than it is in this potentially volatile field of race and culture. If we see race and culture as "nouns", that is, fixed entities with attached meanings, we lose the potential to see them as pauses in ongoing conversations (Krause, 2002). It would be helpful to see terms such as black, white, or mixed race as pauses or stopping points in ongoing conversations about race. The conversations take place in particular contexts containing elements of the past and the future, but if they can be constructed in a dialogical format they acquire the ability to change and develop new meanings. I think we have an ethical responsibility, if we choose to become engaged in this topic, to keep conversations going. So, the focus of this chapter is how to introduce the topic of race and culture into dialogical processes.

However, one thing that makes this such a challenging topic to discuss is that while we, and our ancestors, have all been trying to survive for millennia, survival is often achieved by one group establishing its power over another group, and history is filled with examples of wars, colonization, slavery, labour camps, and ghettoization to prove this point. While we are all trying to survive, there have been, throughout history, the powerful and the powerless, the "haves" and the "have-nots", those who survive at the expense of others.

So, when we sit down to talk to clients about cultural differences, we are also inviting these historical legacies into the room. Why is this important for therapists in the twenty-first century? Because we are not simply therapists and clients of the twenty-first century, and it will help us to do this work if we can see ourselves and our clients as participants in a long-standing exercise in power and the struggle to survive. We carry baggage with us. Having said that, I want to contradict myself by saying we are also living in one moment in the flow of history. Movements such as eighteenth century enlightenment, nineteenth century social reforms, and the abolition of the slave trade made society more aware of abuses of power, just as legislation for civil partnerships and the ordination of women do today. As a society, we become more enlightened and more aware of the experiences of others with increasing exposure to others and the passage of time. I think this is important, because it helps both therapists and clients accept their limitations. We are limited by the power struggles of the past and we are also enlightened by increasing awareness of "the other". The inequities of the past grip our relationships today in a way that will be different twenty years from now. So, we are also trying to create dialogue in the context of the future. (I write this chapter as the mixed-race senator, Barack Obama, is elected as the president of the United States, and his victory has prompted an enormous sense of a future, particularly for many African-Americans.)

Dialogue

How do we begin to construct a dialogical process that allows us to communicate meaningfully with clients from races and cultures other than our own?[1] It is possible to see speech or action in a wider context that also includes all the possible things that were not said or acted upon. The work of Derrida (1982) and Bakhtin (1935) have been influential in highlighting that the thing said acquires its meaning from its relation to "the things not said". In a similar vein, positioning theory articulated by Harré and van Langenhove (1999) goes a step further by suggesting that when we take a position through our words or deeds, we actively position the words not spoken and the deeds not done as "the other". This creates a dynamic of mutual influence between ourselves and others. And when this dynamic model is applied in a social context in which people are vying for the power to compete for limited resources, we very quickly see the emergence of one group holding power at the expense of the "other", who does not.

In relation to this, I want to emphasize two points. First, I want to emphasize the distinction between a dialogue between people of different races and a dialogue between people who have had different experiences based on race. Race and culture are "totalizing" terms and obscure the subtle meanings that these terms have in a particular context. The term race should be used only as a context marker, which alerts us to something potentially powerful and important behind the term. Because race and culture carry such emotionally laden baggage, we can easily fall into the trap of accepting a statement about race as though we know what it means to the speaker, and avoiding the more difficult, perhaps uncomfortable, process of finding out the range of meanings the speaker attaches to the statement. "Race", therefore, needs to be placed in dialogue and I find the concept of "dis-aggregating race" a helpful reminder of the many possible meanings lying behind each encounter.

In order to create dialogue between people who have had different experiences based on race and cultural differences, we need to explore some important aspects of the dialogical process. The prerequisite I have found most important is that each participant feels safe in a dialogue, and I think that people feel safe when they believe their conversational partner acknowledges and respects the reasons they are living their lives as they are (Mason, 1993). This is a tall order, but at least this proviso spares us from the pressure of having to understand, or be fully empathic with, another's experience. I think dialogues are dynamic, fluctuating processes, and, in this context, it means we become more and less respectful during a conversation while seeking over time to reach a more respectful and empathic relationship toward "the other". I use the language of safety, but, over time, I have also moved toward the idea that we need to think about whether someone is "prepared for dialogue". I have found that it is helpful in work with clients to distinguish dialogical conversation from other types of conversation. I explain to clients that a dialogical conversation is a different kind of conversation with its own ground rules that aims to help people understand the positions they speak from and the positions from which others speak to them. Some ground rules which I find helpful are:

- this can be a time-limited conversation that is part of a longer therapeutic session;
- it requires each to listen carefully to the other in order to address the question: "Why is it important to the other to take the particular position they have chosen?";
- the process is structured so that each is listening to the other in sequence, rather than in simultaneous, overlapping conversations . . . (A listens to B, then B listens to A, and so on);
- each should help the other understand the value and meaning of their position, rather than persuade the other of the correctness of their position;
- it might be helpful to use diagrams to graphically represent polarities and positions.

In relation to the issue of safety and being prepared for dialogue, I was interested to read an account of two professional women, one white and one black, who were endeavouring to address their differences in an open and honest relationship (Ayvasian & Tatum, 2004). When the black man, Rodney King, was severely beaten by a group of white Los Angeles police officers in March 1991, the black woman felt such anger against the white community that she could no longer sustain her friendship with her white colleague, and reported that she needed to spend more time with her black friends and their church. This seemed like seeking out, for the time being, the people—her black friends—who would know most what it felt like to be a black person in that society. She felt it was not something a white person could understand. After some months, she then felt able to contact her white friend and re-start their relationship where they left off. For me, this example illustrates the necessity of moving in and out of safe positions in the course of creating a dialogue based on racial experiences, because the dialogue was affected by the external events, or the "racial baggage", that we all carry into dialogue. The example also warns us against the notion that we can understand, or be empathic to, another person all the time. This, I think, goes some way toward lifting the burden on participants trying to create a dialogue across racial difference, and makes it acceptable, even necessary, for each person to step in and out of dialogue.

My second point refers to the way I think we need to employ dialogue. To move toward dialogue is to recognize that the position I hold in relation to race and culture is maintained by the existence of other positions. If I take the position of white privilege, this position gets its various meanings from the complementary position called black lack of privilege. Positions of power exist in relation to positions of powerlessness. When we take a position through our action or utterances, we position others as different, and if the issue at stake is one imbued with power relations, such as class, expertise, or skin colour, we are also positioning others in positions of less power and perpetuating a power dynamic that is favourable for some and not others.

An example

Here is an example, which illustrates the importance of disaggregating experiences of race, and trying to identify the polarity upon which each speaker has taken a position. A white supervisor was working with a group of four family therapy trainees, one of whom was from an ethnic minority, in a live supervision group. The supervisor had been influenced by the discourse about white privilege and the need to be proactive in raising issues of race so that they did not become marginalized in the working of her group. After several weeks of being with the group, she sensed that the ethnic minority trainee felt somewhat different from the others, and surmised that this was due to ethnicity. In order to promote openness and trust, she asked the young woman if there were any issues about race that she would like to raise in the group, to which the supervisee replied, "I don't have any issues about race in this group." The supervisor felt frustrated that her good intention to make it possible to talk about race was not met with approval, and the group drifted on to another topic.

How can we understand what happened? From my conceptual framework, I would argue that each of these persons took positions within different polarities. The supervisor was operating within a polarity that could be labelled "range of interventions to promote discussion of race", and consisted of a myriad number of interventions, some more direct and some more indirect, which she could choose at that moment. Within the myriad possibilities, she chose to take a position I would call "ask the ethic minority trainee directly if she would like to talk about issues".

When polarity lines are drawn out, several things, which were not so clear before, become apparent. Implied is that the supervisor supports and respects all the positions, because they all depend on each other for their very existence. Also implied is that the timing of a discussion about race or respect depends on two people, in this case the supervisor and the supervisee, negotiating the right time to talk. For example, if one person says, "I would like to ask about race here", that is only one position, and rather than necessarily discussing race at this time, both can become interested in how that statement influences the other to take a corresponding position within the same polarity.

Is this a moment to discuss race?

Probably Not yet

If the supervisor/therapist and supervisee/client are united in their adherence to the polarity line, it is more likely each will be interested in trying to connect themselves to the position the other wants to take.

As it happens, I was supervising the supervisor, and, after further discussion with her, we thought the trainee was operating within another polarity altogether, and hers might be labelled "range of things I can do to feel I belong to this group". Within her range of possibilities might be "acknowledge my differences" at one end of the polarity, and "acknowledge my similarities" at the other end of the polarity line. When the trainee was asked about "her issues about race", it might have been difficult for her to take the position "acknowledge my differences" if she was, in fact, more preoccupied with belonging to the group. Within that polarity, it would make more sense to take a position of "acknowledging my similarities" in trying to belong and, therefore, she would need to say, "I have no issues". At the other end of the conversation, for the supervisor, operating within the polarity of "promoting discussion of race", the trainee's reply did not fit, and she felt confused because her efforts seemed to have been in vain. This is an example of positioning others when we try to construct meaning by taking a position on our own semantic polarity. When the supervisor takes the position of "white privilege", she automatically places others in the position of "non-white, less-privileged", but this might not be the position that the other wants to choose for herself, and, as a result, there is a discrepancy that will inevitably lead to misunderstanding. So, as therapists and supervisors, we must be vigilant about our own positions and the way they position others. I think problems of understanding arise when we do not make race and culture acceptable topics for conversation and exploration, but I also suggest that problems arise when we assume race should be discussed at the time and in the manner of our choosing.

Using the positioning model means starting a conversation with the assumption that each of us takes a different position within different semantic polarities. Therefore, we should begin a conversation assuming we want different things from each other and not rush too quickly into a conversation aiming for connectedness. Better to get interested in the other's position, and employ the mantra, "Why is it so important for this person to take this position at this time?", rather than looking for the connections to our own position. Paradoxically, it is the attention to the separateness or the uniqueness of each person's position that encourages each individual to seek out the other and look for the connectedness between different positions. I use this approach in many of my supervisions, because often therapists try too hard to make connections, and, while they are doing so, they fail to see some important aspects of the client's or family members' need for difference, distance, and separateness. I think this is particularly pertinent to the issue of race, for which separateness is so intrinsically bound with a history of abuse of power and the subsequent guilt of those holding power.

Power

Power is a vexed issue. We choose positions (and inadvertently position others) to help us influence conversations and relationships. We would like others to see the world as we see it, or at least not to challenge our view so much that we become uncertain and vulnerable. Therefore, within every conversation there is the subtle negotiation of power to influence relationships (Selvini Palazzoli, Boscolo, Cecchin, & Prata, 1978), and as this occurs over time and within institutions, positions of power are held on to and fought over with consequences for both winners and losers.

When society allocates power, wealth, and status to certain positions, while they do indeed derive their meanings from the existence of the "other", they are difficult to relinquish. Who will willingly surrender power, wealth, or status? This is what we are up against when we encourage people to take responsibility for the "other" position that supports their own. I do not think we can progress with this model until we are able to talk about positions of power and what it might mean to give them up.

However, I also think that changing attitudes about race and culture must not rely exclusively on good works or morality-based charity and love. Rather, here I want to suggest that it is within our own "selfish" interest to review and alter our attitudes toward the other. Our own selfish individual development depends on it. At the heart of my argument is the assertion that we learn and develop as human beings by participating in dialogical communication with the other. If I can define myself in relation to what is "not me", or what lies in the territory belonging to the other, then any expansion of myself and my beliefs will take place, to some degree, within the territory previously allocated to the other. While it is beyond our ability to influence the "system" that creates and maintains racism, we can scale things down and make the issue relevant for therapeutic work by exploring what it means to the therapist–client relationship evolving in front of us. This has been acknowledged by various writers, such as Levinas and Benjamin, who have discussed the idea of having "responsibility" for the other:

> Responsibility for another is not an accident that happens to a subject, but precedes essence in it, has not awaited freedom, in which commitment to another would have been made. [Levinas, 1998[1974], p. 114]

> The notion of intersubjectivity postulates that the barbarism of incorporating the Other into the same, the cycle of destructiveness, can only be modified when the Other intervenes. Therefore *any subject's primary*

responsibility to the other subject is to be her intervening or surviving other. This perspective allows us to move beyond the critique of the thinking subject into the problem of identity as it presents itself in the psychopolitical world. [Benjamin, 1998, p. 99, original italics]

The responsibility to get into dialogue is a moral imperative that lies at the heart of both personal and social change. But what can entice or compel anyone to enter into dialogue with someone, unless there is some self-interest at stake? Are we going to wait for altruism to motivate people to talk and listen to those who are different? I think not. Why should we be interested in another person's position on any particular issue? One reason is that we can enhance our position by readying ourselves to borrow from those who have similar interests, whether they be for alliance or rivalry. We can develop our own wealth, knowledge, and emotional well-being by getting into dialogue with people of similar interests. It is possible to position speakers on the polarity of power. Who has a greater amount of power to define the context? That is, this conversation is about you accepting my point of view or this conversation is about my trying to agree or disagree with your point of view. Are you an employee of the state speaking to someone who feels on the margins of the state? It is then useful to position people on the polarity of how much each is open to being influenced by the other. This is the difference between a *conversation*, in which each has a goal of influencing the other towards their own point of view, and a *dialogue*, in which each is interested in exploring and understanding, and perhaps moving toward the other's position.

I want to clarify here that this positioning model can be used for the therapist to demonstrate the different positions taken by family members, or it can be used for the therapist to demonstrate her own position *vis-à-vis* a client for a particular issue that emerges in therapy. When people are able to listen empathically, their position changes because some of the "others'" position is incorporated into their own, and this signals the emergence of a new position . . . a third position. Another way of representing this might be to say that my position is Context A, and yours is Context B, and the dialogical process allows for the emergence of Context C (Campbell & Grøenbaek, 2006). My experience in managing these dialogues (and they do require active management) is that it is the quality of listening rather than the quality of speaking that facilitates the creation of Context C. Therefore, I emphasize the state of mind for listening by making comments such as these: to the person in the speaking position, "Just try to explain to the other why it is so important for you to take and hold on to your position on this particular issue"; to the person in the listening position, "Try to listen in such a way that helps you come a bit closer to understanding why the other's position is so important to them and why it is so helpful to hold on to their position".

Survival and connectedness

Because we all, chapter-writers and chapter-readers alike, have myriad experiences of race and culture, some of which are highly charged, this discussion will be read through the lens of our own personal and societal meanings. Other writers (see chapters by Daniel, Flaskas, Malik/Mandin, Mason and Pocock, this volume) discuss the necessity of revisiting our own experiences, in order to be grounded and authentic when we raise the topic with clients. I agree that this is a crucial part of the preparation necessary for therapeutic work, but there is one issue I have seldom heard addressed, although I have found this very helpful to me in this effort to "make my own safe environment". This is the issue of *survival*. I think that persons intrinsically want to be connected with, or one might say that persons want to be embedded in, some context that gives meaning to their lives. Another way of saying this might be that persons intrinsically want to be placed in a relationship with the "other" in such a way that allows them to enhance their own position, whether this be a moral, material, relational, or emotional position. This is survival. The problem for us, as therapists, is that we are unrealistic about what people really want to be connected to and we are unrealistic about which "other" our clients want to get to know. This idea of survival might be best understood as an aspect of Maslow's needs' hierarchy (Maslow, 1943), because all thoughts and activities about race and culture differences imply that these are ideas which help us survive.

Concluding thoughts

In this chapter, I have aimed to produce some guidelines for practitioners who try to have conversations across racial and cultural divides. My guidelines have taken the form of processes rather than nouns: being/becoming prepared, being/becoming connected, having dialogues, disaggregating race, positioning oneself and taking responsibility for the "other". These might help to offer different perspectives, but they might also obscure as well as illuminate. Apart from the fact that an iceberg is white, I think the metaphor of the "tip of the iceberg" is helpful in thinking about race and cultural differences. As with skin colour and facial features, that part of the iceberg above the water announces its presence and its identity as an iceberg based on immediate visual features. However, what lies beneath the waterline is much more influential in defining the size and shape of the iceberg and, as we all know from the story of the Titanic, potentially is much more deadly. Similarly, we might make initial judgements about people based on visual cues, unaware of what lies beyond the initial impression. What is this person's history? Why have they come for a consultation? What might they possibly think of finding themselves sitting in front of me? We can only start by taking stock of our own beliefs, attitudes, and prejudices (Cecchin, Lane, & Ray, 1994) and we can only deal with what we "know" about others.

Note

1. Readers who want a more thorough discussion of my use of dialogue and positioning theory can refer to other writings: Campbell and Grøenbaek (2006), and Campbell (2008).

References

Ayvasian, A., & Tatum, D. (2004). Women, race and racism. A dialogue in black and white. In: J. Jordan, M. Walker, & L. Hartling (Eds.), *The Complexity of Connection* (pp. 147–165). New York: Guilford Press.

Bakhtin, M. M. (1935). Discourse in the novel. In: M. Holquist (Ed.), *The Dialogical Imagination* (pp. 259–422). Austin, TX: Texas University Press, 1981.

Benjamin, J. (1998). *Shadow of the Other. Intersubjectivity and Gender in Psychoanalysis.* New York: Routledge.

Campbell, D. (2008). Locating conflict in team consultations. In: D. Campbell & C. Huffington (Eds.), *Organizations Connected: A Handbook of Systemic Consultation* (pp. 79–98). London: Karnac.

Campbell, D., & Grøenbaek, M. (2006). *Taking Positions in the Organization*. London: Karnac.

Cecchin, G., Lane, G., & Ray, W. (1994). *The Cybernetics of Prejudice*. London: Karnac.

Derrida, J. (1982). "*Difference*". *Margins of Philosophy*. Chicago, IL: Chicago University Press.

Harré, R., & van Langenhove, L. (1999). *Positioning Theory. Moral Contexts of International Action*. Oxford: Blackwell.

Krause, I.-B. (2002). *Culture and System in Family Therapy*. London: Karnac.

Levinas, E. (1974). *Otherwise than Being or Beyond Essence*. Pittsburgh, PA: Duquesne University Press, 1998.

Maslow, A. (1943). A theory of human motivation. *Psychological Review, 50*: 370–396.

Mason, B. (1993). Toward positions of safe uncertainty. *Human Systems, 4*: 189–200.

Roth, P. (1997). *American Pastoral*. London: Jonathan Cape.

Selvini Palazzoli, M., Boscolo, L., Cecchin, G., & Prata, G. (1978). *Paradox and Counterparadox*. New York: Jason Aronson.

Shands, H. (1971). *The War with Words*. Paris: Mouton.

CHAPTER THREE

What would (or can) I know? Reflections on the conditions of knowing and understanding in intercultural therapy

Carmel Flaskas

I wrote the abstract for this chapter in the week in which the Prime Minister of the newly elected Labour government of Australia made an apology to indigenous peoples for the wrongs of the past. "Sorry day", with all the talking and the memories and the associations that surrounded it, with all the acknowledgments and the witnessing, had a poignant mix of sorrow, pain, hope, and undeserved tenuous trust. Not for the first time, as a non-indigenous and white Australian, I experienced the generosity in the involvement of Aboriginal and Islander peoples, and felt unworthy and grateful in the face of it. It was a moment of connection and a move toward reconciliation. It was also a time for comprehending the chasm of difference between indigenous and non-indigenous Australia, and the chasm of difference between the tears of indigenous and non-indigenous Australians with respect to our shared past and our shared present.

I feel a kind of fraud writing in this book, for I belong to that group of therapists who are socially and contextually the most illiterate in their personal capacities for intercultural work. I felt nothing but unselfconsciously "at home" culturally and racially in my childhood, growing up in a local milieu of a largely homogeneous culture in the 1960s. With three of my four grandparents coming from different cultures (Irish, Greek, Danish), this would have to stand as a kind of achievement (for better and worse) of assimilation within an immigrant nation, and an achievement of my grandparents and parents. I am still bemused when people ask if I have "gone back" to my heritage—which one, I wonder, and why? I am unaware of any cultural yearnings, and just think of myself as coming from Brisbane. But, although I admit I would be hard-pushed to yearn for Brisbane, I would yearn for Australia if I could not live here, for it is my homeland. And while unconsciously I might have inherited intergenerational orientations to surviving the experience of alienation and cultural bereftness, I have had to learn as an adult, consciously and bit by bit, some literacy in the intimate experience of foreignness and otherness, and some fluency in relating to, through, and across culture and race.

I have had this chapter in the back of my mind for many months, with a number of personal and practice experiences floating through my head. Although the practice musings could open many doors for reflection, I have found myself thinking a lot about the contextual specificity of the conditions of knowing, and the complexity of the therapeutic task of trying to understand. I will settle on these two themes for this chapter. One piece of work with an Aboriginal family from many years ago has stayed with me, for reasons that will be become clear. I will place it at the heart of the exploration, and build the theory discussion around it.[1]

On the power of social immersion: a case study

I began to see an Aboriginal family in a child and family mental health service (CAMHS), referred by one of the Aboriginal services, which was a good referral route, for the therapeutic mandate is clearer when an indigenous service is the first port of call. I learnt this when I worked in an Aboriginal legal service in my fourth-year social work placement, and in my first job in a large psychiatric hospital where we set up an Aboriginal and Islander liaison social work role, which I shared with a colleague. So, the referral route was an auspicious start to the work, even though by then I was in Sydney and with no personal connection to the local indigenous services. The CAMHS service is situated in a multi-cultural and multi-racial area, where 70% of primary school children have English as their second language and where, in those very fine gradations of racism, Aboriginal people were (and still are) the target of the most intense racism.

There was much concern for the child, a boy aged eight, around suicidality and depression. Donny lived with his aunt and her son, aged six. My engagement with his aunt felt quite easy, and, although the boy's cousin could not make much sense of why he was attending, he made himself at home in the family sessions. It was much harder for me to connect with Donny, who was not much of a talker, with or without his family present, and he could not relate very easily to drawing or playing.

There are a number of things I could write about this piece of practice. But, for the purposes of this chapter, there are two parts of the story I want to tell, which expose my limits in a very particular context of social immersion. We had been meeting for a few sessions and the beginning work was around the boy's experience of being bullied at school. The therapeutic system had widened to include changes at school and advice to the boy from some older Aboriginal boys and men. This work was all "on track" and, in a lull in about the fourth session, his aunt said to me, "You know, Carmel, do you think we should have a talk about how Donny feels about being left with me by his mother?" Out came the longer version of the story of his mother's drinking, the coming and going from the country to Sydney with Donny, and now the idea that Donny would be probably be looked after "for good" by his aunt. Donny's mother was part of the stolen generation—she had been removed from her family, and her sister had not, because her skin was lighter than the rest of the family. This social policy was designed explicitly with the entwined interests of assimilation and the destruction of Aboriginality.

I would like to tell you that I had been sensitively biding my time, waiting for the point at which the therapeutic relationship was strong enough to allow me, as a white Australian therapist, to invite an Aboriginal family to talk in front of me of the pain of a child being left by his mother, and a mother being taken as a child from her family, and the effects of this on her and her son's life. Yet, this topic was not even on my agenda—yes, hard to believe, not on the agenda of a family therapist in a child and family mental health service . . .

I understand my situation in this way. Then, and now, I have a politics born of a commitment to the idea that white Australian professionals should "fit", as much as they can, with how indigenous people want to use them. Then, but not now, I thought that there are many ways in which children can be loved and cared for within an extended kinship system, and that a "white" curiosity about what are very common non-nuclear indigenous family arrangements undermines the integrity of these forms of family care (I still believe the first part of this statement, but not necessarily the second part). And I think that then, though I would hope not now, I was unable to find an emotional place within myself to know how to speak of pain and sorrow with Aboriginal people without feeling as if I was (or am still) inflicting this pain, and so this knowing was banished from "my agenda".

It was not just *the difference* between the family and me that created the conditions of this not-knowing—a similar scenario would simply not have occurred had I been relating to a Vietnamese family, or a Lebanese family, or an African family. I could tell you of the layering of my personal history with Aboriginal people—the story of my Danish great-grandparents "allowing" the local Aboriginal people to use their well, my mother's Aboriginal childhood friends in a tiny one-teacher seaside school in the late 1920s, the serious talk from my mother that we should never call Aboriginal people "black" because it would hurt their feelings ("if you have to say anything, say 'coloured'"). I could tell you about my first trip for a funeral to an Aboriginal mission (Cherbourg) when I was a social work student, or the covert subversion of the Palm Island mission management in the psychiatric hospital where I worked. Or I could tell you of the time I found myself going round and round on a ferris wheel, despite my fear of heights, while the patient who routinely absconded back to Palm Island took pity on me and stayed put, waving encouragingly every time I came around (she herself had jumped off the ferris wheel at the last moment, when she remembered that going up high made her sick). But what would all this telling be, if not just one account of the contextual colonial relations that provide the conditions of an otherwise sensible and nice white family therapist finding herself not having in the front of her head something as basic as the importance of a child's loss of his mother in a presentation of depression?

I suspect that a British (but not a Brisbane) audience will disapprove when I say that, although I still blush when I remember this moment, it also makes me laugh—it is a joke at my own expense. For, in the context of the social specificity of my therapeutic relationship with the aunt, and for the historical time, it was "right" that the invitation should come from her and not me. And although the social position I occupied created the conditions of my not-knowing, my positioning of myself "alongside" the aunt none the less provided a safety net, or a good-enough therapeutic relationship, so that she could extend the invitation, and at the right time in the therapy. No harm came from what still stands as a piece of breathtaking stupidity on my part.

But there is a second part to this story, which repeats the same themes, but stays more stubbornly unsettling. Although Donny did not want to play with toys, he would often go to my toy box when he arrived, and bring out the small Chinese parasol, and sit with it in his lap. This was noticed and talked about in a low-key way a number of times, and he told me he liked "Chinesey things". We agreed that we all liked "Chinesey things", and I recall one extended conversation in which his aunt (Lily) said how nice Chinese paintings were, so different to Aboriginal dot paintings, but both so good.

I saw the family regularly for about six months, and every so often after this Lily would ring me to talk about one or other of the boys. In one such talk (*à propos* of what I now cannot remember), she said, "You know, Carmel, his father was Chinese." I did not speak my first thought, which was "Well, Lily, I wish you had told me this a bit earlier . . .!" But this response only momentarily delayed the dawning of my horror at the extent of my own not-knowingness and the power of my immersion in the taboo of Donny's non-indigenous heritage. This taboo was (and is) fuelled by resistance to the history of the physical and cultural annihilation of Aboriginal people, and a determination that the belongingness of Aboriginality should not be lost, regardless of whether you are black, brown, white, or pink with freckles.

The obvious belatedly became obvious. Lily and her son were very dark and clearly looked Aboriginal. Donny was small, brown, and finely featured—he looked, well, kind of Chinese. And just in case, by any chance, any of us missed that he looked kind of Chinese, he collected a small Chinese parasol most sessions, and held it (as a boy) in his lap. His father, and his fantasy of his father and his relationship to his father, still remained eclipsed from view, while his visible Chineseness was rendered invisible. It was small comfort that we had at least all agreed that we liked Chinese things, although I think there could have been a potentially important subliminal message in his aunt's talking about Aboriginal and Chinese paintings, which might have been as close to languaging the boy's cultural and racial beingness as the family could bear at that time.

On knowing and the conditions of dismantling the capacity to know

This piece of practice experience, along with many others, has been formative of some ways I have come to think about therapy practice and the therapeutic relationship, and of how I relate to some theory ideas in the family therapy field. Let me unpack some issues about theory that this practice highlights for me.

Social constructionism is firmly established as part of contemporary systemic therapy theory. Developed in sociology from the 1960s, social constructionist ideas were eventually embraced by family therapy in the context of the postmodernist turn in the early 1990s. The ideas that we are only able to know the social world through a process of social construction, that language constructs what it is we are able to know about the social world, and that we live in a world of dialogue and narrative, are all by now very familiar (Flaskas, 2002). There are two significant "edges" of debate with respect to the limits of any foundational use of social constructionist theory in psychotherapy: the first is whether social constructionism as a theory offers sufficiently complex understandings of realities and realness for the purposes of the activity of psychotherapy, and the second, related, debate is about the way in which the knowing–not-knowing dynamic has come to be cast.

Let me start with the issue of realities and realness. Many discussions within the family therapy literature across the past two decades have signalled some unease with the more extreme anti-realist versions of social construction, where language itself is located as constructing, rather than representing, social and emotional realities (see, for example, Flaskas, 2002; Lannamann, 1998; Larner, 1994; Malik & Krause, 2005; Minuchin, 1991; Pocock, 1995; Speed, 1991). Here, the limits of the social world are understood as lying within the limits of language and the processes of dialogue. This particular position is most heavily associated with the earlier work of social constructionist theorist Kenneth Gergen (for example, 1991, 1994), popularized initially in family therapy through the seminal influence of Harlene Anderson and Harry Goolishian from the late 1980s (1988, 1992).

In the various engagements with this theory within family therapy over the years, one central question has been about whether social constructionism gives sufficient space for the acknowledgement of realities that might exist independent of our consciousness, our languaging, and the processes of social construction (see, for example, Larner, 1994; Minuchin, 1991; Pocock, 1995; Speed, 1991). A related question has been whether social constructionism gives sufficient attention to the "realness" of the intimate lived experience of realities (which might or might not be languaged) as they affect our lives (see, for example, Flaskas, 2002; Pocock, 1995; Malik & Krause, 2005). As Pocock (2009) has noted, these kinds of critiques lean toward a critical realist position. Critical realism acknowledges a complex social world that exists independently of how we come to know it, while still allowing that how we come to "find" and represent that world is a process bounded by language, and that the social world is also mediated and constructed in the process of this representation (see, for example, the discussions in López & Potter, 2001). Within this alternative critical realist theory frame, there is thus no question about whether language constructs *or* represents the world—it always does both.

Critical realism potentially provides a welcome relief from the oppositional dualities embedded in the more extreme anti-realist versions of social constructionist theory. However, the separate and specific issue of the authenticity of the lived experience of realness, so important in any psychotherapy, just barely scrapes into the theory ambit of the different versions of social constructionism, or, indeed, of critical realism. The same could be said for how we might understand and relate to non-conscious and unconscious processes, or to those aspects of human experience that can never really be fully represented by language. If we stay solely within the constructionist/realist theory field, it is also hard to capture the specificity of the social location of the self of the therapist in the therapeutic process, and the nuances of how, as therapists, we might try to mediate and use our social and political and emotional immersion in the process of therapy.

This brings me to the second edge of social constructionist theory, which is the issue of how the knowing–not-knowing dynamic has been cast in our field. Again, we could turn to the work of Anderson and Goolishian, especially their 1992 paper, which first laid out the argument that the therapist should adopt a not-knowing stance in the interest of engaging more fully with the clients' world of language and allowing a richer space for therapeutic dialogue. From one angle, it is peculiar how quickly the idea of adopting a not-knowing stance came to be so influential in family therapy. From another angle, though, it can be more easily understood, especially if we note the very strong congruence with established and developing narrative and Milan-systemic politics and practices. Anderson and Goolishian argued for a collaborative therapeutic position and practices, and for the therapist to actively relinquish her/his expert position in relation to the client/s. The resonance here was very strong, both with the politics of narrative therapy with respect to the power of the therapist and with the depth of the practices of curiosity already embedded in Milan-systemic therapy.

All this led to a casting of the knowing–not-knowing dynamic toward practices of not-knowing and toward minimizing the power differential of the therapist as expert. Across the years, there have been a number of nuanced discussions about the need to hold expertise alongside practices of not-knowing (see, for example, Laird, 1998). Mason (1993) has written of the position of "authoritive doubt", while Larner (2000) has explored the paradox of knowing not-to-know. However, overwhelmingly, the main focus has been on the position of not-knowing. Conversely, there has been very little interest in exploring the barriers to the therapist's "knowing", or the significance of therapist's failure to know.

Abstract though these theory debates I am mapping might appear, they come to life in the world of practice, and no more vividly than in the context of intercultural therapy. What do I learn about the edges of social constructionist theory around realness and knowing–not-knowing when I remember and reflect on my practice experience with Donny and Lily?

First, I come to appreciate the specificity, the power, and the unwordedness of our own social immersion as therapists. The act of relating is simultaneously intensely social and intimately personal, and in intercultural relating there is a special complexity within the therapeutic relationship. To think about engaging across and through difference, and across and through sameness, which is a frame I will call on in the next section of this chapter, is useful in orientating to the challenge of intercultural therapy. Yet, it is hard to capture the specificity of relationship, what is possible and not possible in knowing and understanding, in any particular context of intercultural therapy. In the realness of a shared history and a shared present, regardless of whether it is languaged or not, we are not just engaging with difference. Instead, we are located in social contexts that we simultaneously both know and cannot know.

This was my position in relating to Donny and Lily, and, indeed, their position in relating to me. I would like to claim a wisdom and equanimity about the "pastness" of the practice mistakes I described. But though I believe that, in 2010, there are different social conditions for how I might now "know" and relate to this family and the realness of history, I also believe that the conditions of knowing can never be assumed. Especially where there is a living history of oppression, of which, as therapists, we have been a part, the force of social immersion is invariably much stronger than we are emotionally able to know. This force provides the conditions of a breathtaking not-knowingness on the part of the therapist. When this happens, and we are lucky enough to become alert to it, we need to use every scrap of reflection we can muster. Reflection, and our reflexivity in the way we relate to our reflection, might or might not be good-enough, depending on the particular piece of therapy, the particular therapeutic relationship, and the particular social relationships within which we are embedded.

Second, although social constructionism has helped us to think about the social construction of realities, the "shadow side" of these processes has largely been unexplored. For social processes do not just shape what we come to know and how we come to know it—what we *cannot know* is also shaped by social processes. In other words, social processes do not just construct realities and the experience of realness, they also fragment, dismantle, and, at times, obliterate realities and the experience of realness (Flaskas, 2002, 2009a). Indeed, our capacity to know realness can be powerfully dismantled, in the way that my capacity to know something "obvious" and real about Donny's history was powerfully dismantled.

Psychoanalysis offers some ideas, especially about the unconscious processes of repression and projection, which speak to the most intimate levels of this experience. Foucault generated ideas that spoke to the conditions of possibility of social discourse, and the power of social practices to generate the possibility of ways of thinking, and the spiral of practice and discourse in social process (Gordon, 1980). His work also flagged the capacity of power to create absence (or negative power) as well as presence (or positive power). I do not want to explore here the way in which these different theory frames conceptualize significant absences, but I do want to note that thinking about absence is inevitably harder than thinking about presence.

This might be why, in family therapy, it has been easier for us to think about the dangers of knowingness in the polarity of knowing–not-knowing, but harder for us to think about the dangers of not-knowingness. Yet, it is as important, especially in those contexts of intercultural work, where we are the most deeply immersed in a living history of oppression, to try to think about our not-knowingness and to recognize the extent of our vulnerability to dismantling our own capacity to know. In the case of Donny, who presented as an eight-year-old with depression and some seemingly isolated (suicidal?) acts of risk-taking, my cultural not-knowingness was dangerous.

On empathy and trying to understand

I would like to shift the discussion to a different, though related, territory. So far, I have been exploring the limits and specificity of the social contexts of knowing in intercultural therapy, and will now consider the process of the therapist trying to understand. This lies in the territory of empathy, which has not been theorized very much in family therapy, despite its centrality in everyday practice. Empathy is an intensely relational process. In the therapeutic relationship, we can think of empathy as being the process (on the part of the therapist) of trying to understand, which exists only in relation to the process (on the part of clients) of trying to convey experience and hoping to feel understood (Flaskas, 2009b).

As part of my long-term work on the therapeutic relationship, I have become interested in the therapist's imagination of her self in relation to her clients, and how this imagination influences the form of her connection in the therapeutic relationship and shapes her attempts to understand (Flaskas, 2002, 2009b). I have suggested that there are two kinds of positions we use when we imagine ourselves in relationship to others. Each of these positions relies on a particular kind of fantasy of self-in-relationship-to-other. The first is the fantasy of identification, which assumes that we are sufficiently *like* the other to try to imagine ourselves in their situation and to use whatever resonances come from our own lived experience in our attempts to orientate to our clients' experiences. The second position relies on a different kind of relationship fantasy. Here, rather than imagining ourselves as "like" our clients, we try to imagine ourselves as "the other" in relation to them. We assume that we will not be able to make any easy sense of our clients' experiences and, instead, like an anthropologist in a different culture, or like a foreigner visiting in a different society, we will need to be quite active if we are to try to grasp the experience of the people we are sitting with.

Understandings of empathy that have been produced in the individual therapies tend toward practices (such as reflecting back) that are more associated with the imagination of identification. In the context of individual therapy, the therapist's imagination of identification with the client is often the first, and predominant, fantasy used in nurturing the attempt to understand the universality of the human condition. However, in the context of family therapy, when you have a number of people in the room, all with different experiences and stories, it is harder to rely on the fantasy of identification, even in the early engagement stage of therapy, simply because "plural" identification is more difficult. The challenge of multi-engagement in family therapy means, for example, that the reflecting-back technique of empathy is used far less often.

As Perry (1993) has detailed in his excellent discussion, there are many ways in which empathy is expressed in family therapy—we rely more heavily on the practices of questioning, reflecting teams, opinions, and tasks. The foundational systemic discussions of the position of neutrality/curiosity stressed its practice wisdom in the art of engagement with all family members (see Cecchin, 1987; Selvini Palazzoli, Boscolo, Cecchin, & Prata, 1980). White's (2002) idea of "exoticising the everyday" was one step in the parallel development of narrative practices of curiosity. The systemic and narrative practices of curiosity, generated within the context of the practice challenges of working with families, are strongly aligned with the empathic imagination of difference.

The "rough" distinction can be made, then, that individual psychotherapy tends toward a heavier use of the therapist's imagination of identification with the client, while family therapy tends toward a heavier use of the therapist's imagination of difference. Yet, though this distinction might be seen in the "in the room" practices in individual *vs.* family therapy, I would, none the less, argue that in all contexts of psychotherapy there is a need for the therapist to be flexible in moving between an imagination of herself as the same as, and then as foreign to, her clients. This capacity to use our self to swing between these two positions of imagination potentially allows the conditions for stronger forms of therapeutic connection. In other words, the flexibility of how we think about ourselves in relation to our clients allows us to try to understand both the sameness and the difference of our clients' experience in relation to our own lived experience.

But what has all this got to do with intercultural therapeutic relating, or, indeed, my practice with Lily and Donny? I would agree with the idea that psychotherapy is, to some extent, always an intercultural process, for there is always an engagement with sameness and difference. As the joke about the grounds for gay divorce reminds us, irreconcilable sameness is potentially as corrosive of relationship as irreconcilable difference.

None the less, the historical and present significance of difference in intercultural and interracial therapeutic relating makes special demands on empathic imagination. Although there are many things that could be said about intercultural relating, here I simply want to think about the imagination we have of our "selves" in relation to our clients when we are relating across worlds of difference in lived experience. It is this imagination that provides the ground from which we relate and invite relationship, and it is hard to think of a practice context that is more demanding of a disciplined balance and flexibility of empathic imagination.

Either the fantasy of identification or the fantasy of self-as-other/different can quickly become intensely problematic if used without a back-and-forth movement between the two. In general, it is better to try to imagine oneself as foreign rather than one's clients as foreign, as this leads to more emotionally connected and experience-near practices of curiosity. The therapeutic invitation here is an attempt to signal a desire to understand and connect in the context of an acknowledgement of one's ignorance. However, if one skews too heavily to relying on a fantasy of self-as-other, it can be hard to avoid an interactional slide, when practices of curiosity begin to seem experience-far, not experience-near, and the family and family members feel more firmly constructed by you as the "other". The imagination of identification needs to be held closely alongside the fantasy of difference, a kind of constant scanning for resonance and universality, or a tentative but persistent drawing on what might be "like" our clients' experience in our own lived experience and repertoire of imagination.

In the reverse polarity, stubbornly holding on to an imagination of identification, without the constant counterbalance of the imagination of difference, can lead quite simply to a failure to connect to the difference. In the situation where the therapist is in the dominant cultural and racial position, this can lead to a pernicious closing-down of the space for recognizing or appreciating difference and otherness.

For all sorts of contextual reasons, I had difficulty in negotiating this territory with Donny and Lily. Some things I could have known I was not able to know, and there were huge gulfs in my capacity to understand. I relied on a fantasy of identification and familiarity with Lily, and lined myself up alongside her parenting role in the way that I constructed my invitation in the therapeutic relationship. The mutuality of our relationship allowed it to be good enough for her to step forward about some things that I was not allowing myself to appreciate—the effects on them all of the stolen generation, and the specific lived history of Donny's relationship to, and loss of, his mother.

But the fixedness of the form of my imagination of identification with Lily was no protection when it came to the intracultural taboo of acknowledging Donny's Chineseness, his non-Aboriginality, and the significance of his untalked-about father, the story of his conception, and perhaps even his mother's untalked-about father and the story of her conception. Here, my politics as a white Australian of not questioning that which is not easily talked about within Aboriginal culture collided with an intracultural taboo, and my inability to try to separate out and understand Lily's position from an imagination of difference and curiosity became a major problem.

As happens in family work, how I came to invite a relationship with Lily, and respond to her invitation to me, both affected and was affected by the imagination of myself in relation to Donny. In a reverse polarity, I lost touch with the power of an imagination of identification with Donny, which would have helped me use my own emotional repertoire to relate more easily to his feelings about his mother and unknown father. It was by no means beyond my emotional or professional capacity to tune into the possible meanings and communications of a young boy choosing a Chinese parasol to hold in his lap when he came to see me, a therapist, yet I stayed immovably incapable of thinking about this or of recognizing his visible Chineseness. The tendency for the therapist to split the polarities of imaginative identification and foreignness *between* people in the family, rather than achieving some balance of these imaginations for each member of the family, is a common-enough slide in family therapy.

In retrospect, it is easier to see my failure to be flexible and balanced in how I used the imagination of myself in relation to both Lily and Donny and how this closed down the possibility of trying to understand things that I should have been actively trying to understand. I would have liked, at the time, a source of reflection about the kind of imagination of identification and difference that was orientating me in my attempts to relate to and understand the lived experience of Lily and Donny. It would be omnipotent and just plain wrong to claim that these ideas would have bridged the chasm of my non-understanding as a white Australian. Yet, I do think that another form of reflection would have helped me in the way in which I was using myself and my imagination in trying to understand and relate to Lily's and Donny's experience. It would also have held me more accountable as a (white Australian) therapist.

Conclusion

I am not entirely sure how to conclude this paper. I should follow the tradition of summarizing the theory and practice themes that I have been laying out, using as a base for reflection a flawed and specific piece of interracial and intercultural therapy. I have held this practice against two sets of theory ideas: social constructionism and thinking about the limits on knowing, and the empathic imagination of self-in-relation-to-other in trying to understand and relate to sameness and difference.

There have been many discussions of the dynamics of universality and difference in intercultural relating, and of the challenge of relating to both universality and difference (Krause, 2009). The hope of (a universal) connection stands side-by-side attempts to honour what Frosh (2002) has termed the "incorrigibility of otherness". How this is negotiated in any therapeutic relationship is always specific to that relationship and its embeddedness in the realness of histories and present social contexts. I am inclined to think that the sheer pleasure of interracial and intercultural relating lies in part in the mutual dynamic of knowing and not knowing and understanding and not understanding. Yet, this struggle can be difficult as well as pleasurable. In interracial and intercultural contexts of work, we hope that the mutual attempts we and our clients make to relate through and across difference and sameness will hold the work of the therapy and that the therapeutic relationship will be "good enough". Yet, there can be no neat and easy conclusion about the conditional nature of what is and is not possible, which underlines the importance of nurturing ongoing dialogue and reflection.

I noted in the introduction that I felt "a kind of fraud" writing in this book. Do I feel any less of a fraud now that I have come to the end of the project of writing this chapter? I would have to say no. I find myself resisting the pull to say something more positive here, or maybe even to intone something virtuous about the challenge of intercultural work for therapists like me, whose histories have allowed fairly seamless internal representations of cultural and racial at-homeness. Of course, these representations of seamless at-homeness might be illusions: in my case, I do have to wonder, with grandparents from three far-flung countries, while I sit as a white person with the wrong coloured skin attached to a homeland that should not have come to be mine in the way that it did. Alternatively, these representations might speak to fragile truths, albeit marked by a disavowal of the extent of the social, political, and emotional fragility of someone like me feeling culturally and racially at home. One way or another, I suspect, in my specific context, that I might just have to wear feeling a kind of fraud.

And so, no matter the familiarity of the current multi-racial and multi-cultural context in which I live, there should perhaps always remain a question in my intercultural work that is enabled by my sense of fraud: well, what would I know (about another's) experience, and who am I to think I know? However, as real and useful as this question might be, I am inclined to think that the more important question in terms of my practice and politics is not "what would I know", but "what can I know?" What, in my particular context, with this particular family, are the limits and capacities of my knowing and understanding? And how can I stay alert to the power of my limits while nurturing my capacities to attempt to know and understand the interplay of difference and sameness in intercultural work, and, indeed, in all my psychotherapy work?

Note

1. The theory themes of this chapter overlap with discussions in Flaskas (2002) and Flaskas (2009b). I have also reflected on quite different aspects of this particular piece of practice in Flaskas (2002) and Flaskas (2007).

References

Anderson, H., & Goolishian, H. A. (1988). Human systems as linguistic systems: preliminary and evolving ideas about the implications for clinical theory. *Family Process*, 27: 371–393.

Anderson, H., & Goolishian, H. A. (1992). The client is the expert: a not-knowing approach to therapy. In: S. McNamee & K. Gergen (Eds.), *Therapy as Social Construction* (pp. 25–39). London: Sage.

Cecchin, G. (1987). Hypothesizing, circularity and neutrality revisited: an invitation to curiosity. *Family Process*, 26: 405–413.

Flaskas, C. (2002). *Family Therapy Beyond Modernism: Practice Challenges Theory*. Hove & New York: Brunner-Routledge.

Flaskas, C. (2007). The balance of hope and hopelessness. In: C. Flaskas, I. McCarthy, & J. Sheehan (Eds.), *Hope and Despair in Family Therapy: Adversity, Reconciliation and Forgiveness* (pp. 24–35). London: Routledge.

Flaskas, C. (2009a). Narrative, meaning-making, and the unconscious. In: C. Flaskas & D. Pocock (Eds.), *Systems and Psychoanalysis: Contemporary Integrations in Family Therapy* (pp. 3–20). London: Karnac.

Flaskas, C. (2009b). The therapist's imagination of self in relation to clients: beginning ideas on the flexibility of empathic imagination. *Australian and New Zealand Journal of Family Therapy*, 30: 147–159.

Frosh, S. (2002). *After Words: The Personal in Gender, Culture and Psychotherapy*. London: Palgrave.

Gergen, K. J. (1991). *The Saturated Self: Dilemmas of Identity in Contemporary Life*. New York: Basic Books.

Gergen, K. J. (1994). *Realities and Relationships: Soundings in Social Construction*. Cambridge, MA: Harvard University Press.

Gordon, C. (Ed.) (1980). *Power/Knowledge: Selected Interviews and Other Writings 1972–1977 by Michel Foucault*. New York: Pantheon.

Krause, I.-B. (2009). In the thick of culture: systemic and psychoanalytic ideas. In: C. Flaskas & D. Pocock (Eds.), *Systems and Psychoanalysis: Contemporary Integrations in Family Therapy* (pp. 167–184). London: Karnac.

Laird, J. (1998). Theorizing culture: narrative ideas and practice principles. In: M. McGoldrick (Ed.), *Revisioning Family Therapy: Race, Culture and Gender in Clinical Practice* (pp.20–36). New York: Guilford Press.

Lannamann, J. W. (1998). Social constructionism and materiality: the limits of indeterminancy in therapeutic settings. *Family Process, 37*: 393–419.

Larner, G. (1994). Para-modern family therapy: deconstructing postmodernism. *Australian and New Zealand Journal of Family Therapy, 15*: 11–16.

Larner, G. (2000). Towards a common ground in psychoanalysis and family therapy: on knowing not to know. *Journal of Family Therapy, 22*: 61–82.

López, J., & Potter, G. (Eds.) (2001). *After Postmodernism: An Introduction to Critical Realism*. London: Athlone.

Malik, R., & Krause, I.-B. (2005). Before and beyond words: embodiment and intercultural therapeutic relationships in family therapy. In: C. Flaskas, B. Mason, & A. Perlesz (Eds.), *The Space Between. Experience, Context and Process in the Therapeutic Relationship* (pp. 95–110). London: Karnac.

Mason, B. (1993). Towards positions of safe uncertainty. *Human Systems: The Journal of Systemic Consultation and Management, 4*: 189–200.

Minuchin, S. (1991). The seductions of constructivism. *Family Therapy Networker, 15*(5): 47–51.

Perry, R. (1993). Empathy – still at the heart of therapy: the interplay of context and empathy. *Australian and New Zealand Journal of Family Therapy, 14*: 63–74.

Pocock, D. (1995). Searching for a better story: harnessing modern and postmodern positions in family therapy. *Journal of Family Therapy, 17*: 149–174.

Pocock, D. (2009). Working with emotional systems: four new maps. In: C. Flaskas & D. Pocock (Eds.), *Systems and Psychoanalysis: Contemporary Integrations in Family Therapy* (pp. 93–110). London: Karnac.

Selvini Palazzoli, M., Boscolo, L., Cecchin, G., & Prata, G. (1980). Hypothesizing-circularity-neutrality. *Family Process*, 6: 3–9.
Speed, B. (1991). Reality exists OK? An argument against constructivism and social constructionism. *Journal of Family Therapy, 13*: 395–405.
White, M. (2002). *Narrative Practice and Exotic Lives: Resurrecting Diversity in Everyday Life*. Adelaide: Dulwich Centre Publications.

CHAPTER FOUR

Objectification, recognition, and the intersubjective continuum

David Pocock

I will begin with a poor question: what is culture? The idea that culture can be something (some "thing") without a reflexive concern for definition led, during the period of my family therapy training in the late 1980s, to "culture" becoming a corrective to ethnocentric assumptions of universality implicit in the theories of family structure and process that had proliferated in the preceding two decades. The predominant message to trainees was that cultural differences were to be respected, honouring culture being a good thing. Simultaneously, late 1980s UK family therapy was preoccupied with gender. However, here the message was strikingly different. Skewed gender roles were not to be respected but challenged, patriarchy being a bad thing. It is a testament to the feasibility of Foucault's (1975) notion of the disciplinary power of discourse that I do not recall the obvious question being framed by any of us trainees: given that most cultures could be judged to be patriarchal, and notions of equality imply a mostly Euro-American ethnocentricity, which message should predominate—do we honour and respect patriarchy or challenge it? Since the denigration of otherness (to consolidate a comfortingly superior togetherness) is also a feature of most dominant cultures, the same dilemma becomes even more acute for racism;

surely we should not honour that? With the linguistic turn in family therapy of the 1990s, one way of managing the discomfort of moral relativism that these issues raise was to allow in marginalized discourses—to give the other a voice. But, as Burr (1999) argues, this mostly sidesteps the issue; would we wish to further legitimize the voices of paedophiles and holocaust deniers, are these not also cultural groups?

This muddle of paradox and idealization derives from the "what is culture" question and how the answer has been implicitly constructed in the development of a family therapy discourse that was forced to catch up after an impoverished start. As Krause (2007a, 2009) shows, Bateson's ideas on culture (e.g., Bateson, 1958, 1972) did not find their way into early family therapy theorizing, which focused on mechanistic forms of cybernetics, much to Bateson's irritation (Harries-Jones, 1995). The omission was a 1980s discovery and had, therefore, to be added on to the existing body of family therapy teaching. This, I suggest, was undertaken in a spirit of regret and guilt at the previous neglect and devaluation and, accordingly, "culture" acquired a compensatory idealized gloss, a corrective script (Byng-Hall, 1995).

Around the same time, there were other late add-ons, including gender, race, class, and sexual orientation, which created the aforementioned potential for paradox. Listing race, gender, class, and sexuality at the same hierarchical level as culture gives rise to the equivalent confusion of logical types (Whitehead & Russell, 1927) as grouping parrots, rats, cows, and animals generally together. What part of gender, for example, is not culturally constructed? Furthermore, since "culture" was a corrective to the normative blind-spot of Euro-American theory builders (who were themselves assumed to be culturally homogeneous) then the term tended to become associated with equivalently large communities; the imported paradigm being the relatively isolated tribe historically studied by social and cultural anthropologists.

I will begin again with what I hope will be a better question: what is the most helpful way for systemic family therapy to define culture? This way of framing the question owes a good deal to Wittgenstein (1953), who understood the meaning of a word to be dependent on its usage within a language game. In other words, the meaning of "culture" depends on how we use it in practice. Since Wittgenstein's later philosophy was a key influence on social constructionism (Gergen, 1999; Shotter, 1993), it might be assumed that I will promote a fully constructionist and relativist view of these issues. However, as Collier (1999) indicates, language does not just create social perceptions which we come to take for granted (and forget this taking for granted and treat such perceptions as given and real); it is also about the external world. If language, for all its constitutive capacity, did not have this quality of *aboutness*, then humans would barely have survived one day, let alone managed a couple of hundred thousand years. When early humans were able to shout, "Many lions come this way, run for your lives!", a response "How, exactly, are you using the term 'run'?" would be somewhat perilous, reality literally having the capacity to give us a nasty bite if we do not accept that, in practice, words quite often adequately describe things once we agree on definition.[1] Words create social maps so that we can co-ordinate our being with others. But a map also stands and falls by its success in orientating the users to the territory. For these reasons, I identify with critical realism (Krause, 2007b; López & Potter, 2001; Pocock, 2008) rather than strong versions of social constructionism.

An intersubjective continuum

Culture might be better defined as no different from relationship other than in matters of scale. In the remainder of this chapter, I use "relationship" to signify a little intersubjective domain and "culture" to signify a bigger one. Although "culture" is still commonly used in reference to large communities (e.g., Sikh culture), I prefer Falicov's (1983) multi-contextual view in which the term is also applied to the intersubjective product of smaller groups, avoiding the misleading rubric "subculture". This position allows greater visibility to be given to the acculturating influences of, for example, the workplace, political affiliation, gang, religion, school, sport, and sexual reference group. These are not necessarily sub-divisions of a dominant culture, but are frequently multiple and competitive in their influence, especially given the contemporary conditions of globalization and postmodernity (Gergen, 1991; Lyotard, 1979).

Pakes and Roy-Chowdhury (2007) show, through discourse analysis of therapy sessions, how the reification of culture of the other can turn a fluid and complex set of issues into a monolithic entity, closing down the possibility of understanding. An encounter between two people might, instead, be cross-cultural in aspects of their ethnicity, intracultural in privileged aspects of their gender role and class, cross-cultural in their political affiliations, intracultural in their love of UK premiership football, and so on. In Falicov's (1998) words, each participant brings a subjectivity constructed within "rich cultural borderlands": most of us are cultural mutts. However, a useful default position is that all human encounters, even in apparently homogeneous communites, begin as—and to some extent always remain—cross-cultural: otherness may be bridged but never fully transcended (Frosh, 2009).

One aim of this chapter is to deconstruct the sense of strong categorical difference that the terms "relationship" and "culture" have acquired. In all other respects than size, I argue, they can be treated as synonyms: both involve the co-ordination of certain regularities between subjects that allow them to go on reasonably well together. Attachment is a strategy for safety and belonging; so is culture, by this definition. It is, therefore, quite meaningful to speak of all intersubjectivity, including early intersubjectivity, as cultural. Indeed, Bateson (1972) comes close to doing just this:

> I suggest that we should consider under the head of "culture contact" not only those cases in which contact occurs between two communities with different cultures . . . but also cases of contact within a single community. In these cases the contact is between differentiated groups of individuals, e.g., between the sexes, between old and young, between aristocracy and plebs, between clans etc. . . . I would even extend the idea of "contact" so widely as to include those processes whereby a child is moulded and trained to fit the culture into which he was born . . . [Bateson, 1972, p. 64]

Here, Bateson points to a complex multiplicity of cultural experiences; culture is placed at the heart of the matter from the start of life, and throughout, and the distinctions "intra-cultural", "cross-cultural", and "relational" all lose sway. With this in mind, I am drawn to the following sketch of the system of self,[2] relationship, and culture.

1. I conceive the concepts of relationship and culture flowing into each other in a continuum of intersubjectivity. From this position,

it would make sense both to describe a relationship between two persons as developing its own culture and to describe any culture of any size as the creation of the relationships between social members operating in a domain of mutual—although not necessarily symmetrical—influence. Similarly, a family, kinship group, or other social network could be equally well described as a set of relationships or as a culture.

2. There is a continuous dialectic between subjective and intersubjective domains in which the self both co-creates—and is changed through—intersubjective experiences on the relational–cultural continuum: such self experiences having simultaneously a here-and-now (synchronic) dimension and a developmental (diachronic) dimension. In shorthand it might be designated thus: subject ⇔ intersubjective. I would differentiate this dialectic from, for example, the drive theory of classical psychoanalysis, on the one hand, which downplays the intersubjective, and strong versions of social constructionism on the other hand (e.g., Rosenbaum & Dyckman, 2004), which downplay the idiosyncratic experiencing subject (Layton, 2008).

3. Self is constructed from multiple relational–cultural experiences. The self may be, in a single moment, a father, son, husband, brother, football player, friend, enemy, colleague, American TV-watching, British, Islamic, Conservative, Asian factory worker.

4. Relational–cultural experiences do not write themselves on to a passive blank-screen self (Rosenbaum & Dyckman, 2004), but are constructed and internalized idiosyncratically (Krause, 1995). However, idiosyncrasy also has its limits, since the self cannot stand outside relationship and culture.

5. Identity has both a relatively conservative aspect (I recognize myself as "I" when I awake each morning) and a relatively fluid aspect (I recognize that I am different in differing relational–cultural contexts).

6. The self has conscious and non-conscious dimensions; no one can ever give more than a partial account of his or her matrix of historical and contemporary relational–cultural influences.

7. The self is embodied and located in a material world, both aspects giving rise to needs, and anxieties that such needs will not be met. Embodiment, in the form of genetic endowment, and materiality place constraints on relational–cultural variation.

Feeling right: feeling wrong

In *Naven*, Bateson (1958) describes the important role that headhunting had, until recent times, played in the culture of the male Iatmul. On reading this, I found myself experiencing a sense of shock and revulsion, the origin of which was not immediately obvious. On reflection, it was not the headhunting itself that particularly bothered me; in truth, I found that rather exciting and exotic. The disturbance came from what I can only describe as my perception of a lack of fair play in the manner of the killing. Bateson records that it made no difference at all to the Iatmul men if the victims were killed in a fair fight or whether they were stabbed in the back. In Bateson's phrase, my emotional reaction arose from "news of a difference" (Bateson, 1979, p. 68). I had no idea that this feeling of wrongness about such matters lurked in me—it is stored out of conscious awareness. Even now I cannot fully map these internalized experiences which had been brought forth by coming up against that reported aspect of the male Iatmul culture,[3] but I think they are probably made up of an unconscious identification with my father's white colonial association of Englishness with fair play (unpleasantly tinged with a racist sense of superiority) reinforced by a childhood watching, and acting out with peers, war and "western" movies in which "cowardly" acts by various "baddies" legitimized their ultimate demise, providing some guilt-free excitement and re-establishing the moral order.

In turn, it is quite possible that an Iatmul man of that period would be no less shocked with aspects of my relational–cultural assumptions of what feels right—for example, the idea of intimacy between a father and his grown-up son.

> While I was on Sepik, a European father and son settled together on the Ceram River many miles away, where they started a small isolated tobacco plantation. The Iatmul heard of this and were surprised and shocked. They came to ask me if the two were really father and son and were disgusted when I told them it was so. They said, "Has the father no shame." [Bateson, 1958, p. 41]

A side effect of the neglect of Bateson's ideas on culture was the downplaying of emotion (Krause, 2009; Pocock, 2005, 2009, 2010a,b) which, for a family therapy culture bent on revolution, was perhaps too much associated with the psychiatric–psychoanalytic paradigm dominant in North America at that time. As we can see in the examples above, a response of rightness or wrongness ascribed to the behaviour of self or other is primarily an emotional one. As Krause (2007a, 2009) outlines, Bateson felt that he had misunderstood the meaning of the naven ritual until the moment when he grasped its emotional aspect: that the *wau* (actual or nominated maternal uncle) was a figure of fun. His enduring interest in the emotional emphases of a culture—what he called "ethos"—is revealed in an interesting anecdote (Bertrando, personal communication[4]). Selvini Palazzolli, the leader of the original Milan Group, wrote to Bateson, near the end of his life, giving written examples of the group's interventions and asking his view on whether they were systemic. He wrote back to say that he was unable to judge this from her letter, since the text alone could not provide him with the emotional tone. For Bateson, behaviour, structure, and belief are not understandable outside of the emotional context.

Through what processes do particular behaviours, beliefs, and emotions come to feel right or wrong? Fonagy and colleagues (Fonagy, Gergely, Jurist, & Target, 2004) show how the infant takes in not simply the experience of the relationship with the care-giver, but, more crucially, the infant's experience of *how he or she is experienced* in the mind of the care-giver. Emotional attunement by the care-giver gives rise to a capacity in the child (mentalization) to reflect on states of mind of self and others. But how the care-giver responds to a particular affect or behaviour in the infant will be contingent on the emotional acceptability of these displays to that care-giver (Krause, 2002) within the context of the care-giver's relational–cultural matrix. There is evidence of divergent encultured behaviour in babies as young as fourteen weeks emerging through brain–body co-ordination between care-giver and infant—well before the first uses of language at around ten months (Cowley, Moodley, & Fiori-Cowley, 2004). The infant develops a sense of what is emotionally acceptable and unacceptable to the care-giver, co-constructing the range of what feels right and what feels wrong. For Crittenden (2000, 2008), this gives rise to a range of attachment strategies which include the balancing, inhibition, or emphasizing of negative affect. Development brings new capacities: for example, the ability to falsify positive affect in order to fit in, to feel acceptable in the mind of the other.

Maturity also brings a wider intersubjective world of siblings, new kinship relationships, and peers. By the time of adolescence, and then throughout life, a multiplicity of intersubjective experiences become available and secondary identification (Meissner, 1970), in which an individual consciously and unconsciously identifies with the norms of various cultural groups, might increasingly play a role. Such processes, preconsciously or unconsciously embodied in implicit memory systems (Borofsky, 1994), become taken for granted guides to appropriate actions, thoughts, and feelings: the "habitus", using Bourdieu's (1977) term.

The therapeutic encounter

Malik and Krause (2005) give the following vignette from a family therapy session.

> The therapist, an African-American man, was meeting with a Muslim family from Rwanda consisting of a mother, her sister, and three daughters. There was also a team of therapists observing through the one-way screen. Before the session, the African-American therapist had greeted the Muslim Swahili-speaking interpreter in the waiting room in front of the family by shaking her hand in a friendly manner. The interpreter was clearly disconcerted but shook the therapist's hand in return. Several of the colleagues behind the screen reprimanded the therapist for this during the break, pointing out that this was against Muslim practice. You do not shake hands in a greeting and women certainly do not shake the hand of a strange, non-related man. The therapist conducted a sensitive and interested interview. [At] the end of the meeting the mother in the family, who was a thoroughly traditional woman, got up, walked over to the therapist, took his hand and shook it. Her daughters followed her example. [p. 99]

I will contrast this with a recent experience of my own. A white professional family from the North American mid-west was referred to me (white British) because the eldest teenage son appeared depressed. The family had moved recently to the UK because of father's work. The father telephoned me in advance of the session and asked me if he and his wife could meet me without the children, since he needed to talk to me about how I proposed to conduct the therapy. He seemed not to want to discuss this further on the telephone and I agreed to his suggestion, feeling somewhat apprehensive about what lay ahead. When we met, the father did most of the talking and carefully explained that "his" family were Baptists and that it was his responsibility to ensure they were not subject to any bad influences that would be contrary to their religion. Was I, he asked, a Christian? My reply—that I was brought up in the Baptist tradition, was no longer a person of religious faith, but tried to be understanding of the beliefs of those I worked with—did not satisfy him. He was willing to consider me referring them on to another family therapist who is a practising Catholic.

The therapeutic encounter depends on whether a feasible new transitional attachment can be made from the intermingling of relational–cultural subjectivities of family members and therapist. An essentialist and monolithic view of culture (Krause, 1995)—that culture dictates to the self—might predict more difficulties in forming a therapeutic alliance in the first case than the second, especially given the cross-cultural "error" of the African-American therapist in shaking the Muslim woman interpreter's hand. On the face of it, there were far greater overlaps in the subjectivities of therapist and family members in my case. My lapsed faith was clearly an important issue, but I am still unsure that this was the single crucial issue in the decision not to engage, especially in view of the apparent flexibility of the father in being willing to meet with a Catholic therapist.

I think the key to understanding the different outcome in the two vignettes is that the intersubjective therapeutic encounter takes place at both conscious and non-conscious levels. Notions of the unconscious and preconscious lie outside the cultural comfort zone of mainstream family therapy, but traditional models of psychoanalysis, which underplay the moment-to-moment influence of the analyst on the patient, also fall short of a fully systemic understanding of the therapeutic relationship. I prefer the language of interaction in the term "co-transference" (Orange, 1995), in which the therapeutic space is seen as organized by the interacting subjectivities of all participants, to the language of action and reaction inherent in the terms "transference" and "countertransference".

Even with the limitations of a textual account, I am moved by the description of the traditional Muslim mother initiating a handshake with the African-American therapist. Her willingness to move toward the other in both an emotional and bodily sense suggests to me that she in turn had felt, during the session, some movement towards her by the therapist, a generosity of understanding and recognition that had temporarily bridged the relational–cultural otherness. The therapist was, we learn, "sensitive and interested"; something happened beyond technique or other forms of correctness that allowed them to meet each other. Of course, this is speculative on my part.

I can shed a little more light on my meeting with the Baptist parents. I was relieved that the father took "his" family elsewhere. I had extricated myself from the Baptist Church in my late teens and have not overcome a low tolerance to its religious literalism and patriarchy. I did not like the father because, on reflection, I never really got to meet him. Instead. I projected on to him some of my earlier experiences of patriarchy, both religious and familial. The difficulty, I believe now, was not otherness, but a distorting sameness created by my projective identification. I saw something of me in him and he became an internal object that prevented recognition of him as an external subject (Benjamin, 1999; see also Frosh (2009) for a summary of Benjamin's position on recognition and a wider discussion on the challenges and limitations of knowing the other). In addition, I suspect the antipathy was mutual, that I was also an object to him: perhaps a personified devil capable of seducing his family from the true path.

I suggest it is this failure of mutual recognition in the second case that distinguishes it from the first. The African-American therapist seems to have moved beyond his unconscious assumptions of sameness or shared habitus (implicit in the automatic handshake offered to the Muslim interpreter) to find some recognition of the Muslim mother as a unique subject and fellow human, whereas the Baptist father and I seemed to remain as objects to each other, stuck in cross-projections of what we already assumed about the other in the co-transference, with no way forward.

My point here is that otherness is not the problem, but unacknowledged assumptions of sameness drawn from a lifetime of relational–cultural intersubjective experiences stored largely out of awareness. Treating others as objects rather than discovering them as subjects is not just a matter of wrongly assuming they are the same as us: objectification includes the assumption that *the other will fit our assumptions of their otherness* as in cultural stereotyping. As the traditional Muslim mother shows us in the first example, we have to be ready to be surprised, to stay open for news of a difference and, paradoxically, looking out for difference might allow the discovery that we sometimes have more in common across cultures than we think.

News of a difference can easily be misunderstood and the common therapeutic mantra "respect difference" can be a dubious guide. Racists perceive ("project" is more accurate) "racial" difference very readily, for example. What they do not receive is news on the unique subjectivity of the other, which includes a shared humanity. What is at stake is whether our existing conscious—and especially non-conscious—assumptions can be changed by new information. The point here is that the therapist needs to reflexively monitor her assumptions of other(s) *and* self, since both will need regular revision if the therapy is to be helpful.

As in my textual encounter with the male Iatmul, news of a difference can be striking, disturbing, and immediate, allowing the therapist to discover more about the self and, potentially, something new about the other. However, because assumptions of sameness and knowing are frequently non-conscious, such news can sometimes take a long time to arrive.

In individual therapy with Nina, a bright, engaging, Brazilian trainee solicitor who was depressed and convinced that she was failing in her career, we had struggled to understand how she had become convinced that she was deficient in mental capacity. It seemed to me that her investment in the belief that she had less "brain power" than her peers robbed her of motivation to work for her exams, in which she frequently under-performed. In turn, she interpreted her under-achievement within the same low-brain-power schema: her beliefs and behaviours formed a closed, self-reinforcing loop. Explorations of the potential origins of this led to a traumatic memory of failing some school exams as a nine-year-old. She had been told by her deeply disappointed parents that, because of this failure, she would not be allowed to accompany the family on holiday, but would have to stay with relatives to do summer school. Although this punitive sanction had later been lifted, her predominant memory was that of shame and the associated idea that she was not clever enough.

This adaptation to her parents' sanction seemed understandable to me in the light of an apparently insecure attachment to them both. She had been raised by her maternal grandmother for the first few years of her life and struggled to find her place in the family when returned to her parents at the age of five, around the time of the birth of the second child. It seemed to me that a more secure child would have felt entitled to be angry with the parents about this sanction, and that her self-blame and the specific assumption that there was something wrong with her brain were an adaptive unconscious avoidant strategy of turning the negative affect against herself in order to fit in (Crittenden, 2008; Pocock, 2010a,b). This way of thinking of these experiences felt right to Nina, but made no real difference to the strength of her self-blaming schema. Little progress seemed to be made on this key issue and the work began to feel stuck.

Only slowly, over many sessions, did news arrive of a more pervasive sense of shame in relation to the circumstances of her birth. She was illegitimate, a fact we knew but had not sufficiently understood emotionally, since initially it seemed to mean little to Nina and does not have strong emotional significance in my relational–cultural history. What took time to slowly and painfully emerge was a never spoken shame about this illegitimacy that needed to be understood in the context of the family's Catholicism, poverty, and an internalized self-denigration which was gendered and linked to her "dark" skin and "inferior" indigenous status.[5] The shame of educational failure, which I had assumed we had the measure of, seemed to be fed by this more corrosive subterranean shame from earlier unprocessed relational–cultural experiences.

The stuckness was caused by the apparent irrelevance of her illegitimacy being "in the bag". It had slipped there, unbeknown to either of us, through the seductive illusions of knowing and sameness. Nina had been temporarily colonized in the therapy by an account in which both of us had failed to recognize the importance of the emotional issues that gathered around the circumstances of her birth. (The extent to which echoes of European colonization of Brazil contextualized that process between us—a Brazilian patient and a European therapist—remains an open question.) I thought I had understood her, and she thought she had been understood, but we were both wrong; the narrative fitted too poorly with her unformulated experience (Flaskas, 2009) and the therapy stalled. The gradual realization of this error was much needed, allowing a revival of curiosity, a rebalancing of knowing with not-knowing, and, eventually, some recognition and progress.

Summary

To conclude, I will draw together the arguments in this chapter in a few key points.

- To protect against cultural essentialism and subsequent objectification of the other, it is helpful to deconstruct the category differences between "relationship", "sub-culture", and "culture". Instead, these are seen as fluid, overlapping areas on a continuum of intersubjective experiences, from small to large.
- Self is an idiosyncratic, dynamic, and complex internalization of these multiple relational–cultural experiences.
- Finding a place of belonging within a relational–cultural system is primarily a process of internalizing "rules" of emotional acceptability; such "rules" can then be taken for granted and lost to conscious awareness.
- Recognition of the other as a subject requires one's conscious and non-conscious assumptions to, at least partly, break down (the arrival of news of a difference). Without this, the other remains an object, a projection of the self. No alliance or collaboration is possible without some mutual recognition (each "feeling felt"); participants will simply talk past each other.
- It follows that a productive psychotherapy will require new discoveries of self and other to be made by all participants.

Notes

1. On the other hand, I doubt any systemic psychotherapists would take the phrase "this child has got oppositional defiant disorder" at face value. Such unexamined constructions can also have a nasty bite, and we need our postmodern tools to at least put the term into inverted commas, a good minimum starting point being, perhaps, "this child has got a diagnosis of 'oppositional defiant disorder'", a diagnosis being a very different thing to a disorder.
2. The terms "self" and "subject" are used as synonyms.
3. My emphasis here is on the difference between my self-narrative before reading Bateson's passage about the male Iatmul and afterwards. In other words, it was news about my hitherto hidden ethics of killing, and not news about an essential difference between Euro-American culture and

male Iatmul culture, waging total indiscriminate war on whole populations being, for example, a particular characteristic of the former (Hobsbawn, 1994) and not the latter.

4. Paolo Bertrando heard this from Luigi Boscolo, one of the original Milan Associates, who assured him that the anecdote was genuine. There does not seem to be a written account of this story, although Boscolo indicated to Bertrando that the original letter from Bateson might be still in the archives of the Milan Centre for Family Therapy. During a brief attempt to research the story, I also heard from Carlos Sluzki, who had been given a very similar account by Gianfranco Cecchin, another of the Milan Associates.

5. This, in turn, is likely to be linked to complex "race" and "ethnic" status hierarchies deriving from a history of Portugese colonization and intermarriage or sexual liaison between people of different backgrounds. At the time of the work, these were unfamiliar to me and did not form part of Nina's conscious narrative.

References

Bateson, G. (1958). *Naven: A Survey of the Problems Suggested by a Composite Picture of the Culture of a New Guinea Tribe Drawn from Three Points of View* (2nd edn). Stanford, CA: Stanford University Press.

Bateson, G. (1972). Culture contact and schizmogenesis In: G. Bateson, *Steps to an Ecology of Mind* (pp. 61–72). Balantine: New York.

Bateson, G. (1979). *Mind and Nature: A Necessary Unity*. New York: E. P. Dutton.

Benjamin, J. (1999). Recognition and destruction: an outline of intersubjectivity. In: S. Mitchell & L. Aron (Eds.), *Relational Psychoanalysis: The Emergence of a Tradition* (pp. 183–200). Hillsdale, NJ: Analytic Press.

Borofsky, R. (1994). On the knowledge and knowing of cultural activities. In: R. Borofsky (Ed.), *Assessing Cultural Anthropology* (pp. 331–347). New York: McGraw-Hill.

Bourdieu, P. (1977). *Outline of a Theory of Practice*. Cambridge: Cambridge University Press.

Burr, V. (1999). Overview: realism, relativism, social constructionism and discourse In: I. Parker (Ed.), *Social Constructionism, Discourse and Realism* (pp. 13–25). London: Sage.

Byng-Hall, J. (1995). *Rewriting Family Scripts: Improvisation and Systems Change*. London: Guilford Press.

Collier, A. (1999). Language, practice and realism. In: I. Parker (Ed.), *Social Constructionism, Discourse and Realism* (pp. 47–58). London: Sage.

Cowley, S., Moodley, S., & Fiori-Cowley, A. (2004). *Mind, Culture, and Activity*. New York: Lawrence Erlbaum.

Crittenden, P. (2000). A dynamic-maturational approach to continuity and change in pattern of attachment. In: P. Crittenden & A. Claussen (Eds.), *The Organisation of Attachment Relationships: Maturation, Culture and Context* (pp. 343–357). Cambridge: Cambridge University Press.

Crittenden, P. (2008). *Raising Parents: Attachment, Parenting and Child Safety*. Cullompton, Devon: Willan.

Falicov, C. (1983). *Cultural Perspectives in Family Therapy*. Rockville, MD: Aspen.

Falicov, C. (1998). From rigid borderlines to fertile borderlands: reconfiguring family therapy. *Journal of Marital and Family Therapy*, 24: 157–163.

Flaskas, C. (2009). Narrative, meaning-making, and the unconscious. In: C. Flaskas & D. Pocock (Eds.), *Systems and Psychoanalysis: Contemporary Integrations in Family Therapy* (pp. 3–20). London: Karnac.

Fonagy, P., Gergely, G., Jurist, E., & Target, M. (2004). *Affect Regulation, Mentalization, and the Development of the Self*. London: Karnac.

Foucault, M. (1975). *Discipline and Punish: The Birth of the Prison*, A. Sheridan (Trans.). London: Allen Lane.

Frosh, S. (2009). What does the other want? In: C. Flaskas & D. Pocock (Eds.), *Systems and Psychoanalysis: Contemporary Integrations in Family Therapy* (pp. 185–201). London: Karnac.

Gergen, K. (1991). *The Saturated Self: Dilemmas of Identity in Contemporary Life*. New York: Basic Books.

Gergen, K. (1999). *An Invitation to Social Constructionism*. London: Sage.

Harries-Jones, P. (1995). *A Recursive Vision. Ecological Understanding and Gregory Bateson*. Toronto: University of Toronto Press.

Hobsbawn, E. (1994). *Age of Extremes: The Short Twentieth Century, 1914–1991*. London: Abacus.

Krause, I.-B. (1995). Personhood, culture and family therapy. *Journal of Family Therapy*, 17: 363–382.

Krause, I.-B. (2002). *Culture and System in Family Therapy*. London: Karnac.

Krause, I.-B. (2007a). Reading *Naven*: towards the integration of culture in systemic psychotherapy. *Human Systems*, 18: 112–125.

Krause, I.-B. (2007b). Gregory Bateson in contemporary cross-cultural systemic psychotherapy. *Kybernetes*, 36: 915–925.

Krause, I.-B. (2009). In the thick of culture: systemic and psychoanalytic ideas. In: C. Flaskas & D. Pocock (Eds.), *Systems and Psychoanalysis: Contemporary Integrations in Family Therapy* (pp. 167–184). London: Karnac.

Layton, L. (2008). Relational thinking: from culture to couch and couch to culture. In: S. Clarke, H. Hahn, & P. Hoggett (Eds.), *Object Relations and Social Relations: The Implications of the Relational Turn in Psychoanalysis* (pp. 1–24). London: Karnac.

López, J., & Potter, G. (2001). After postmodernism: the new millennium. In: J. López & G. Potter (Eds.), *After Postmodernism: An Introduction to Critical Realism* (pp. 3–16). London: Athlone.

Lyotard, J.-F. (1979). *The Postmodern Condition: A Report on Knowledge*, G. Bennington & B. Massumi (Trans.). Manchester: Manchester University Press.

Malik, R., & Krause, I.-B. (2005). Before and beyond words: embodiment and intercultural therapeutic relationships in family therapy. In: C. Flaskas, B. Mason, & A. Perlesz (Eds.), *The Space Between: Experience, Context and Process in the Therapeutic Relationship* (pp. 95–110). London: Karnac.

Meissner, W. (1970). Notes on identification. I. Origins in Freud. *Psychoanalytic Quarterly*, 39: 563–589.

Orange, D. (1995). *Emotional Understanding: Studies in Psychoanalytic Epistemology*. New York: Guilford Press.

Pakes, K., & Roy-Chowdhury, S. (2007). Cultural sensitive therapy? Examining the practice of cross-cultural family therapy. *Journal of Family Therapy*, 29: 267–283.

Pocock, D. (2005). Systems of the heart: evoking the feeling self in family therapy. In: C. Flaskas, B. Mason, & A. Perlesz (Eds.), *The Space Between: Experience, Context and Process in the Therapeutic Relationship*. London: Karnac.

Pocock, D. (2008). Be dragons here? Why family systems therapy needs a new operating system. *Context*, 97: 20–23.

Pocock, D. (2009). Working with emotional systems: four new maps. In: C. Flaskas & D. Pocock (Eds.), *Systems and Psychoanalysis: Contemporary Integrations in Family Therapy* (pp. 93–109). London: Karnac.

Pocock, D. (2010a). Editorial: emotion as a systemic issue. *Context*, 107: 1–3.

Pocock, D. (2010b). Emotions as ecosystemic adaptations. *Journal of Family Therapy*, 32: 362–378.

Rosenbaum, R., & Dyckman, J. (2004). Integrating self and system: an empty intersection? *Family Process*, 34: 21–44.

Shotter, J. (1993). *Conversational Realities: Constructing Life through Language*. London: Sage.

Whitehead, A., & Russell, B. (1927). *Principia Mathematica, Volume 1* (2nd edn). Cambridge: Cambridge University Press.

Wittgenstein, L. (1953). *Philosophical Investigations*. Oxford: Blackwell.

PART II

EXPANDING REFLEXIVITY IN SYSTEMIC PSYCHOTHERAPY

CHAPTER FIVE

With an exile's eye: developing positions of cultural reflexivity (with a bit of help from feminism)

Gwyn Daniel

> "What seems to you
> so nimble and fine,
> like a fawn,
> and flees
> every which way,
> like a partridge,
> isn't happiness.
> Trust me:
> my happiness bears
> no relation to happiness"
>
> (Taha Muhammad Ali, 2006)

Cross-cultural work most starkly reminds therapists not to be too ready to attribute meaning to the utterances of others, a tendency which probably constitutes one of our profession's "occupational hazards". The tightrope we walk between connecting with the meaning systems of others and staying aware of the all the nuances that constitute difference is a never ending one. It involves making the imaginative leap into others' worlds to search for meaning and coherence, especially in what may seem strange and inaccessible (Krause, 2002b), as well as acknowledging that difference is inevitable, and requires respecting "the other *as other* with whom one has connections but whose inner space cannot be colonized" (Frosh, 2009, p. 189). The ability to communicate across difference involves risk taking and extending ourselves beyond our own cultural comfort zone; in fact, these very processes bring forth information about what *are* "taken-for-granted" comfort zones. Thus, we are required to be aware both of our current prejudices (Cecchin, Lane, & Ray, 1994) and to recognize constraints in our thinking that might be indicative of prejudices we have yet to recognize or articulate. This can be defined as being self-reflexive, but self-reflexivity in a context of cultural diversity does not seem to be an adequate concept. I prefer to think about cultural reflexivity.

I define cultural reflexivity in psychotherapy as an attention to the processes through which we negotiate cultural identities, through which we bring forth cultural meanings and the ways in which we engage with aspects of "otherness" and difference. For my own practice, as a therapist most readily identified with the majority (and more privileged) culture in Britain, it raises two questions. First, how do therapists from the dominant culture[1] engage with ideas about "otherness" in ways that show how, through seeing ourselves in the eyes of others, we locate aspects of our own "habitus" (Bourdieu, 1990) that might otherwise remain invisible? Second, in attempting to develop such processes of mutuality within cultural interactions, how do therapists monitor the operation of power practices and the ways that histories of oppression, racism, and marginalization have an impact upon the present, and are all too often enacted in the present?

How can we use these two requirements of cultural reflexivity in the service of openness, transparency, mutuality, and, indeed, intimacy in therapy? How can therapists who are sensitive to the ways that "othering" operates in the interests of dominant groups remain unafraid to engage openly and reflexively with their own cultural selves, values, and beliefs? The risk in cross-cultural encounters can be that of withholding aspects of self because differences are, in this society, that is, in "post-colonial", contemporary Britain, so readily constructed in hierarchical terms that there can be a fear that taking a clear position of beliefs and values is seen as being judgemental or insensitive. In this way, opportunities for encounters and robust dialogue between people constructing themselves as equals are so easily lost.

Much of this chapter will be devoted to "teasing out" aspects of this dilemma and, in doing so, I argue that, for systemic thinkers, there are important aspects of feminist theory that can provide points of connection. Evoking the interface with gender is important, first because gender and culture sit, often uneasily but always intertwined, on the borders of each other's domains and are occasionally evoked as competitive contexts from which to narrate experiences of inequality or oppression. Second, and more importantly, because the feminist project itself has lent so much richness to enhance thinking about and challenging "otherness" that it adds texture to the attempt to unpack the complexities of cultural identities and "othering" (Bhavnani & Phoenix, 1994; Krause, 2002a; Mama, 1995; Sampson, 1993).

"Othering" and being "othered"

In her chapter in the book *Representing the Other* (Wilkinson & Kitzinger, 1996), Rosalind Edwards writes about her experience as a white woman researcher wanting to interview black and white women about their experiences of being single mothers and her shock at the suspicion this engendered among black women. She writes of being

> jolted by the meeting of my own identity – Ros Edwards, approachable woman researcher who had been a mature student and a lone mother, and was "on their side" – with a racialised categorisation of an untrustworthy white institutional figure ... not resonant with my experiences and conception of self. [Edwards, 1996, p. 85]

It is this kind of process that calls forth contextual/cultural reflexivity, an experience of how we and our contexts are viewed from another vantage point and how privileging one aspect of identity (lone parent) can mean losing sight of how another (white woman) might be privileged by others. A lack of awareness of the wider political contexts which shape cross-cultural encounters, an insistence that benign intentions count for more than they do, an inability to reach into the complexities of institutional racism can, because of their subtlety, be as oppressive as some of the more obvious manifestations of racist practice. Those from minority cultures will be highly skilled at reading these nuances; those from the majority, much less so. How can majority therapists maintain a reflexive stance on their own cultural positions without disempowering themselves by becoming so cautious and tentative that opportunities for close engagement are lost? It seems to me that we can do so by being willing to learn from the conditions that those from the minority have long been accustomed to. This means reaching into our own experiences of "othering" and being "othered", by creating contexts where we receive feedback about blind spots and/or by actively seeking out opportunities to be in a cultural/racial minority, to feel disqualified by lack of understanding of cultural norms or by limited language use. To do so means "problematizing" exactly that which is the main source of privilege and domination, which is the way that, if the society in which you live reflects your ethnic and cultural norms, you might never learn the art of living life at different levels, of "double consciousness" (Du Bois, 1903; Gilroy, 1993). While the concept of "double consciousness", that is, of having to incorporate a view of yourself through the eyes of others, arose out of contexts of extreme racist oppression and stereotyping, I also think of it as a positive skill that emerged from adversity and one that enhances the ability to be culturally reflexive. While much has been written about how "othering" acts as a way for dominant groups to maintain a unifying sense of their own identity (MacKinnon, 1989; Sampson, 1993) the extent to which dominant groups have wanted to learn from this has been highly variable (Thomas, 2002).

Said, in *Orientalism* (1978), one of the founding texts of post-colonial studies, analysed the relationship between telling the history and mores of colonized subjects and establishing hierarchies of knowledge and power, laying bare the processes through which western colonialism depended for its own unitary identity on defining and categorizing a subjugated, exoticized, oriental "other". However, he also issues an invitation to reverse this process: for the dominant culture, too, to read itself against another's narrative. In later writing which explores experiences of exile, Said invites readers to "Regard experiences then as if they were about to disappear: what is it about them that anchors or roots them in reality? What would you save of them, what would you give up, what would you recover?" (Said, 1993, p. 407) "Liberation", he wrote, as an intellectual mission, born in the resistance and opposition to the confinements and ravages of imperialism, has now shifted from the settled, established and domesticated dynamics of culture to its unhoused, decentred and exilic energies, energies whose incarnation today is the migrant and whose consciousness is that of the intellectual and artist in exile, the political figure between domains, between forms, between homes and between languages. [1993, p. 403]

While Said is careful to say that he is not remotely suggesting that the consciously chosen theoretical position of the intellectual (or therapist) can be compared to the miseries of forced displacement, he is, nevertheless, pointing to a moral stance which is that of situating oneself among the *potentially* displaced.

Exile, far from being the fate of nearly forgotten unfortunates who are dispossessed and expatriated, becomes something closer to a norm, an experience of crossing boundaries and charting new territories in defiance of the classic canonic enclosures, however much its sadness should be acknowledged and registered. [1993, p. 384]

This, for me, means that, rather than focusing on the condition of marginalization or dispossession as somehow vested *within* those who are especially vulnerable, in which case it will be subtly "problematized", the state of never having to think of such vulnerability could, arguably, be viewed as more problematic. How majority therapists take on this position without making phoney or patronizing assumptions of equivalence is the theme of this chapter, and it goes to the heart of how we understand the politics of identity, to the relationship between self and other, and to the learning that can take place through all the different levels of engaging with the positions of others. This is where feminist thinking has a great deal to offer, as cultural theorists have reminded us (Hall, 1996; Mama, 1995).

Gender and culture

In exploring gender and culture, it seems to me there are two intersections. First, there is the interplay between what we might call "essentializing" and "constructionist" discourses. While "essentializing" is almost a term of abuse in postmodern/social constructionist scholarship, in practical terms we find ourselves drawing upon both of these discourses according to the contexts in which we are engaged. When we wish to deconstruct a theoretical perspective or therapeutic position as being gender or culture bound, we usually do so by highlighting the experiences that are not represented. We are then

> faced with the paradox that we cannot demonstrate what is missing without defining the 'something' that is left out: but in defining this, we run the risk of an alternative view of reality that may become equally limited, unitary and static. [Burck & Daniel, 1995, p. 27]

So, for example, feminist critiques of certain types of discourse evoking the idea of the "unitary rational subject" might involve highlighting "women's ways" of thinking and knowing (Belenky, Clinchy, Goldberger, & Tarule, 1986; Gilligan, 1982), or cultural assumptions about identity formation as a process of individuation or self-realization might be challenged by evoking an ethos of "collective identity" attributed to non-Western societies. All of these descriptors run the risk of reducing the complexity and dynamism of gendered and cultural identities to an alternative, but equally enclosed, space. However, there are still many contexts where we feel the need to evoke the "essentializing" concept of identity, bearing in mind Hall's (1996) invitation to use it as a term "under erasure". While we think of our identities as inescapably plural, we still have to decide on "the relative significance of the different affiliations which could vary depending on the context" (Sen, 2006, p. 29) and, even more importantly, we need to be aware of the identities ascribed to us by others.

Second, feminist theory has the capacity to deconstruct power and, by laying bare the operation of power practices, to amplify the voices of those who are "othered" and to reverse the gaze to those doing the "othering" (MacKinnon, 1989). Feminism, as Frosh (personal communication) has said, has provided an opportunity for men, too, to see themselves as "other", in other words to "problematize" masculinity and its constructs and constraints. Feminism has laid bare the taken-for-grantedness of patriarchy to expose it in all its gender partiality, as Spender (1980) argued in her analysis of how the English language can be seen to have encoded a "male" view. While these arguments run all the risks of over-simplifying and essentializing mentioned above, as a *process* it involved a liberating and often painful struggle that I, as a woman, could feel that I was on the "right side" of. I could talk happily about the stupidity and shallow thinking that emerges from positions of unquestioned gender privilege. As a white person, my struggle is to locate and question those taken for granted aspects of the way "my" world is reflected in mainstream discourse and to interrogate this. The reversing of the gaze makes "whiteness" and privilege objects of study (McIntosh, 1998) and takes apart all the "wes" and "theys" and "yous" that slip around in our discourses. Indeed, as I have already become aware in writing this chapter, how I, as a white British woman, use "we" creates interesting dilemmas. How do I talk about oppressive practices and take some collective responsibility for them (hence the "we") without entering into an exclusionary discourse? The problem with talking about "othering" is that we are so likely to repeat it in the very process of deconstructing it. Not so long ago, I was having a conversation with a black friend about the stereotyping of Muslims and we were both objecting to the government's glib use of the phrase "the Muslim community". "After all," I said, "we don't talk about the white community." "But we do," said my friend.

Feminism and "othering"

"Othering" is a form of discrimination when it categorizes certain groups as "other" (for example, highlighting ethnicity only in relation to minorities), when it either excludes them from "mainstream" thinking or responds to them as stereotypes or representatives of categories. However, rather than only thinking either of "othering" simply as a "bad thing" to be avoided or, alternatively, "the other" as a cause for celebration (Sampson, 1993), it is perhaps important to address the question of what can be learnt from analysing the experiences of being "othered", the purposes that it serves for dominant groups, and all the ways in which understanding these processes can enhance theory and practice in wider contexts. This has been at the heart of the feminist project over the past fifty years. From Simone de Beauvoir to Catherine MacKinnon, Judith Butler, Jessica Benjamin, and many others, the relationship of self and other has been explored both within intimate relational contexts and located within the practices, performances, and politics of gender and power.

Benjamin (1998, 2000), in challenging the way that psychoanalytic theory represents male–female relationships in terms that reflect patriarchal inequalities, has developed an intersubjective theory which emphasizes mutuality. She posits the relationship between self and other as the foundation of all our emotional and cognitive development.

> The tension between recognising the other and wanting the self to be absolute (omnipotence) is, to my mind, an internal conflict inherent in the psyche; it exists independent of any given interaction – even in the most favourable conditions. It is not interpersonally generated but is, rather, a psychic structure that conditions the interpersonal. The problem of whether or not we are able to recognise the other as outside, not the sum of our projections or the mere object of need and still feel recognised by her or him, is defining for intersubjectivity. [Benjamin, 2000, p. 294]

Other feminists have drawn upon Lacan's theories of early development. Segal describes the "mirror phase" in terms that resonate with ideas of double consciousness. She describes how infants gain a sense of self through their reflection in the mirror of their mother's gaze, but adds, "However, this is not the beginning of a 'true self' but of an inevitably constraining and alienating ego, a self-for-others, always 'referential to the other' and therefore distanced from the infant's inner drives and desires" (Segal, 1994, p. 131).

This suggests that there is inevitably a threat to the self from the relationship with the other. Yet, the particular form of relationship that is posited in intersubjective theory involves a "certain handling of the trope similarity/difference in which neither is collapsed into the other. Recognition staves off the absorption of self into the other, just as it prevents the other being colonized by the self" (Frosh, 2009, p. 188). Identities are, therefore, constructed through and not outside of difference and, crucially, we are always dependent on the representations of the "other" to define who we are.

Benjamin has developed her concept of recognition into the political domain—in the field of Israeli–Palestinian relations—where she emphasizes the ethical necessity of taking responsibility for the hurts inflicted on others (Benjamin, 2009).While theories which extrapolate outwards from the psychological to the social and political are always open to criticism, since, as in the above example, they can so often fail to properly address the impact of power imbalances, systemic theory is well adapted to teasing out the complexities of power in both intimate and political contexts. Both of these are reflected in the relationship between power and dependency: the extent to which our dependency on representations *of* others and on feedback *from* others to define who we are is overt or hidden. These representations are inevitably embedded within the cultural. Thus, in societal contexts of structured inequality, whether of class, of race, or of gender, the idea that we know ourselves through our relationship to others so often carries with it the corollary that the other's experience has to be delegitimized and silenced, since

> when these selves are dominant in a given society, they can construct the other so as to affirm a particular kind of self for themselves ... if I find myself in and through you but no longer control the you that grants me myself then I am forced to deal with a self that is beyond my control and I may not always enjoy this self with which I must now contend. [Sampson, 1993, p. 155]

The way that power is embedded within these processes is crucial, since, in hierarchical contexts, recognition of others is so often dependent on the "other" accepting those representations. MacKinnon explores this in relation to pornography and Benjamin, in her earlier work, explores the sexual politics of domination within contexts of sexual inequality and violence, contexts which serve to sustain the fantasy that women have to be controlled in order for men to maintain their rigid attachment to certain tropes of masculinity (Benjamin, 1990; MacKinnon, 1989). When women resist these formulations, they are likely to experience a violent response, which objectifies them and reflects a refusal to acknowledge the reciprocal nature of the relationship.

In a recent article on honour killing, Rose explores the complex and paradoxical nexus of extreme domination and equally extreme dependence within particular cultural contexts. "The honour killer is a stalker marking out his territory and policing a boundary between the sexes on which he cannot rely ... he has placed his masculinity in her hands. We could say he needs her too much" (Rose, 2009, p. 7). Here, she depicts gendered and cultural beliefs interacting at the extremes, but which offer illumination about processes whereby the greater the context of inequality, the greater can be the fear and denial of complementarity. She also places this within the context of displacement and exposure to rapid social change that influences both men and women and their differential access to power and privilege. This lays bare the social processes through which some groups come to be in a position to define and represent others and are, therefore, able to withhold recognition of the other by blocking feedback or by refusing to challenge categories of domination.

Awareness of how "othering" is used to confirm and reinforce the boundaries of dominant cultural norms raises the necessity to turn the gaze back on those with the power to perform "othering" in such oppressive ways. This becomes a question of ethics, as Levinas (1969) argues:

> A calling into question of the Same—which cannot occur within the egoistic spontaneity of the Same—is brought about by the Other. We name this calling into question of my spontaneity by the presence of the Other, ethics. [p. 33]

"Spontaneous" acts can be defined as those that appear not to need to be thought about because they stem from deep-seated and unquestioned assumptions about the world. These assumptions are most likely to be maintained when others are voiceless, when they are not physically present, or when they are not held in mind.

Identities and meeting places

The necessity to be aware of how processes of "othering" operate within contexts of inequality raises important questions for therapeutic practice. At the same time, they can carry the risk of calling up a rather static and polarized model of selves and identities. Recognition, as Butler (2004) reminds us, can go "over the edge into knowledge as mastery" (p. 215). That this is a particular risk in therapeutic contexts, since the "client" or family is always available to be understood as "other", reinforces the importance for systemic practitioners to keep thinking of the mutual influences that evolve between us and our clients, that evoke different views of selves and others, and that shift in meaning within different contexts. As Hall reminds us, identities involve questions of using the resources of history, language and culture in the process of becoming rather than being; not "who we are" or "where we came from" so much as what we might become, how we have been represented and how this bears on how we might want to represent ourselves. [Hall, 1996, p. 4]

He suggests looking at identity not so much in terms of a return to roots, but of a coming to terms with our "routes". Ideas about our identities, as shifting, as performative (Butler, 1990, 1997, 2004), but always contingent on the availability of representation, are neatly encapsulated in Hall's concept of identity as a point of "suture": a stitching together/a meeting point between those discourses and practices which attempt to interpellate and hail us into place as subjects of a particular discourse and of the processes which construct us as subjects. Identities are, thus, points of temporary attachment to the subject positions that discursive practices construct for all of us (Hall, 1996).

The idea of a meeting place has obvious resonances for therapy as a location where "questions about personhood are raised and negotiations about identities take place" (Burck & Daniel, 1995, p. 77). However, for systemic therapists, it is also a space where we reflect on the feedback we receive about ourselves as cultural/gendered beings, feedback that is not merely understood in terms of projections emanating from clients or families, but as providing therapists with the possibility to learn and to be changed. How we reflect on our positioning in the gaze of the "other" depends on how attuned we can allow ourselves to be to the feedback we receive, and this, in turn, depends on the kinds of experiences to which we are exposed. In the cultural domain, I argue that, for obvious reasons, minority therapists will have developed this finely tuned skill to a much greater degree of expertise than majority therapists. It is, after all, likely to be an experience replicated in many other areas of life. For majority therapists, it generally calls forth much more of a learning process.

In the gaze of others: two case examples

First example

I worked in individual therapy with Carla, a woman with a Black British mother and a Jamaican father. Our initial sessions were taken up with exploring family of origin issues, especially around her very contentious relationship with her mother and sister, which reached crisis point after her father died. Carla was incensed at how marginalized and demeaned she felt by her family. In our sessions, she would become angrier and angrier and her performance of rage sometimes made it hard for me to feel I was able to open up any space for reflection. While there were many things going on in the work, one effect of the way Carla passionately expressed herself was how I began to experience it as positioning me culturally. I felt shrivelled up, repressed, and increasingly limited in my freedom of expression. I felt myself, in Carla's eyes, to be staid, overly rational, middle class, and stereotypically "English". Over the course of my working with Carla, I made a visit to Italy, where I experience other aspects of myself more strongly, where, paradoxically, I *feel* my Welshness in a way that I struggle to feel in either England or Wales. During this period, Carla made a visit to her family in Jamaica, and on her return she described her enormous relief that there were so many people with a similar "style" to her, where she was able to challenge her idea that she was "loud", and how feedback about her "loudness" had acted as a constraint on her in Britain, which she resented and which further fuelled her anger. I never talked directly about my own experience, but I wondered whether accessing it helped me to be more appreciative of Carla's relationship to her identity and to how she experienced her identity differently in another country. Both of us, it emerged, had negative experiences of our cultural positions, were experiencing ourselves in cultural transition and the excitement of new reflections on selfhood.

Second example

I had been working with this couple—a Palestinian woman and a Welsh man—for several months. Much of the initial work had focused around gender constructions, with Nadia complaining about David's inability to show his feelings and David describing himself as "all reason" and Nadia as "all emotion". He considered reason to exist on a much higher moral sphere than emotion. Nadia both took up this stereotyping of her and defended herself in relation to it by commenting on how out of touch with his feelings David was. They were both gradually able to access more complex views of themselves, with Nadia commenting on how different she was in other contexts, such as at work, where she was well able to draw upon her instrumentality.

David, meanwhile, was able to talk about his sadness at his lack of closeness to their children and his struggle to think positively about himself as a father.

I asked in more depth about their experiences of growing up and the culture of their families of origin. Nadia spoke at length and very movingly about her Palestinian identity, describing the complex emotions of loss, of pride, and of shame. She now attributed her "emotionality" more to her cultural roots than to her gender. At one point, when she was speaking with great passion and lyricism about her family in Palestine and their dispersal, her experience of visiting them, and her profound sense of loss about the past, she said, "I know I'm going on a bit and I can't expect you two (me and her husband) to understand because you are English." I found myself saying, quite spontaneously, "Excuse me, but just who are you calling English?" While they both laughed at this, it led us to explore, in a more nuanced way, what it feels like to be categorized in ways that do not do justice to your own complex sense of yourself, as she did to him (and me) regarding culture and they did to each other in relation to gender. It also invited a new and more connected conversation about the meaning for David of being in a culture within Britain that is frequently stereotyped and how he had distanced himself from this aspect of his identity. At the same time, it was possible to recognize that neither David nor I had experienced the profound upheaval and loss that Nadia had: of land, of country, of way of life, and of language, that these were losses that were indeed worthy of strong emotions, but that she had also accessed the instrumental, rational side of her as she created a new life within Britain.

In both these examples, as the therapist, I experienced a perturbation in a sense of myself as a cultural being, occasioned by direct or indirect communications from clients. My experience was not "like", let alone "equivalent" to, theirs, but, on each occasion, highlighted some processes that seemed useful in teasing out the complexities of how we view ourselves through the eyes of others.

Mono-culturalism as "deficit":
learning cross-cultural competence

Thomas (2002) offers the following challenge to majority therapists:

It would appear to be the case that few majority white therapists would choose to explore issues around a falsely acquired superior identity . . . a great contribution can be made by minority therapies to the body of systemic and psychodynamic therapists. The very fact that they are minority therapies will make it difficult for majority therapists to feel able to learn from them. It would after all defy all logic that any other than majority-group therapists could contribute anything of worth. [p. 54]

This leads me to the question of how "majority" therapists can create contexts in which to learn. I find the idea of cross-cultural competence invaluable here. However, by cross-cultural competence, I am not referring only to therapists' abilities to learn about and work with clients/families from other cultures. This can create a limited and hierarchical position in cross-cultural work, which, whatever the intention, maintains those hierarchies. I am more interested in something that is surprisingly under-discussed in psychotherapy, which is all there is to be learnt from those who have developed themselves in contexts of hybridity, who locate their identities across geographical, linguistic, and cultural spaces, who take a position of "Culture's in-between" (Bhabha, 1996). What learning has taken place in these contexts that is unavailable to those who remain rooted in unitary experiences of place, cultural context, or language? Pakaslahti, the Finnish psychiatrist, director of the film *Kusum*, whose upbringing was multi-lingual and cross-cultural, describes how, in his life and work, he hears "a polyphony of voices in space and time" (Pakaslahti, 2006). This Bakhtinian metaphor resonates with Said's musical metaphor of living life "contrapuntally" (Said, 1999).

We might regard those who do not have cross-cultural experiences, who have not lived in other countries, learnt other languages, lived with or loved a person from a different culture, as deprived or lacking in some way rather than, however benignly and subtly, "problematizing" those who have. Just as a form of stupidity can envelop those who have the power to isolate themselves from the feedback of others (think of the decision making during the Bush administration), so there is a loss involved in never facing the challenge of having to observe and adapt to (or reject) the culture and mores of a majority. So, without romanticizing, it seems important not only to celebrate the skills and ingenuity involved in cross-cultural living (Mama, 1995), but, more importantly, to learn from them. While none of us is responsible for the narrowness of our childhoods, we all have a responsibility to develop our own "polyphony", to embed cross-cultural thinking into our everyday lives, rather than regard it as a position we adopt when we see families who are "different". Cross-cultural competence incorporates all those experiences of living life at different levels, but, in my opinion, is rarely presented in the systemic psychotherapy literature as a skill that has been learnt and that can be learnt from diverse acts of living.

Language

Anyone brought up with English as a first language already has a built-in advantage in that they are less likely to need to learn other languages to survive. (In the UK, in 60% of state schools, fewer than half the pupils take a foreign language at the age of fourteen.) Uncontested language dominance brings a particular responsibility to think about unearned privilege in all contexts (Borstnar, Mocnik-Bucar, Rus-Makovec, Burck, & Daniel, 2005). However, while many commentators bemoan the lack of foreign language teaching in schools, the focus is rarely on the numbers of British children who actually are already bilingual. Among the advantages of speaking several languages discussed by Burck (2005) is the way that it creates a sense of contingency, an awareness of the different constructions of self that emerge through language use. Burck draws upon Ricoeur's connection between awareness of the cultural genres that are taken up and the telling of one's life story to suggest that this enables individuals to take up an ironic position, conscious enough of the discursive cultural order to make transgression, critique, and change possible.

Unlike other members of my family, I did not grow up bi-lingually and have needed to call up experiences to help me think about the complexities of positioning in relation to language use. Three have been helpful. First, as a child growing up in the English home counties, but visiting my Welsh-speaking extended family every summer, I became aware of a sense of exclusion and distance, of something lacking in me and my siblings that was hinted at but never actually articulated. Second, living in Israel for a year when our two-year-old daughter was learning to speak bi-lingually in English and Hebrew, I became aware of how my own very limited Hebrew language skills constructed certain kinds of interactions with her Israeli friends which fell far short of those I wanted to have with them. (For example, if I had to say "no" to a request, I could rarely explain my reasons why!) Third, last year, for the very first time, I gave a professional presentation in another language. My struggle with inarticulateness, clumsiness, and constraint, coupled with the generosity of my colleagues, led me to reflect yet again on how much those who speak a dominant language take this for granted, and how rarely we celebrate the skills of bi-lingualism. Living with different, and, at times, contradictory, language perspectives means living with a sense that there never was one singular truth, and Burck's research subjects vividly describe their radical doubts about what Rorty (1989) calls the "final vocabulary" (Burck, 2005).

While it is, of course, impossible to provide hard evidence that living bi- or multi-lingually, or in contexts of cultural hybridity, is better for our mental health, our ability to be self-reflexive, or for our intellectual development, some studies do show that growing up bi-lingually has positive effects on children's cognitive skills as well as their creativity and social attunement (Burck, 2005). Another study finds that, for immigrants, a flexible, slow, and hybrid acculturation seems to be better for mental health than either rigid adherence to, or rapid shedding of, the original culture and language (Escobar, 1998, quoted in Falicov, 2003, p. 384). It is a fair proposition that attending to the dimension of positive skills and outcomes creates a valuable way of thinking for therapists working in a multi-cultural society.

Contextual reflexivity

Opportunities for learning are created in every encounter with those who use our services and from their unique perspectives on us as therapists and the organizations in which we work. Systemic therapists have been particularly sophisticated in addressing therapy as an encounter between different belief systems rather than privileging those of the therapist. While it is always good practice to address this at the beginning of therapy, it also remains an ongoing dynamic as therapy progresses, and can perhaps be usefully described as a way of thinking in which therapists should think of themselves as constantly under scrutiny and of needing to be accountable. Privileging the therapeutic relationship (Flaskas & Perlesz, 1996) can sometimes be at the expense of a focus on the wider societal and cultural contexts within which it is embedded and those from which clients will scrutinize therapists.

Third example

I met with a mental health professional, referred for private therapy by a colleague. At the initial session, I did what I usually do, which was to ask if he had any questions to ask me about my approach. He said that he did because, as a gay man who knew I worked at the Tavistock Clinic, he was troubled by the attitudes to homosexuality among psychoanalysts, which he found discriminatory. He wanted to know what my position was in relation to this. My first reaction was shock that he could think that I, whose personal views were so different, could possibly be associated with an approach to therapy which I also considered to have been homophobic. My second reaction was to disassociate myself from these views and to say only what my own position was. However, I then thought that I had to take responsibility for belonging to an institution which had this history and which, in my opinion, continues to have a problematic stance in relation to sexuality. That meant that in my response I was also careful to position myself critically within the institution rather than dismissively as if outside it. I later reflected that my immediate (unvoiced) responses were of a similar order of stupidity to the white policeman who declared after the publication of the McPherson report, "I am not an institutional racist."

Fourth example

A therapist in my supervision group was working with a Black British woman who had moved to this country from Africa and now lived with her three sons, two of them teenagers aged fifteen and seventeen, while the third was aged six. The mother had had a period of illness and depression during which she had relied hugely on the two older boys, and she felt very anxious about the effect this had had on them, as her ex-husband had failed to give the family any support at this difficult time. Now that she was stronger, she came to therapy to give her sons the chance to talk about what it had been like for them. She worried about how they had coped with the outside world when she was not available to support them and, having experienced racism herself, was afraid that they would not have been able to talk to her about these experiences. She had been in therapy herself and had found it very helpful. The therapist was also Black British, and her family was from a different African country. I supervised the work as part of a training group, sometimes from behind the screen, sometimes in the room.

In an early session, the therapist and the mother were talking about the older two boys and their experiences, and they both seemed to agree on how important it was for the boys to be able to talk about their feelings. Sitting in the room, I became aware of how detached the young men were from this discourse and that the therapist was really struggling to engage them. I was also mindful of my powerful position, both as supervisor and as the only white person in the room. I remembered a description the older boy had given of himself as "the strong and silent type". Deciding to offer some reflections, I said to the sons that I was aware that having the triple disadvantages of being older, female, and white, I could hardly claim to speak on behalf of young black males, but I wondered what they made of the conversation that was going on between their mother and the therapist. What did the idea of their "needing" to talk mean to them? If strength and silence went together, could it imply that they were seen as weak? They must have been incredibly strong and resourceful to keep things together when their mother was ill. Perhaps their mother wanted to give something back, but they were not sure how it would affect them. Could they feel that their mother thought they could not handle difficulties in the outside world? Could experiences of racism be one of the hardest things to talk to their mother about because they knew what a struggle she had had?

In a later session, when the two young men had laid claim to the therapeutic space and each had met with the therapist individually, they told her and their mother about some very distressing experiences of racism which they both felt they had handled well and which they tended to minimize more than their mother did. In a reflecting team discussion, the white members of the team spoke about our own shame, as white people, in witnessing the young men's account of their experience, and reflected both on the mother's pain that this continued to afflict the next generation and on the young men's pride at how they had responded.

In this work, naming differences—race, gender, age and experience, and deciding as white members of the team to position ourselves as we could be seen in the gaze of the family, as representatives of a racist society—seemed to enhance a sense for all of us, including the therapist in her relationship both to the family and to the team, of collaborating across difference without attempting to collapse it.

Conclusion

The need to hold on to difference within communication is emphasized by Bakhtin (1981, 1986) when he writes that the possibility to see the world through the other's eyes "is a necessary part of the process of understanding . . . but if this were the only aspect of this understanding, it would merely be duplication and would not entail anything new or enriching", thus "only outsiderness creates the possibility for an enriching dialogue" (Bakhtin, 1986, p. 7). In all therapy, cross-cultural or otherwise, the therapist makes moment-by-moment judgements about how much of our inner conversation (Rober, 2005) we reveal and in what ways we should do this. However, what often can get lost in therapists' reflections on cultural difference is the degree to which the gaze of others has the potential to expose a lack—indeed, one could say the very lack that "othering" is designed to conceal. Feminism has challenged the illusion of the autonomous (male) subject that is buttressed by the process of depicting women as vulnerable. This serves both to protect the male by concealing his dependency and to perpetuate her "vulnerability" so that she remains easy to dominate. Men who engage with this analysis are likely to reflect in many more nuanced ways about how they perform vulnerability, dependency, and connectedness, as well as, of course, privilege. I have argued that it is also incumbent on those of us from a culturally dominant group to think about what similar processes we might be engaged in and what we can learn from them. For example, to what extent, by failing to question the implications of language and cultural dominance, do we conceal our own lack of ability to manage multiple cultural and linguistic identities?

Intersubjectivity as a psychological theory and dialogism as a philosophical position both stress the importance of interactions as meeting grounds between those who have the capacity to influence each other. What I have aimed to highlight in this chapter is how majority therapists can develop a way of thinking in which they can show that they are being influenced by the client/family in this dialogic process quite as much as the other way round. This involves paying attention to how we are viewed by others, and how others' views of us organize the way we speak and act in the therapeutic relationship, but also create perturbations for us from which we can learn. This way of thinking is likely already to have been developed to a far more sophisticated degree by minority than majority therapists, and this is where thinking about cultural diversity and hybridity have been both challenging, productive, and exciting for majority therapists. As the Arabic poet Samie Ma'ari said, "Identities are highly complex, tension filled, contradictory and inconsistent entities. Only the one who claims to have a simple, definitive, clear-cut identity can be said to have an identity problem" (quoted in Gergen, 1991, p. 155).

Note

1. When I use the terms "dominant culture" or "majority therapists", I am doing so in the British context only. It is helpful, as Ani (1994) and Afuape (2011) discuss, to call European cultures the "Minority World" to emphasize their minority position globally.

References

Afuape, T. (2011). *Power, Resistance and Liberation in Therapy with Survivors of Trauma: To Have Our Hearts Broken*. London: Routledge.

Ani, M. (1994). *Yurugu: An African-Centered Critique of European Cultural Thought and Behaviour*. Trenton, NJ: Africa World Press.

Bakhtin, M. (1981). *The Dialogical Imagination*. Austin, TX: University of Texas Press.

Bakhtin, M. (1986). *Speech Genres and Other Late Essays*. Austin, TX: University of Texas Press.

Belenky, M. F., Clinchy, B. M., Goldberger, N. R., & Tarule, J. M. (1986). *Women's Ways of Knowing. The Development of Self, Voice and Mind.* New York: Basic Books.
Benjamin, J. (1990). *The Bonds of Love. Psychoanalysis, Feminism and the Problem of Domination.* London: Virago.
Benjamin, J. (1998). *The Shadow of the Other. Intersubjectivity and Gender in Psychoanalysis.* New York: Routledge.
Benjamin, J. (2000). Response to commentaries by Mitchell and by Butler. *Studies in Gender and Sexuality,* 1: 291–308.
Benjamin, J. (2009). Commentary at Psycho-Political Resistance in Israel/Palestine Conference, Birkbeck University.
Bhabha, H. K. (1996). Culture's in-between. In: S. Hall & P. du Gay (Eds.), *Questions of Cultural Identity* (pp. 53–60). London: Sage.
Bhavnani, K., & Phoenix, A. (1994). *Shifting Identities Shifting Racisms. A Feminism and Psychology Reader.* London: Sage.
Borstnar, J., Mocnik-Bucar, M., Rus-Makovec, M., Burck, C., & Daniel, G. (2005). Co-constructing a cross-cultural course: resisting and replicating colonising practices. *Family Process,* 44: 121–131.
Bourdieu, P. (1990). *The Logic of Practice.* Cambridge: Polity Press.
Burck, C. (2005). *Multi-Lingual Living.* Basingstoke: Palgrave Macmillan.
Burck, C., & Daniel, G. (1995). *Gender and Family Therapy.* London: Karnac.
Butler, J. (1990). *Gender Trouble, Feminism and the Subversion of Identity.* New York: Routledge.
Butler, J. (1997). *Excitable Speech: A Politics of the Performative.* New York & London: Routledge.
Butler, J. (2004). *Undoing Gender.* New York: Routledge.
Cecchin, G., Lane, G., & Ray, W. A. (1994). *The Cybernetics of Prejudices in the Practice of Psychotherapy.* London: Karnac.
Du Bois, W. E. B. (1903). *The Souls of Black Folk.* Chicago, IL: Chicago University Press.
Edwards, R. (1996). White woman researcher–black women subjects. In: S. Wilkinson & C. Kitzinger (Eds.), *Representing the Other* (pp. 83–88). London: Sage.
Escobar, J. (1998). Immigration and mental health. Why are immigrants better off? *Archives of General Psychiatry,* 55: 781–782.
Falicov, C. (2003). Culture, society and gender in depression. *Journal of Family Therapy,* 25(4): 371–387.
Flaskas, C., & Perlesz, A. (1996). *The Therapeutic Relationship in Systemic Therapy.* London: Karnac.

Frosh, S. (2009). What does the other want? In: C. Flaskas & D. Pocock (Eds.), *Systems and Psychoanalysis* (pp. 185–202). London: Karnac.

Gergen, K. (1991). *The Saturated Self*. New York: Basic Books.

Gilligan, C. (1982). *In a Different Voice; Psychological Theory and Womens' Development*. Cambridge, MA: Harvard University Press.

Gilroy, P. (1993). *The Black Atlantic: Modernity and Double Consciousness*. Cambridge, MA: Harvard University Press.

Hall, S. (1996). Who needs identity? In: S. Hall & P. Du Gay (Eds.), *Questions of Cultural Identity* (pp. 1–18). London: Sage.

Krause, I.-B. (2002a). *Culture and System in Family Therapy*. London: Karnac.

Krause, I.-B. (2002b). Uncertainty, risk-taking and ethics in therapy. In: B. Mason & A. Sawyerr (Eds.), *Exploring the Unsaid* (pp. 34–48). London: Karnac.

Levinas, E. (1969). *Totality and Infinity*. Pittsburg, PA: Duquesne University Press.

MacKinnon, C. (1989). *Toward a Feminist Theory of the State*. Cambridge, MA: Harvard University Press.

Mama, A. (1995). *Beyond the Masks. Race, Gender and Subjectivity*. London: Routledge.

McIntosh, P. (1998). White privilege: unpacking the invisible knapsack. In: M. McGoldrick (Ed.), *Re-Visioning Family Therapy* (pp. 147–152). New York: Guilford Press.

Muhammad Ali, T. (2006). Warning. In: P. Cole, G. Levin, & Y. Hijazi (Trans.), *So What: New and Selected Poems* (p. 7). Port Townsend, WA: Copper Canyon Press.

Pakaslahti, A. (2006). Bio-sketch on website of World Psychiatric Association Transcultural Psychiatry Section. www.wpa-tps.org/Pakaslahti-A.htm

Rober, P. (2005). The therapist's self in dialogical family therapy: some ideas about not-knowing and the therapist's inner conversation. *Family Process*, 44: 477–495.

Rorty, R. (1989). *Contingency, Irony and Solidarity*. Cambridge: Cambridge University Press.

Rose, J. (2009). A piece of white silk. *London Review of Books*, 31(21): 5–8.

Said, E. (1978). *Orientalism*. London: Vintage.

Said, E. (1993). *Culture and Imperialism*. London: Vintage.

Said, E. (1999). *Out of Place: A Memoir*. London: Granta Books.

Sampson, E. (1993). *Celebrating the Other*. London: Harvester Wheatsheaf.

Segal, L. (1994). *Straight Sex: The Politics of Desire*. London: Virago.

Sen, A. (2006). *Identity and Violence*. New York: Norton.
Spender, D. (1980). *Man Made Language*. New York: Routledge & Kegan Paul.
Thomas, L. (2002). Ethnic sameness and difference in family and systemic therapy. In: B. Mason & A.Sawyerr (Eds.), *Exploring the Unsaid* (pp. 49–68). London: Karnac.
Wilkinson, S., & Kitzinger, C. (1996). *Representing the Other*. London: Sage.

CHAPTER SIX

Cultural and family ethos in systemic therapy

Paolo Bertrando

> "The aspects of things that are most important for us are hidden because of their simplicity and familiarity. (One is unable to notice something—because it is always before one's eyes.) The real foundations of his enquiry do not strike a man at all. Unless that fact has at some time struck him.—And this means: we fail to be struck by what, once seen, is most striking and most powerful"
>
> (Wittgenstein, 1953, p. 29)

In this chapter, I will outline the evolution of my own practice in the light of my experience with other cultures, both in supervision of cases around the world, and in my everyday work—however limited—with minority or ethnic groups. Such experiences have made me slightly suspicious of my own attitude toward "simple" or "taken-for-granted" cases—cases where I think I know everything about clients because I have the (erroneous) feeling they are "just like me". In order to deal with this phenomenon, we have to reflect on the nature of families, on the one hand, and of culture, on the other.

Families and therapies: a co-evolution

Families, first of all. The idea of a crisis of the family has been quite commonplace in Western professional literature for a long time (Coontz, 1992). The fact is, though, that forty years after David Cooper (1971) had prophesized "the death of the family", the family is still prominent in all societies, albeit in different forms. The very notion of "family" has changed today: it is probably better to speak of "families" rather than "family" (Fruggeri, 1997). The families I see in my everyday practice are more and more manifold, less and less constrained by one norm. Multiplicity has become commonplace, and the most important sources of family multiplicity are ethnicity and culture (Walsh, 2003). All this implies that today it is more frequent for me—as for any other therapist—to deal with complex families, where ethnic and cultural, as well as other, factors play a significant role. This creates difficulties, but is not impossible to deal with for a systemic therapist. I will give a small example.

It happened in Perth, Western Australia. Among other things, I was there for a live demonstration of a systemic family interview, a task which usually does not create excessive problems. On the morning of the interview, while she was giving me minor details so as not to begin the interview too blindly, the colleague in charge of the case added, almost casually, "Oh, and besides, it's an Aboriginal family." I felt a moment of bewilderment. What did I know about Australian Aboriginals? Probably just those few notions that any traveller in Australia can extract from accidental readings and travel guides, nothing more. For a moment, I wondered whether, from the vantage point of my own ignorance, I could draw something meaningful from this consultation. Then I decided to take a risk and go on anyway.

I will not give too many details here. Suffice to say that I conducted my interview more or less as usual, observing and listening to family members as I do with all my patients. I was slightly more wary and cautious, more keen-eyed in watching their reactions. Apparently, no member of the family resented me, and the discussion about the case, with the presenter and the training group, helped something new emerge. Discussing with the group, I learnt I had missed most of the cultural and political subtleties. Then again, perhaps the very fact that my viewpoint was an alien one had some use. After all, the family had already been seen by colleagues well versed in Aboriginal meanings;

if some difficulties remained, maybe they were also due to their metaphorical lenses, which hindered the emergence of other views. (Anyway, the family remained in therapy; so my ignorance was not harmful and what I was able to trigger was later elaborated in a more cross-cultural and safer context.)

One interesting fact remains: it was not necessary for me to become a cultural mediator, although some basic general knowledge of cultural difference would not have been harmful to the process. My usefulness as a therapist probably lay in my being "other" to that family's culture. Otherness, of course, is the very condition for therapy. But I had the distinct feeling that my "increased otherness" in this case had prevented me from seeing the family as a stereotypical case of an "Aboriginal family": I was so ignorant about that subject that I was not even able to create a proper stereotype. How often, however, do we use stereotypes when we see patients whose background we take for granted? And to what extent was my feeling of uneasiness and wariness during the interview the fuel for the consultation to develop?

I think this is true of the very essence of the therapeutic enterprise: it is our otherness in itself—to an extent, at least—that makes us therapeutic. This is the idea or assumption I would like to explore in this chapter. I will use the vantage point of emotions, because I think that emotional communication is the most immediate and least intentional and meditated, and this implies that emotional misunderstandings are the most difficult to process. In addition, emotions have very interesting and relevant cultural implications.

Ethos: emotion and culture

In Western thinking, emotions tend to have very definite features. First, they are considered as pertaining to the individual; second, they are considered as something essential, unchangeable in nature. Recent biological, neurological, and evolutionary research tends to consolidate such assumptions (Panksepp, 1998). Of course, I cannot argue with the findings of such an impressive body of research; however, I want to point out that what biological research classifies as "emotion" does not necessarily coincide with what we consider an "emotion" in everyday language, and both of them, in turn, are different from what therapeutic culture calls "emotion".

We can date the modern study of emotion back to Darwin's (1872) classical study. Darwin believed that emotions were not exclusive to humans, and were shared with animals: his book is full of examples, which testify his intense sympathy toward the animal world (Ekman, 1998). The idea that the range of emotions available to humans is limited and universal is today justified by neurophysiologic interpretations of emotion: if emotions originate from cerebral circuits, and if in this respect our brains are basically the same, there cannot be any cultural variation, and the effect of psychotherapy would lie in a rewiring of brain structures, rather than in the creation of new meaning (LeDoux, 1996).

Actually, relying on the early work by Bateson and Mead (1942), as well as on Birdwhistell's (1970) work on kinesics, the first systemic thinkers took for granted that emotions were culture bound. Such a belief was shaken by Ekman's studies (Ekman, Sorenson, & Friesen, 1969), which demonstrated that the recognition of emotional expression appears to be universal, both in literate and pre-literate cultures.

According to Ekman (1998), Bateson questioned the Darwinian idea of the expression of emotions, because he considered emotions as forms of communication rather than expression (in his view, communication was alternative to expression). Ekman, instead, considers emotions as signals of internal states that have proved useful through evolution—an idea close to the theories of evolutionary psychology (Cosmides & Tooby, 2000). In contrast, the communicational peculiarity of emotions is the emission of unintentional communicative signals, which, as such, are different from most human (intentional) communication.

Later systemic authors, the ones who actually influenced systemic therapies, like Watzlawick, Jackson, and Beavin (1967), eluded this problem through their concept of the black box, putting aside the very concept of intentionality. As Krause (1993) has pointed out, the emphasis on behaviour, and on an observation of systems "from the outside"—von Foerster's (1982) "observed system"—led them to consider emotions as universal motivating forces, thus putting culture out of the field.

As far as the universality of emotions is concerned, the more general dispute is between authors who tend to pay attention to primary or basic emotions (the customary list comprises joy, surprise, fear, anger, disgust, and sadness, although different authors tend to build slightly different lists (Ekman, 1992; Plutchik, 1980), and authors who consider the more complex world of secondary and even tertiary ("social") emotions, such as jealousy, embarrassment, shame, and so on (Parrott, 2001). Such emotions can also be considered as basic emotions put into context.[1] Possibly, even this dispute depends on the tendency to use the same word to define very different entities.

However, even a passionate advocate of the universality of emotional expression, such as Paul Ekman, recognizes that emotions are "embedded in a context; they may be elicited by different stimuli, be operated upon by different display rules, be blended by other affects, and be followed by different behavioural consequences" (Ekman, 1998, p. 386). Even if there is a biologic programming of emotions, it is an open programme, where programmed emotions might be deeply moulded and modified by environmental influences: "To have shown that there are universals in facial expression of emotions does not mean that expressions are universal in every regard . . . There are a number of ways in which cultures do differ in their emotional expression" (Ekman, 1998, pp. 391–392).

Ekman (1972) and his collaborators conducted an important experiment. By showing either videotaped travelogue or stressful film (accidents, surgical operations), they tried to establish how American and Japanese subjects reacted to these events, either when alone or in the presence of an observer dressed in a white coat:

> A very high correlation was found between the particular facial movements shown by the American and Japanese students *when they were alone*. Virtually the same repertoire of facial movements occurred at the same points during the film. But when there was another person present the Japanese and Americans, as predicted, showed entirely different facial expression. The Japanese showed more smiling than the Americans to mask their negative emotional expression. [Ekman, 1998, p. 385]

This was due to the fact that, in Japanese culture, it is judged as improper to show negative emotions in the presence of an authority figure (see also Ekman, 1973). Here, we can again see the twofold meaning of emotion: a basic level, probably untouched by cultural difference, and a second level, where expression and its decoding is modulated by culture.

There are several examples of the same process in the work of ethnographers and anthropologists. Levy (1973) observed that the Tahitians had no word or concept for what we call "sadness". When something happened that we could call "a sad occurrence", for example, being abandoned by a lover, the Tahitians acted in what for us would be a sad way—loss of appetite, inactivity and a sad expression—but they explained this as a kind of physical sickness, rather than relating their experience to the abandonment.

Briggs (1970), in her study of an Eskimo (Utku) family, discovered that the very idea of expressing anger was socially condemned (she actually experienced ostracism after she had showed ill temper toward one of her Utku hosts):

> Expressions of ill temper toward human beings (as distinct from dogs) are never considered justified in anyone over the age of three or four; and even when one expresses hostility toward dogs one must define it as a disciplinary action. [Briggs, 1970, p. 328]

The Utku neither denied the possibility of being angry, or even deeply hostile, nor failed to recognize an angry attitude when they see it. But they did not accept the free expression of anger: their entire value system was against it.

In her experience on the atoll of Ifaluk, Lutz (1988) discovered that one emotion, *ker* (roughly translatable as something similar to our "happiness"), is considered immoral. Of course, she was stunned at learning this, not only because she had learnt something she had not anticipated about Ifaluk people, but also because she felt challenged in her "implicit American ethnotheory of the person and emotion" (p. 44), that is, the assumption that pursuit of happiness is a socially desirable (and even commended) goal. Understanding emotional words in full means to be able to envisage a very complex set of performances, with multiple levels of meaning and action. As Geertz (2000) states, one of the most promising dimensions of cultural psychology is the study of emotional keywords among cultures. It shows that emotions described through different words acquire different semantic halos, as if those emotions actually were discrete "life forms" (Wittgenstein, 1953).

We can find traces of this very multiplicity if we look at the evolution of our own Western culture, rather than at the differences between cultures. For example, the sense of the word "apathy", the "absence of passion" advocated by ancient Stoics (Gross, 2006). For the Stoics (and for Descartes), apathy was a desirable condition, and humans were supposed to struggle in order to get to it. For Thomas Hobbes, a political activist, passions were necessary for civil life, therefore apathy should be proscribed. For present-day psychologists (Oatley, 2004), apathy is a signal of depression, sometimes even of psychosis, therefore of pathology: our times prescribe the free expression of emotions.

In short:

> If we accept that emotions are simple psychophysiological states univocally linked to facial expressions, working on the intercultural aspects of emotions is simple (this is what actually Ekman did).
>
> If, however, emotion is seen as woven in complex ways into cultural meaning systems and social interaction, and if emotion is used to talk about what is culturally defined and experienced as "intensely meaningful", then the problem becomes one of translating between two different cultural views and enactments of what is good and proper. [Lutz, 1988, p. 8]

Individual emotion, then, can be considered as standardized—to an extent, at least—by culture, as Mead (1935) and Benedict (1934) envisaged many years ago. Bateson referred to such a process as the "ethos" of a culture, "which we may define as the expression of a *culturally standardised system of organisation of the instincts and emotions of the individuals*" (Bateson, 1958[1935], p. 118, original italics).

Bateson arrived at the notion of ethos during his own fieldwork on the naven ritual developed by the Iatmul people of the Sepik river in New Guinea. He observed that his understanding of the rituals he saw was incomplete if he did not take into account, on the one hand, the emotional state of the Iatmul while performing the ritual, and, on the other, his own emotional reactions to it (Krause, 2007). He soon discovered to what extent his description was (unavoidably) biased. And his biases were the stronger the more his own emotions were involved, because it was harder for him to detach himself from his own emotions.

A more thorough understanding could only come from some experience of conflicting ethos. Bateson himself, though, was, from the beginning, aware of the slippery state of his very concept of ethos. "Ethos" is a category we create to give sense to what we see, rather than a fact existing in objective reality: "People can be influenced by emotions, but 'ethos' is itself not an explanation, it is a class of explanations adopted by the scientist" (Krause, 2007, p. 118).

Now, any therapist finds herself facing the very same difficulty Bateson had to face with the Iatmul people in New Guinea: she observes emotional states in her patients, and experiences emotional states in herself. If she imagines that she immediately understands the meaning of such emotional exchanges, she is taking for granted that she and her patients are sharing exactly the same ethos, an assumption that is questionable even if they actually share the same cultural background, and that is completely wrong if they do not, as we will see in the clinical case that follows.

A clinical example: Emily and her mother[2]

A school psychologist requested a family session for Emily, a fifteen-year old girl from the Philippines. Emily was an only child, who had immigrated to Italy when she was twelve. Her school marks were good, but she was isolated from her classmates and generally found socializing difficult. This was the therapist's first session with Emily, although she had already attended another family session, conducted by another therapist with an ethnopsychoanalytical approach.[3] The family had refused further sessions.

The family was invited to the first encounter, together with the school psychologist and a Filipino female cultural mediator. The father was absent, apparently for work reasons. At the beginning of the session, the mother spoke, while Emily was silent, looking at the floor, and answering all questions in monosyllables.

Mother's talk was clear and bitter. Emily had been disrespectful to both parents in the preceding session, mother had felt ashamed, and she did not want any more of this. She also did not want other people in the community to "talk behind their backs". Therefore, she and her husband refused to participate in the therapy. Having made this clear, the mother left for work, and Emily, alone in the room with the psychologists and the mediator, finally began to talk about herself.

Mother had come to Italy, alone, when Emily was four. Emily had lived with her maternal grandparents in the Philippines, while her father lived in another home. The family was reunited in 2006, when Emily and her father joined her mother in Italy. Initially, the mother had seemed very close and affectionate to Emily, but she soon became indifferent: the parents seemed interested only in themselves, and barely talked to Emily. This was in contrast to home, where Emily had a good relationship with her maternal aunt, in whose home she felt listened to and understood. This, in turn, made her mother angry and she accused Emily of being even more intractable when she came home after a visit to this aunt.

The sexual relationship between her parents was another problem for Emily: the three members of the family shared the same bedroom and the parents made love when they thought she was asleep, without perceiving the signals she sent to communicate she was awake. When she had tried to tell her mother something about this, her mother had slapped her, telling her it was none of her business.

The therapist felt that Emily was putting her to a test, postponing meetings, sometimes on the very day of the appointment. She accepted her motives, but, at the same time, refused to change the hour within the same day, instead postponing to another day. After this negotiation, possibly feeling accepted by the therapist's firm affection, Emily participated in weekly sessions.

Emily's mother responded to another invitation to the family by coming alone, and repeating that her daughter showed her no respect. "She gets back at me, walks noisily, bangs doors, she is angry." Most of all, Emily refused to use the linguistic formula which, in Tagalog,[4] indicates respect towards adults. The mother cried when she remembered that, when she briefly went back to the Philippines after seven years, Emily, who on the phone had seemed affectionate, was distant and angry with her. Only at the airport, when the mother was leaving, Emily had desperately clung to her, to the point of tearing her trousers. Amid tears, the mother remembered that she said, "It's too late now, you had forty-five days, but now it's late." "I tried to be patient with Emily when she came to Italy," she said, "I tried in any way to communicate, but to no avail. Emily does not speak to me, does not answer when I ask why she is so angry, and asks me to buy her anything she wants, without any concern for money. She is sweeter only when, in the evenings, we sit on the couch to talk, but when I want to go to bed, because I work and I get tired, she tries to make me stay." Emily seemed jealous of the parents' relationship, and the mother felt divided between husband and daughter. She was also sad because Emily said that her grandmother was her real mother, and that she wanted to go back to the Philippines. She wondered whether she really had not given Emily enough.

After a few days—to the therapist's utmost surprise—the mother called to cancel the next meeting and also asked to terminate Emily's individual therapy because Emily had not shown any improvement. The therapist was able to keep the individual therapy going, but with a growing sense of unease, because Emily tended to refer to the mediator rather than to her, answering in Tagalog without looking at the therapist, even when she was able to answer in Italian. Moreover, when the therapist wanted to give an emotionally charged message to Emily, the mediator translated only the content, without conveying either the emphasis or the intonation.

The therapist's attempt to solve this problem by asking the mediator—now perceived as an obstacle to her relationship with Emily—to stay outside the session for a while brought no result; the themes remained the same, with Emily now wanting to contact the social services in order to leave her own family and move in with her aunt. Finally, after the latest session, Emily again called the mediator because her father had kicked her and hurt her, after she had screamed at him. The therapist felt stuck in an impasse, and asked for supervision.

The supervision focused on the following themes:

1. Emily and her parents hardly appeared to listen to each other. Emily desperately wanted to be listened to but refused to use the traditional respectful linguistic formula that she used with the mediator with her mother, thus closing communication rather than opening it.
2. In the therapist's perception, Emily did not take responsibility for what she was doing and saying. She appeared self-centred, and unable to accept other persons' points of view.
3. The most important considerations, though, regarded the therapeutic process. The referral to the ethnopsychoanalytical therapy had apparently overestimated the similarity between this family and other families from the Philippines encountered before by

the same team (a sort of intercultural prejudice: the similarity among Filipino families are more relevant than their differences). In this specific case, mother, especially, experienced deep shame in the face of other members of the community, most of them strangers, which reinforced her unbearable sense of being surrounded by witnesses to her own inadequacy. Shame put her on a spot even in her Filipino community, enhancing rather than reducing her sense of isolation.

4. Father had refused therapy from the beginning. Possibly, his attitude might also reflect the refusal of an Italian woman psychologist who put the family's choices into question. Mother had apparently accepted the therapeutic setting, but in the end she never participated properly in the process. All in all, the parents were not available to participate in therapy and any attempt to involve them was pointless and possibly harmful to Emily's therapy.

5. It was mandatory to clarify the triadic relationship between Emily, the therapist, and the mediator. Since Emily needed and looked for the mediator's presence, it was impossible for the therapist to get rid of her. At the same time, to work together with the mediator, the therapist had to find a new cohesion and a common direction, possibly by making the difficulties created by nonverbal aspects of translation explicit. (There was also the possibility that the relationship between the therapist and the mediator mirrored the one between mother and aunt, as the solution proposed by the therapist paralleled the one chosen by the mother, exclusion rather than integration and co-operation.)

6. All in all, the therapeutic work could become more profitable by focusing on the here and now of each session, especially on emotional interaction between Emily and the therapist, rather than on the repetitive account of what happened outside. Also, the therapist could be more open in stating her opinions, even if they were totally different from Emily's. By doing so, she could confront Emily's dichotomy, feeling either unconditionally accepted or unconditionally refused.

Shortly after the supervision, Emily again called the mediator, crying and saying she wanted to run away from home. The therapist called her back, and made an appointment for that very afternoon. At the same time, the mother called the therapist too, extremely worried and crying. She said that she did not want to send Emily back to the Philippines, but she was desperate about changing the state of affairs. In the session, Emily was aggrieved and furious: nobody ever talked about the kicks, as if they had never happened. Emily now wanted to go back home, tell her parents "everything", and go and live with her beloved aunt. The therapist focused on the idea of "telling everything", which for Emily apparently meant to pour out her accusations and anger on her parents. By focusing on Emily's emotion, she tried to presentify the parents' reactions,[5] and to imagine a way of talking to them, taking their feelings and responses into account. Emily began to reflect on the possibility of saying "something" rather than "everything", and to look at her parents' reactions before continuing. What could it be like for Emily to communicate her feelings and, at the same time, observe her parents' emotions towards her?

After the session, the therapist called the mother at home, to let her know about Emily's fears about going back home. In the two final sessions, Emily explained that that very day she had clarified her feelings and reciprocal expectations with her mother, generating relevant changes. Emily began using the formal respect her mother demanded and also to be more obedient. The parents bought a sofa bed in order to sleep in the living room, leaving the only bedroom to Emily. She also felt that her mother was kinder to her, scolding her less, and for her birthday she bought her a new mobile phone.

This brief therapeutic snapshot about Emily and her family shed some light on working with cultural differences (while, at the same time, putting into question the meaning of "cultural differences"). First of all, the role of shame both in East Asian culture and in the case of Emily's family had been underestimated. One can wonder whether the ethnopsychoanalytical methodology, created to deal mainly with the needs of African families (Nathan & Stengers, 1995) can work as well with families from East Asia. Although Benedict's (1946) idea that Japanese culture specifically, and East Asian culture in general, is based on shame rather than guilt has been criticized for its categorical stance (Doe, 1973), the fact that shame plays a key role in those cultures is widely accepted (You, 1997). Moreover, shame was important in Emily's family and especially for her mother.

The therapist tried initially not to fall into the trap of cultural prejudices. But, in doing so, she tried to suppress difference rather than enter into dialogue with it. This is exemplified by her attempt to remove the cultural mediator from the sessions. In retrospect, she attributed this to her emotional distress within the sessions, which she had tried to "cure" by treating Emily as if she were an Italian adolescent—an attempt made possible by Emily's own assimilation in the host culture, which, however, could not be complete. Thus, the mediator became a key figure, a Filipino woman who was the bridge between Emily and her culture of origin (she was the one toward whom Emily showed the deference mother wanted). Her removal probably made Emily think that the therapist did not care about the importance to her of this woman, who also had been involved well before the therapist herself.

Besides such critical points, the therapy had, quite suddenly, a very positive effect. Possibly, one of the main therapeutic factors lay in the very availability of the therapist to listen to anybody: in this case, Emily and her mother, but taking into account also relevant third parties (Bertrando, 2002) such as the father, the aunt, the grandparents, the Filipino community, and, finally, the mediator. The therapist's active listening, and her attempts to promote further listening might have provided a different interactional model from the one that appeared to be prevalent in the family, which was demanding attention without being open to listening to the others. The possibility of focusing on the other, while expressing her own feelings, seemed to bring a positive feeling to the clarification between mother and daughter.

Something relevant had happened in the relationship between mother and therapist. The latter had to force herself to listen to the mother's complaints, suspending judgement about their content and their cultural consistency. The therapist could choose a relativistic position (her demands are legitimized by her culture) or an ethnocentric position (her demands are too rigid for an adolescent daughter in the Italian context). Both positions would have been simplistic, in the face of such a complex reality. Actually, the culture that mother advocated was not the only possible version of Filipino culture (the mediator emphasized that other Filipino parents had very different positions toward their children). Probably the mother, who had emigrated many years before, was still faithful to a cultural standard that in the present-day Philippines had changed. Emily had grown up in a live culture that had changed in time, whereas her mother had crystallized it in her memory. But the suspended judgement that the therapist had been able to develop had allowed her to become a relevant figure for both mother and daughter, thus paving the way for the development of family relationships.

In this, the supervision had a role, especially in helping the therapist to feel her own emotions and make sense of them (Bertrando & Arcelloni, 2009). This, in turn, gave her a different awareness of her relationship with the mediator, and of the link between expressing oneself and listening to others.

Ethos and the therapist's inner dialogue

All this brings our attention to the prejudices. Prejudices are manifold and include all kinds of ideas, emotions, knowledge, and so on, which therapists and patients bring into the therapeutic encounter (Cecchin, Lane, & Ray, 1994). Among them there is a category with a privileged status: premises.[6] "Premises", as Luigi Boscolo told me more than once, "are like the soles of your feet: you can't see them, because you are standing on them." If we accept the Batesonian notion that our premises organize our world vision, this implies that we are so embedded in them that we fail to see them, as the quote from Wittgenstein in the opening to this chapter suggests, albeit from a different position. Of course, our premises are deeply embedded in our cultural identity (Bateson created the concept while reflecting on how to understand aspects of Iatmul culture). Similarly, doing systemic therapy means being able to guess our patients' premises, without losing sight of our own, and, one hopes, to help our patients to change aspects of theirs.

Premises are linked to our own cultural identity, too. To what extent, though, is any "cultural identity" specific or pure? The cultural heritage of each of us is mixed and complex. I am part of a culture for sure—but, exactly, of which one: Italian, European, intellectual, medical, psychiatric, systemic culture? As a systemic therapist, I share part of my culture with psychiatrists, and I am partly alien to them, and vice versa. I claim my Italian identity with other Europeans, in some instances, but I claim my European identity with other Italians. The issue of culture becomes complex as soon as we acknowledge that we participate in several cultures at the same time, and we cannot explain ourselves to ourselves (not to mention others) simply in terms of one culture. And what is true of ourselves is, of course, true of others, too. Any distinction of the kind "us/them" presupposes a clear, univocal definition of who are "we" and who are "they", which, however, is slippery: we are Italians, Europeans, Western people, a football team's supporters, and so on. So, our individual (and family) identity is the variable sum of several different group (cultural) identities. To have just one identity can be considered as pathological, as it were, to be only a mental patient or only a psychiatrist.

Besides, the very word "culture" can be a trap because no culture can be seen as a consistent whole. Such a fictitious cultural unity has been a problem for anthropology itself (see, for example, Carrier (1995) and his critique of the very concept of "Western culture" as a consistent whole). It can be a problem for therapy, too, because, as we know, patients coming from the same "culture" can be as different from each other as members of a distant culture. As an Italian colleague who had lived and worked in Chile for twenty years told me, "The most relevant migration in my life was my migration from Southern to Northern Italy when I was fifteen. Compared to that, moving to Chile as an adult was nothing!"

To some extent, we manufacture our cultural identity, and, in doing so, we manufacture the others' cultural identities as well. In positioning theory terms (Harré & Moghaddan, 2003), we position the other as alien, and the other is induced, in turn, to position us as aliens. To an extent, cultural differences (or, at least, the degrees of cultural difference) originate from a deliberate choice. This is true in therapy, anyway, where reciprocal emotional positioning is a complex process that involves the entire selves of both therapists and patients (Bertrando, 2009).

Probably, when families coming to therapy were comparatively culturally homogeneous, it was possible for the therapist to take culture for granted, understanding them against the background of a grid of some implicit normative sociology, like Talcott Parsons' functionalism (Parsons & Bales, 1956) advocated by Minuchin (1974). Along the same lines, Jay Haley could salute in Milton Erickson a therapist who "was very American in his views. . . . He had a basic understanding of growing up in the United States that clarified for him the stages of family life and the processes of normal living" (Haley, 1982). This can be one of the reasons why emotions were undervalued in systemic therapy for most of its history (Krause, 1993). Today, though, such social homogeneity is rapidly disappearing, due to the nature of the postmodern world (Gergen, 1991), coupled with the growing multicultural environment we live in. Normative solutions to the dilemmas of family living are no longer available. Actually, if one looks for them in one's tradition (as Emily's mother did) or in the surrounding social standards (as Emily did), one is likely to fail. If we see families from a cultural as well as an emotional standpoint, we can say that any family develops—to some extent, at least—its own, idiosyncratic ethos. Such an ethos will be conditioned by cultural tradition, social status, affective relationships, degree of formal culture, and so on, but it will not be fully determined by any of those. And I, as a therapist, have some possibility of intervening in it with a degree of success only if I accept a substantial absence of guide in dealing with it. I will have to discover it through a preliminary acceptance of my own (emotional) ignorance: what I have, in the encounter, are the emotions I can observe or infer, and my own reaction to them. I cannot properly know the client's ethos, and I am partially blind to my own, too.

We should remember that—as any anthropologist working in the field can testify—our culture is as important as the culture of the other. Since therapy is a kind of fieldwork where we bring our emotional biases together with other biases, we should take this relativism into account in our practice. Therapists' and patients' emotions are a part of any specific therapeutic interaction, and are modified and moulded during the course of it, in the very act of communicating them (Planalp, 1999). If we feel wary of our own emotions, we (at least) diminish the risk of taking them for granted, and consequently automatically considering some patients' emotions as "wrong" or "inappropriate" or "pathological". Or, better still, we might consider them inappropriate or pathological, but immediately we might ask ourselves how this is happening, what is the process through which we decide about that inappropriateness or pathology. Ideally, patients, too, might begin to wonder about their own emotions.

This can, incidentally, be one of the reasons why psychotherapy can be effective. The therapist is important if she can be experienced as another person, radically different from her client. Through this position of otherness, she can be useful. Empathy in itself is not enough, as Bakhtin (1923) clarified a long time ago:

I must empathize or project myself into this other human being, see his world axiologically from within him as he sees this world; I must put myself in his place . . . But in any event my projection of myself into him must be followed by a *return* into myself, a return to my own place outside the suffering person, for only from this place can the material deceived from my projecting myself into the other be rendered meaningful ethically, cognitively. If this return into myself did not actually take place, the pathological phenomenon of experiencing another's suffering or one's own would result—an infection with another's suffering, and nothing more. [Bakhtin, 1923, pp. 25–26]

In the tradition of systemic and family therapy, empathy has been somewhat taken for granted, since emotions were considered as cultural universals (Krause, 1993). If we do not share this view, then empathy should be constructed from scratch every time: the therapist should be suspicious toward her own prejudices (Bertrando, 2007)—and prejudices about emotions are the hardest to suspect, because of the immediacy of our own feelings.

It is essential to my functioning as a therapist to be *other* to my patients. But how can I guarantee my otherness, if I share with them most of my premises? If I follow this pathway, I reverse the common sense ("I can understand my patients only if I share their premises, feelings, values . . .") into its opposite ("I can be useful to my patients only if I don't share their premises, etc."). I must, rather, try to discover them and, paradoxically, this is easier if I come from a different culture. What I need in this process is a sufficient degree of curiosity, openness, awareness of (some of) my prejudices and, of course, some awareness of their prejudicial nature. And, most of all, a willingness to go on with such a quest.

Elsewhere, I have compared psychotherapies at large (and systemic therapy specifically) to what Foucault (1988) defined as technologies of the self (Bertrando, 2007). It is easy to see in therapy a technology of the self for patients, but we should remember that this is true for therapists, too. A cultural awareness of my emotions could have such an effect on my own "self" through inner dialogue.

According to Rober, inner conversation (the term he favours over "inner dialogue") is "a negotiation between the self of the therapist and his role. In this process of negotiation, the therapist has to take seriously, not only his observations, but also what is evoked in him by these observations" (Rober, 1999, p. 209). In my experience, this implies: I talk to somebody, or do something with somebody, and I am immersed, embedded in dialogue. At the same time, though, I (another "I", another version of my being "I") am observing myself doing this, asking why and how I am doing this, sometimes even disagreeing with myself (that first "I"). In a sense, I am working at the same time in experience and description of experience. This is very similar, again, to an anthropologist in the field, constantly comparing her own feelings to what she observes in her informants, and drawing from the comparison some aspects which help her to go on. From such a standpoint, systemic psychotherapy can be considered as a technology of the self that generates or facilitates the emergence of a more open, more flexible self. In a way, the therapist should become, like Borges's (1952) Shakespeare, "equal to all men"—and, of course, women.

An anthropological stance for systemic therapy

Let me give another Australian example, from the opposite side of the continent, in Sydney. A colleague working in a free clinic brought a Japanese client, the wife of a manager transferred from Tokyo to Sydney, who had asked for some support, for consultation. "The problem is," said the therapist, "that this woman speaks minimal English, and my work is difficult, tiring, although she really tries to do her best, with the help of a dictionary she brings to sessions. I tried to tell her that there are several colleagues of Japanese descent, who could work with her in her mother tongue, but she refused. She also declined the participation of her husband—who speaks perfect English—in the sessions. She wants me . . ."

In the course of supervision, we discovered that the young woman's story was as strange as it was sad. Years before, during a car trip with her best woman friend, she had had an accident when she was driving. Her friend had ended up in an irreversible coma, and she had remained in hospital for weeks to look after her, all the time having to face the mute but unrelenting reproach of her friend's parents, especially her mother, who could hardly stand her being the survivor. She had not rebelled, feeling worse and worse and in time developing serious depressive symptoms (losing weight and sleep, becoming more and more sad and guilty, and so on)."Why didn't you say anything? Why did not you rebel?" the therapist had answered. "Because I couldn't," the patient had protested. "I could not abandon my friend. And in our culture it is not permitted to criticize senior persons." The arrival in Sydney had been a liberation that, however, had not completely freed her from the burden of her guilt.

This clarified the seemingly inexplicable request for an English-speaking, very Australian therapist. For the young woman, it was necessary, rather than merely advisable, to choose a therapist who was completely alien to her culture, with no contact with her past and her mother tongue, so as to be freed from all reminders of Japan—including her guilt, and the prohibition against criticizing her friend's elderly parents. Her very otherness made the therapist indispensable. (And my own distance from both cultures was probably useful in the supervisory process.)

I think that any therapist should be, independently from the culture of her patients, somewhat of an ethnologist (in the sense of Geertz (1973)), of somebody who tries to enter into dialogue with people whose premises she hardly knows or guesses. If, as therapists, we can manage to do that, we can attain a state described by Bakhtin as "the inexhaustibility of the second consciousness, that is, consciousness of the person who understands and responds: herein lies a potential infinity of responses, languages, codes. Infinity against infinity" (Bakhtin, 1971, p. 136).

Notes

1. "Anger can be brought forth by something that is provocative, insulting, or frustrating, to name just a few of the anger themes, although what you find provocative, insulting or frustrating may not be the same without or within culture" (Ekman, 1998, p. 392).
2. This case was presented by Francesca Fantini, who was the systemic therapist in charge of it. I acted as her supervisor.
3. In such an approach, the patient or family are seen in a setting where several co-therapists act together, contributing to the creation of a "community" similar to the one they left in their country of origin: the community is considered as the place where suffering and distress "make sense" for the persons who experience them (see Nathan, 1993).
4. The Austronesian language spoken by a third of the population in the Philippines (Gonzalez, 1998).

5. This is an example of the presentification of the third party in systemic individual therapy: trying to make absent others present in the dialogue, as if they were in the therapy room (Boscolo & Bertrando, 1996).
6. A premise, according to the meaning given by Bateson, can be described as "A generalized statement of a particular assumption or implication recognizable in a number of details of cultural behaviour" (Bateson, 1958[1935], p. 24). In other words, a basic assumption, which we can consider unconscious.

References

Bakhtin, M. M. (1923). Author and hero in the aesthetic activity. In: M. Holquist & V. Liapunov (Eds.), *Art and Answerability. Early Philosophical Essays by M. M. Bakhtin* (pp. 4–256). Austin: Texas University Press, 1990.

Bakhtin, M. M. (1971). From notes made in 1970–71. In: C. Emerson & M. Holquist (Eds.), *Speech Genres and Other Late Essays* (pp. 132–158). Austin, TX: University of Texas Press, 1986.

Bateson, G. (1958[1935]). *Naven*. London: Wildwood House.

Bateson, G., & Mead, M. (1942). *Balinese Character: A Photographic Analysis*. New York: Special publications of the New York Academy of Sciences, Vol. 2.

Benedict, R. (1934). *Patterns of Culture*. Boston, MA: Houghton Mifflin.

Benedict, R. (1946). *The Chrysanthemum and the Sword*. New York: Meridian Books.

Bertrando, P. (2002). The presence of the third party. Systemic therapy and transference analysis. *Journal of Family Therapy*, 24(3): 351–368.

Bertrando, P. (2007). *The Dialogical Therapist*. London: Karnac.

Bertrando, P. (2009). Emotional positioning and the therapeutic process. *Context, 107*: 17–19.

Bertrando P., & Arcelloni, T. (2009). Anger and boredom. Unpleasant emotions in systemic therapy. In: C. Flaskas & D. Pocock (Eds.), *Systems and Psychoanalysis* (pp. 75–92). London: Karnac.

Birdwhistell, R. L. (1970). *Kinesics and Context. Essays on Body Motion and Communication*. Philadelphia, PA: University of Pennsylvania Press.

Borges, J. L. (1952). *Otras Inquisiciones* (English version, *Other Inquisitions 1937–1952*), R. L. C. Simms (Trans.). Austin, TX: Universtity of Texas Press, 1976.

Boscolo, L., & Bertrando, P. (1996). *Systemic Therapy with Individuals*. London: Karnac.

Briggs, J. L. (1970). *Never in Anger. Portrait of an Eskimo Family*. Cambridge, MA: Harvard University Press.

Carrier, J. (1995). *Occidentalism. Images of the West*. Oxford: Oxford University Press.

Cecchin, G., Lane, G., & Ray, W. A. (1994). *The Cybernetics of Prejudices in the Practice of Psychotherapy*. London: Karnac.

Coontz, S. (1992). *The Way We Never Were. American Families and the Nostalgia Trap*. New York: Basic Books.

Cooper, D. (1971). *The Death of the Family*. London: Penguin Press.

Cosmides, L., & Tooby, J. (2000). Evolutionary psychology and the emotions. In: M. Lewis & J. Haviland (Eds.), *Handbook of Emotions* (2nd edn) (pp. 91–115). New York: Guilford Press.

Darwin, C. (1872). *The Expression of Emotion in Man and Animals*. London: Murray [3rd edn, with an Introduction, Afterword and Commentaries by Paul Ekman. London: HarperCollins, 1998].

Doe, T. (1973). *The Anatomy of Dependence*. Tokyo: Kodansha International.

Ekman, P. (1972). Universals and cultural differences in facial expressions of emotion. In: J. Cole (Ed.), *Nebraska Symposium on Motivation, 1971* (pp. 207–283). Lincoln, Neb: University of Nebraska Press.

Ekman, P. (Ed.) (1973). *Darwin and Facial Expression*. New York: Academic Press.

Ekman, P. (1992). An argument for basic emotions. *Cognition and Emotion*, 6: 169–200.

Ekman, P. (1998). Afterword. University of emotional expression? A personal history of the dispute. In: C. Darwin, *The Expression of Emotions in Man and Animal* [1872] (pp. 363–393), with an Introduction, Afterword and Commentaries by Paul Ekman. London: HarperCollins.

Ekman, P., Sorenson, E. R., & Friesen, W. V. (1969). Pan-cultural element, in facial display of emotions. *Science*, *164*: 86–88.

Foucault, M. (1988). Technologies of the self. In: P. Rabinow (Ed.), *Ethics. Essential Works of Foucault 1954–1984, Vol. 1* (pp. 223–251). Harmondsworth: Penguin, 2000.

Fruggeri, L. (1997). *Famiglie. Dinamiche interpersonali e processi psico-sociali*. Roma: La Nuova Italia Scientifica [II Ed. Roma, Carocci, 1998].

Geertz, C. (1973). *The Interpretation of Cultures*. New York: Basic Books.

Geertz, C. (2000). *Available Light. Anthropological Reflections on Philosophical Topics*. Princeton, NJ: Princeton University Press.

Gergen, K. (1991). *The Saturated Self*. New York: Basic Books.

Gonzalez, A. (1998). The language planning situation in the Philippines. *Journal of Multilingual and Multicultural Development*, *19*: 487–488.

Gross, D. M. (2006). *The Secret History of Emotion. From Aristotle's Rhetoric to Modern Brain Science.* Chicago, IL: University of Chicago Press.
Haley, J. (1982). Erickson's contribution to therapy. In: *Jay Haley on Milton Erickson* (pp. 38–60). New York: Brunner-Routledge, 1993.
Harré, R., & Moghaddan, F. (Eds.) (2003). *The Self and Others. Positioning Individuals and Groups in Personal, Political, and Cultural Contexts.* London: Praeger.
Krause, I.-B. (1993). Anthropology and family therapy: a case for emotions. *Journal of Family Therapy*, *15*: 35–56.
Krause, I.-B. (2007). Reading *Naven*: towards the integration of culture in systemic psychotherapy. *Human Systems*, *18*: 112–125.
LeDoux, J. (1996). *The Emotional Brain. The Mysterious Underpinnings of Emotional Life.* New York: Simon and Schuster.
Levy, R. I. (1973). *Tahitians: Mind and Experience in the Society Islands.* Chicago: University of Chicago Press.
Lutz, C. A. (1988). *Unnatural Emotions. Everyday Sentiments on a Micronesian Atoll and Their Challenge to Western Theory.* Chicago, IL: University of Chicago Press.
Mead, M. (1935). *Sex and Temperament in Three Primitive Societies.* New York: Morrow.
Minuchin, S. (1974). *Families and Family Therapy.* Cambridge, MA: Harvard University Press.
Nathan, T. (1993). *Fier de n'avoir ni pays ni ami, quelle sottise c'était. Principes d'etnopsychanalyse.* Grenoble: La Pensée Sauvage.
Nathan, T., & Stengers, I. (1995). *Médecins et sorciers. Manifeste pur une psychopathologie scientifique. Le médecin et le charlatan.* Paris: Les Empêcheurs de penser en rond.
Oatley, K. (2004). *Emotions. A Brief History.* Oxford: Basil Blackwell.
Panksepp, J. (1998). *Affective Neuroscience: The Foundations of Human and Animal Emotions.* New York: Oxford University Press.
Parrott, W. G. (Ed.) (2001). *Emotions and Social Psychology: Essential Readings.* Philadelphia, PA: Psychology Press.
Parsons, T., & Bales, R. T. (1956). *Family Socialization and Interaction Process.* Glencoe, IL: Free Press.
Planalp, S. (1999). *Communicating Emotion: Social, Moral, and Cultural Processes.* Cambridge: Cambridge University Press.
Plutchik, R. (1980). *Emotion: Theory, Research, and Experience: Vol. 1. Theories of Emotion.* New York: Academic Press.
Rober, P. (1999). The therapist's inner conversation in family therapy practice: some ideas about the self of the therapist, therapeutic impasse, and the process of reflection. *Family Process*, *38*: 209–228.

Von Foerster, H. (1982). *Observing Systems*. Seaside, CA: Intersystems Publications.
Walsh, F. (Ed.) (2003). *Normal Family Processes. Growing Diversity and Complexity* (3rd edn). New York: Guilford Press.
Watzlawick, P., Jackson, D. D., & Beavin, J. (1967). *Pragmatics of Human Communication*. New York: Norton.
Wittgenstein, L. (1953). *Philosophical Investigations*, G. E. M. Anscombe & R. Rhees (Ed. & Trans.). Oxford: Basil Blackwell, 2001.
You, Y. G. (1997). Shame and guilt mechanisms in East Asian culture. *Journal of Pastoral Care, 51*(1): 57–64.

CHAPTER SEVEN

Developments in Social GRRRAAACCEEESSS: visible–invisible and voiced–unvoiced[1]

John Burnham[2]

The importance of being aware of, sensitive to, and competent in working with issues of social difference has a rich history in the systemic and narrative approaches to therapy and training and is specified in the AFT learning outcomes in the training for therapists and supervisors. (AFT website). The "Social GGRRAAACCEEESSS" is a mnemonic developed jointly with Alison Roper-Hall (Burnham, 1992, 1993; Roper-Hall, 1998) and has, in its various forms, been making a practical contribution to this movement, in the systemic field, since 1990. This chapter describes its history, presentations, applications, and exercises. It introduces the distinction between Personal and Social GGRRAAACCEEESSS, and explores the differences within SG, along the dimensions of visible–invisible and voiced–unvoiced.

History

From DISGRRACCE to SOCIAL GRRAAACCEESS and/or Social Graces

In 1990, I was, as a therapist, supervisor/trainer, and director of systemic training programmes, struggling along with many others to manage the complexity that was involved in engaging and working with those aspects of experience and practice that were, at that time, referred to as the "isms" (e.g., racism, sexism, ageism). As a personal prompt, I created a mnemonic called DISGRRACCE to remind me of these important aspects of difference. It stood for Disability, I, Sexuality, Gender, Race, Religion, Age, Class, Culture, and Ethnicity. I used it as a personal reminder, a teaching tool, and I included it in student handbooks as a guideline for writing case summaries. In a teaching session, I might put the mnemonic across the top of the board as a visual context/guideword for myself and the participants. I used to say, "It's a DISGRRACCE if we do not include these issues in our therapy/training, etc." The "I" was inserted to make up the mnemonic, but when I asked audiences to guess what the I stood for, many people said "identity", and proposed that identity was created from and within these different aspects of lived experience. This idea of identity was "lost" when the mnemonic was later altered. It might be said that these aspects of difference are constitutive of a person's identities and, recursively, the communities in which they live and where and with whom they story their experiences.

This idea/practice was useful to an extent, but the negative implications of the word "DISGRRACCE" sometimes led to misunderstandings of my positive intentions in using the mnemonic. One black female student said, "Are you saying these issues are disgraceful?" This response triggered a change in my practice, and, in Burnham (1992), I proposed "An extension of this ('DISGRRACCE') may be to think about becoming GRACEFUL through the evolution of therapies and trainings which actively develop approaches, methods and techniques that enhance abilities in these areas" (p. 27). Around 1993, Alison Roper-Hall suggested amending the mnemonic by putting "social" in front of GRRACCES, to emphasize the social construction of these aspects of experience. In the view of both Alison and myself, it is important to retain the prefix of "social" as a context for these issues of difference. However, in writing this chapter, I have wondered whether it might be useful to also use the distinction of *Personal* GRRAAACCEEESS (PG), as well as *Social* GRRAAACCEEESS (SG). This might draw our attention both to the social contexts in which differences are constructed (SG), and the shaping of individual experience within those contexts. Our curiosity might include both SG and PG and the recursive relationships between them. Social GRRAAACCEEESS was introduced as a practical tool, not a theoretical position. Although it is grounded in social constructionism, it can be used by any practitioner.

Spelling and presentation

Over time, the mnemonic has been presented and used in a variety of ways. In Alison Roper-Hall's teaching and writing (Roper-Hall, 1998), she prefers the grammatical spelling of "Social Graces" and uses it in a "mind map" format for audiences to generate suggestions about different aspects of experience. This enables new GRACES to be added according to the experience and imagination of the reader/audience. I prefer to use the eccentric spelling, which has now extended to Social GGRRAAACCEEESSS, as it draws attention to it as a word made for a particular purpose, and avoids the connotation of "correctness" associated with the dictionary definition of social graces. The mnemonic can be presented in different ways, including a linear list, and what I call a "collide-scope". These two ways of presenting might be seen as grounded in Bateson's dictum that "we shall know a little more by dint of rigour and imagination, the two great contraries of mental process, either of which by itself is lethal. Rigour alone is paralytic death, but imagination alone is insanity" (1980, p. 233).

As such the relationship between them should be seen as reflexively complementary. Each contributing to our work in a different way. Moving between the two can enable practitioners to gain the advantages emergent from "double description" (Bateson, 1980, p. 21). A list can promise or offer rigour, clarity, and order, to the point of tempting us with certainty. Alternatively, the collide-scope suggests difference, variety, movement, complexity, fluidity, and can excite our imagination. It can also prompt doubt, danger, uncertainty, confusion, and frustration, which are not unfamiliar feelings in our practice.

A linear list of Social GGRRAAACCEEESSS: what does it currently "stand for"?

Gender
Geography
Race
Religion
Age
Ability

Appearance
Class
Culture
Ethnicity
Education
Employment
Sexuality
Sexual orientation
Spirituality

Each named difference can be regarded as being part of, and making a contribution to, the construction of social realities, as well as being a significant punctuation within a person's experience, shaping of their identity, and reflexively influencing their positioning within family, and other social relationships, and society and broader cultural contexts. This clear, equal, yet artificial separation of the constitutive aspects of a person's experience can facilitate a rigorous exploration of each aspect. It can afford each aspect a consideration that they might not otherwise receive, if a practitioner, team, or organization goes forward on the basis of what is usual, preferred, or "common-sense" practice. When the term common-sense is used, I am likely to ask: "In what framework does this make *sense* and who is that framework *common* to?" Systemic practitioners often have an allergic reaction to linearity, but this separation might allow for a skills analysis that can show which areas need particular development in the endeavours of therapy, training, supervision, and organizational practice.

Making the phrase "Personal/Social GRRAAACCEEESS", a rigorous part of planning for conversations with clients, between colleagues, and in training programmes increases the chances that each aspect will "have its turn", and be featured as a context to systematically describe and evaluate practice/agency development. Formal examples of systematically using SG include Birmingham MSc Course Handbooks, and Northumbria University personal and professional development (PPD) sessions undertaken in the context of their MA in Family Therapy and Systemic Supervision courses. Elsewhere, University of Newcastle uses SG as a four-bar "Diversity Grid" applied across the clinical psychology training programme. The Relate Institute includes it as a writing guideline and in the marking criteria on MA and MSc Relationship Therapy courses. Jersey's Early Years & Childcare working group on Social Inclusion have utilized the Social

Grraacceees acronym to provide a focus on social difference in their self-assessment tool on inclusion to be used by anyone working with children and families to help them consider their attitudes and working practice within the social inclusion and equlity agendas. Referring to the mnemonic regularly, on your desk, across the top of a one-way screen, on a notice board, might prompt practitioners to give an account of how they are attending to each of these aspects in their work, and can promote inclusion when otherwise differences may disappear, be ignored, and excluded. However, people do not live in a simple clear list, and a more imaginative, diagrammatic kind of presentation can hint at the complexity involved in the relational aspects of the Personal or Social GGRRAAACCEEESSS.

Collide-scope

In an attempt to demonstrate the rich, complex, sometimes random, unpredictable relationship between the different aspects of a person's experience within the complexity of social relations, I devised this diagram in Powerpoint (Figure 1).

Figure 7.1.   Collide-scope.

What should I call this? Tapestry was tempting, but lacked movement. Kaleidoscope (different visions created through multiple reflections) was more attractive, but too symmetrical. How about a collide-scope? In this non-symmetrical, sometimes colliding vision of relations between socially produced differences, there is a greater sense of what Pearce (1989) defines as mystery.

> Mystery is the recognition that the human condition is more than any of the particular stories that make it coherent, or any of the particular patterns of coordination that construct the events and objects of the social order. [Pearce, 1989, p. 23]

Compared to the visual clarity of the list, viewing the collide-scope is not easy, nor is it intended to be. It might also be interesting, confusing, exciting, and frustrating. The collide-scope is intended to generate curiosity and an awareness of your relative positioning in relation to the aspects of difference for yourself, and to the positioning of your colleagues/clients. You might immediately see some aspects which go unseen by a colleague. In workshops, using this image with PowerPoint leads to participants often having to *physically change their own position* in relation to the diagram, before some aspects become visible to them. Some people leave their chairs, move closer, bend themselves, develop conversations with other participants in which they learn something about what they are observing and themselves as observers, and, thus, visualize and experience what might happen in any episode of social interaction or conversation. In PowerPoint, these aspects are then moved around in the "collide-scope". Relations between these differences change. They expand and contract, collide, become foregrounded for a while, and then temporarily move into the background, faded, yet always remaining present. What is obscure might become clearer, what is clear becomes uncertain. This can sound as if each aspect takes an equal and fair turn in the limelight, with the same degree of opportunity to be the highest context marker. Life, left to its own devices, seems not to be like that. At different times and in different contexts, some aspects will, unjustly, remain in the background and be almost invisible and perhaps never spoken about. It may be foregrounded in a negative and unfair light. This is perhaps when the rigour of lists in the forms of specific training policies, procedures, practices, and exercises can remind us to examine each one specifically and develop the specific skills that are necessary to (a) bring each one forth, (b) show that it can be discussed in this context, and (c) to evaluate its contribution to the issues being discussed in any particular context.

Applications and exercises

Many imaginative exercises have been created to explore the more complex relationships between practitioners and the Social GRRAAACCEEESS, and to enable them to be more practically competent in using them. These include: Burnham (1993); Roper-Hall (1998, 2008) working clinically with older adults; Heaphy (2000) in training exercises; Burnham and Harris (2002) to address culture in supervision; Divac and Heaphy (2005) giving "Space for GRRAACCEES" within training for supervisors; Karamat Ali (2007) hypothesizing in a context where the participants are mostly white middle class; Mills-Powell and Worthington (2007) inviting students to choose one letter from SG and to say something about themselves and how the identity it represents informed their life and influences the hypotheses they make and questions they ask; Burnham, Alvis Palma, and Whitehouse (2008) deconstructing the differences within a training group to facilitate reflexive discussion, and focussing on the gendered significance of who holds the remote control during video supervision; Partridge and Lang (personal communication) using structured exercises to help doctoral students connect "their personal graces" to different stages in the research process. Partridge found it was necessary to "warm the context" (Burnham, 2005) by making connections between research and the graces. In an unpublished dissertation, Totsuka (2010) describes an exercise that she calls "Which aspects of Social GRRAAACCEEESS grab you most?" Supervisees found it useful to explore what *does not* grab them, "because then we have to ask why, don't we?" Some feedback from participants was: "personal stories contextualized people's preferences"; "thought provoking and made me think outside the box"; "some people talk about things that I kind of take for granted"; "you can't challenge everything, so you challenge what's organizing you".

Each of these exercises invite, facilitate, require, and nudge practitioners to extend their practice outside their current preferences. Another way of developing and extending abilities is to explore the differences between the social differences, in particular where they appear on a continuum between visible and invisible, and where they are heard on a continuum between voiced and unvoiced. How might this influence the ability of practitioners and families to raise these differences for discussion?

Differences among the differences
(not all differences are the same!)

During the applications and exercises referred to, practitioners often reflect on personal and professional experiences and generate stories from these experiences. They often tell of their dilemmas and uncertainties about how including aspects of the SG in the conversations are personally affecting them. These dilemmas can often be situated along the dimensions of visible–invisible, and voiced–unvoiced. Juxtaposing these two continua creates a set of four quadrants, shown in the heuristic graphic below (Figure 2).

Initially, I thought that, as in other graphics, such as Barry Mason's "towards safe uncertainty" (1993) and Karl Tomm's "empowerment" (workshop, 2008), there was a ranking of the quadrants in terms of being more/less preferred as a context for therapeutic or supervisory practice. I imagined that "invisible and unvoiced" was the least preferred and that practitioners would want to work towards "visible

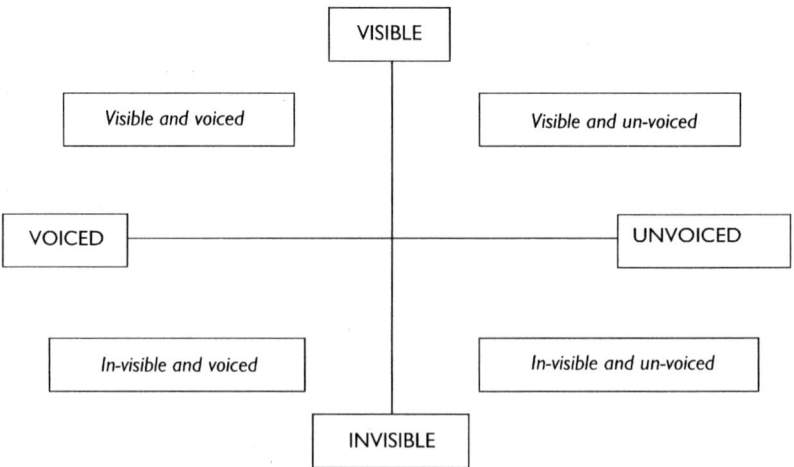

Figure 7.2. The four quadrants of visible–invisible, voice–unvoiced.

and voiced". This still has some attraction, but I think that it is important to adopt a reflexive approach to the potential value of each quadrant as a context for working in any particular milieu. Voicing the unvoiced, or bringing the invisible into the conversation might contribute to transparency that is therapeutic, or exposure that becomes unhelpful. Roberts (2005) addresses these issues relating to transparency in some detail.

I realise that these terms do not fit for all practitioners, including those with impairments of sight, hearing, or speech. Neither do they fully or adequately describe all the ways there are to experience aspects of social difference and construct social realities. These issues might well be developed in further publications, in collaboration with practitioners with expertise in those areas (Petters, 2011). For the moment, however, I want to observe that it is an ongoing aspect of practice in which relational reflexivity (Burnham, 1993, 2005) is required in order to make decisions with each client/family/supervisee/colleague about what is relevant in their/our particular circumstances, and what metaphors and language helps to describe the story lived. Porter (personal communication) described her experience: "I think the quadrants works in the written form as it invites your own imagination to consider ways you would incorporate into practice. Immediately I think about supervision groups, individual pieces of work, so as a reader the tone and voice is included." The quadrants are arranged in a particular order, but they could be read or used in a different order that makes more practical sense for you.

Visible and unvoiced

Visible aspects of SG might be about self/other, anything in the room, or visual "clues" about such aspects as race, gender, age, ability, culture, and other aspects of appearance. This might be about a particular person: clothes, body shape, colour, height, hairstyle, hair length, glasses, body markings, jewellery, badges, and so on. These might go unvoiced (by comment, reflection, or question) by anyone in the session. This might happen for a range of reasons. For example, being outside awareness; seeing but not noticing; perception of relevance; not realizing the significance; taken for granted; cultural rules of politeness; not having words to name/describe, or not having a culturally appropriate question/grammar; waiting for someone else to say something; or if the practitioner does not mention it then it cannot be important. For example, Totsuka (2010), uses the schema within her SG exercise, and the feedback illustrates this section very well. For example: Ruth (supervisee) described how she wondered if her client did not return because she saw a Jewish symbol in her house. Due to her appearance (she is blonde and has blue eyes), Ruth thinks her clients assume that she belongs to the majority white group in the UK context. This poses a dilemma for her when she works with clients of ethnic minority background. She wonders if her clients assume that she belongs to the dominant group and, therefore, cannot relate to their experience. When she works with the clients of white UK background, the dilemma is that they might assume that she is the "same", but she is "feeling different inside".

There is so much that can be commented on in any session/course of work that, perhaps inevitably, there is more that is unvoiced than voiced. It is often difficult to know what is relevant, necessary, appropriate, or has therapeutic potential. If the differences are not particularly relevant to the work, then it might not matter that they go unvoiced. However, practitioners might be anxious that they are missing something important. They might not be content merely to hope that they have done what they can to create a context where the clients feel that differences of significance can be discussed. They might also feel they need to develop the ability to notice their noticing and take the initiative in giving voice to that noticing. If the therapist experiences themselves as regularly noticing but not voicing particular SG that the client has not raised, then it may indicate a possibility to develop what I will call their vis-abilities. A practitioners "vis-abilities" are those abilities to notice what is visible, and step outside their preference/prejudice and generate curiosity. They might graciously invite them into a spoken domain to indicate that this is a place where these issues can be discussed if and when appropriate. While it is significant when a client raises these aspects, in this chapter I will focus on the practitioner's abilities to take the initiative in bringing forth these issues.

Visible and voiced

Developing vis-abilities might involve different levels of relational risk taking (Mason, 2005) and relationally reflexive conversations

(Burnham, 1993, 2005) between practitioner and client/supervisee. Depending on the content, any conversation could be brief or prolonged, easy or difficult. Vis-ability might be restricted by assuming meaning, as in "it's obvious", and it can be enhanced by the "discipline of curiosity", asking questions, even when you are sure you know the answer (Burnham, 2005). Vis-ability might be decreased when working with people who are similar to you in some ways (appearance, class, culture, age), and increased when you are working with someone who shows a visible difference of which you become aware. Vis-ability may vary with clients over time and with different people in the same room. How one voices what is visible can have significant effects. For example, to say about a person that you notice that they are *in* a wheelchair, is quite different to saying that you notice they are *using* a wheelchair. Practitioners might value rehearsing the words they might use so that they do not sound too inexperienced or embarrassed. For example,

> *Therapist*: "I notice you are wearing a cross. Is that symbolic of something religious, or something you like to wear, or both?"
>
> *Therapist*: "It looks as if we are of different ages, genders, and racial origins. Shall we talk about that as a way to start, or talk about it when it seems relevant?"

In supervision, Porter described a difficult piece of work with an unaccompanied minor who was seeking asylum and who had experienced multiple carers and social workers. I proposed that she ask the question, "When you look at me, who do you see?" After a period of silence, the girl replied, "I see all of the social workers and professionals who promised to stand by me and support me, but eventually let me down." This seemed to open space for a relationally reflexive (Burnham, 2005) conversation which explored the young woman's hopes and expectations and the abilities, or otherwise, of their relationship to realistically achieve these.

The voicing of the visible SG might open up stories that can be deconstructed and with different possibilities. It might also lead "nowhere in particular", be seen as irrelevant, or be disruptive to a therapeutic process. For example, a young woman seemed to use her hair as "curtains" in sessions one and two and then "opened the curtains" in session three. My usual comment would often voice this visible difference with a variation on "I was wondering when you would come out to play?", often leading to a humorous response and emergent possibilities. On this occasion, she promptly "closed the curtain" and did not reappear until session five, by which time I had learnt a lesson about not always voicing what is visible (readers can insert their own version of what they think I should have learnt from that episode!). The British Association for Sexual and Relational Therapy intentionally include the reference "sexual" in their visible and voiced title, so that clients do not have to risk embarrassment by asking, "Do you do sex therapy?"

Invisible and voiced

Many cultures will have interpretations of phrases such as: "There is more to this than meets the eye", or "Don't judge a book by its cover" (Islamic Words of Wisdom, 2010), indicating "that you shouldn't prejudge the worth or value of something, by its appearance alone" (Hirsch, 2002). Aspects of SG/PG that are not, or not necessarily, obvious to the eye include: geography, religion, ability, class, culture, ethnicity, employment, education, sexuality, sexual orientation, and spirituality. Clients might speak of invisible aspects of SG/PG in a variety of ways, including request for therapy: "Differences in our class backgrounds is causing trouble in our marriage"; informing a practitioner, "I need you to know that . . ."; prompting of one family member by another, "Go on, tell them about . . ."; questioning a practitioner, "Do you have children of your own?" An example from Totsuka (2010): Patrick (supervisee) talked about hidden aspects of self, and contexts in which he might or might not choose to make his invisible aspects voiced. He always tells people he is gay when he attends job interviews because he does not want to work in a homophobic environment. This led to reflection from the observers as to how he might manage invisible aspects of his personal self in his working context and acknowledgement that some aspects of personal selves are harder to disclose in some contexts.[3] Practitioners and agencies can contribute to creating contexts in which clients feel this is a place where these aspects of their experience can be discussed, both by how they respond to initiatives taken by clients and by the initiatives they take to bring forth these issues. My colleague, Dr Queenie Harris, received a telephone request: "I am looking for a family therapist who is a Christian and I was given your name. Are you a Christian?" Queenie replied, "Yes, I am Christian, but I might not be the kind of Christian that you are looking for. Shall we talk about it first?"

Taking the initiative could include:

- routine questionnaires inviting/requiring clients to give us information about themselves;
- routine questions that might help to bring forth the invisible:

    "Are there are any things that are not immediately obvious about you, that you think it is important for me to know?"

    "In my work with people and families I am interested in how different aspects of their life influence their well-being and help them to overcome the problems they are facing, for example, their cultural belongings, their religious or spiritual beliefs, the job they do, the class they come from and belong to ... how about you?"

    "Is there anyone special in your life at the moment?" (As an alternative to "Do you have a girlfriend/boyfriend?", given their visible gender.)

    "What idea has to die, so that you can live?"

    "I am interested to know if there are any spiritual or religious values that might be a resource to you in facing this problem?"

See also Griffith and Griffith (2002) and O'Hanlon (2006).

Impressions drawn from what is visible and voiced might trigger a prejudice or create an assumption that stifles the discipline of curiosity and the ability to hypothesize about what is invisible. The term "invis-ability" does not work in the same way as "vis-ability". So, what kind of ability is required? One ability might be learning not to be "put off" or mesmerized by what is visible, not to fall under the spell of immediate visceral feelings or immediate thoughts "that x (something visible) says it all". If you think someone looks "unapproachable", ask them anyway, and use this information about this prejudice to trigger a self-reflexive conversation with colleagues or in supervision. Keep the SG in mind somehow: because you cannot see some SG, it does not mean to say that they are not important. I have, myself, made many mistakes in this area, and hope that I have learnt to be braver and more skilful from those episodes that have come to light. For example, six siblings (8–15 years old) were separated and living in a variety of placements, with no intention/hope of being physically reunited with one another or with their parents before they were legally able to make that decision for themselves. As part of rehabilitating their emotional relationships with one another, they wanted something practical that they all could do, no matter what their age was. I asked each person to make something which could be shared among them, so that when they each looked at that object, it might remind them of their love and affection for each other and their family identity, even when they are physically separate (making their love for one another visible). In the next session, the children looked excited about showing and sharing the things they had brought to share ... all except one boy, who was said to have reduced abilities to learn and communicate and was often on the periphery of sessions. I could not see that he had brought anything, and I (and his siblings, perhaps) was concerned not to embarrass him, or his social worker, by asking him. I assumed that he perhaps lacked the abilities to complete the task. As the session was drawing to a close, he said, "What about mine?" It turned out that he had bought eight white plates from the market, and written the name of each family member around the edge, and the name of their family in the middle. The plates had a device that meant they could be hung on a wall and displayed. After a significant silence, everyone gave him a round of applause and agreed that his was the "best of all". My fear/sensitivity to his assumed lack of ability almost led to his invisible ability not being brought forth. Thank goodness that he felt able to remind us!

These are not hard and fast distinctions. For example, there are times when a person's gender might be uncertain (Iantaffi, 2010), or there might be a visible clue about a person's religion in their dress/symbols.

Sometimes, the voicing of an aspect of experience makes it difficult to discuss and sometimes not. For example, a father who said in a family session, "I am a racist, I suppose" (voiced). From the response of the other family members, I was unable to tell what their position was in relation to his statement (invisible). I was somewhat taken aback by this, but proceeded by asking, "Do you think other people in the family share your views?" As he imagined what their positions might be, and then each person responded, the invisible became voiced. Each person had a different position: some felt they used to share his views, but not now, others felt they were more strongly influenced by racist values than their father. They felt that the influence of these strong prejudices were related to the reasons they were coming for therapy, and so we then considered how each person had arrived at this position, what had led people to change, and how they might change to different positions.

Invisible and unvoiced (can we resist temptations of curiosity?)

The aphorism "Out of sight, out of mind" (we might forget about things we cannot see) makes a different sense in reverse: "Out of mind, out of sight" (if we do not think about things, we tend not to see them). Aspects of difference might remain invisible and unvoiced by both the client and the practitioner for a variety of reasons, within or outside of people's awareness. In some contexts, experience might not be volunteered, asked about, explored, and can sometimes be explicitly declared "out of bounds". I thought that while this might be the least preferred and most difficult quadrant to work in, it might be the easiest and potentially the shortest section to write about. Yet, it has been the most difficult to write about, and the most reflexively demanding. The main difficulty I have experienced in considering these possible contexts in which some aspect of SG is not visible and never voiced is what I would call the temptation of curiosity. This would be the kind of *compulsive curiosity* that might lead me to drift into, or attempt to push the conversation into, the invisible and voiced quadrant as an unquestioned/taken for granted routine. Amundson, Stewart, and Valentine (1993) wrote about the dangers inherent in the "temptation of certainty", while curiosity (Cecchin, 1987) is so often posited as a desirable therapeutic asset. While I would support that position in general, and have committed myself to the posture of curiosity in practice, in writing this section I have, gradually, come to think that curiosity, or certain kinds of curiosity, might be problematic. It might be that curiosity that is used *routinely or non-reflexively* draws practitioners to continue exploring aspects of difference that clients prefer not to, are unaware of some "taken for granted" aspects of their lived experience (it is only the fish that does not know (until they are out of it) that they swim in water). For example, it might be only when a person moves to another country/culture/organization that they realize what values/practices they take for granted in their practice routines. It might be that non-reflexive or premature curiosity, based on unquestioned professional beliefs about the goodness of, for example, openness, transparency, and honesty, could contribute towards a problematic pattern. For example, the more a client/supervisee declines to discuss an issue, the more the practitioner hypothesizes/believes that declining to discuss is evidence of its immediate relevance, and generates curiosity and further, sometimes unwelcome, premature exploration.

Two adult sisters (aged thirty and twenty-seven) came to therapy to work on their relationship following a reconciliation after being estranged for five years due, as they described it, to the drug-saturated lifestyle of the younger sister. According to them, the work was going well, and then the younger sister said she felt spiritually ready to confess to her sister everything, and get it "off her chest" about what she had had to do to maintain her drug habit. The older sister said she did not want/need to know, and was happy to "draw a line" under that period of their relationship, and get on with being grateful for how things were now. The therapist had what might be called a bias towards healing through forgiveness, and, on reflection, considered that he/she influenced the conversation towards enabling the younger sister to make her confessions. The confessions included content that the elder sister found she could not tolerate/forgive, and this response had a deleterious effect on their relationship with each other and with the therapist. The therapy was resumed sometime later, but only following a session in which the therapist proposed to co-create new ground rules for the conversations. A relationally reflexive approach to openness was held, which looked at questions to be considered by all members of the therapeutic system, including both the sisters and the therapist. The questions included: "When I want to introduce something into the session, have I thought about the effects that it might have on me, on others, and on what we are trying to achieve in our work together?" "How might 'speaking out' about things that I am finding it hard to bear alone be a resource to our work together, and how might it be a restraint?" "How might I know when 'getting things off one's chest' could best be considered in an individual session, before deciding how, or whether, to confess it to others, who might find hearing it too difficult?" In this way, each person, including the therapist, was prompted to think relationally about something that seemed like a personal decision. This relational consideration seemed to have reflexive effects on how each person then conducted themselves personally.

This example is not intended necessarily to show that it is always a mistake to persist in helping people to give voice to painful issues, or aspects of difference whose significance they are not yet aware of. It could indicate that a therapist's prejudice/passion about openness, or the influence of a non-reflexive belief in curiosity, or any other therapeutic concept, as an unquestioned virtue, can lead to an anti-therapeutic effect, even with therapeutic intentions. Warming the context (Burnham, 2005) is a practice that is intended to be used at different turning points or junctions in the work with any client, not only at the beginning. The more I write about what is invisible and unvoiced, the more I feel tempted to give in to the influence of compulsive (non-reflexive) curiosity, which, alongside overwhelming optimism, continues to be the most troublesome aspect of my approach to therapy. Fellow sufferers from this kind of condition might seek a suitable antidote by growing reflexive curiosity into a second-order skill. This growth can be helped through practices such as: exploring your own relationship with an aspect of SG by asking yourself (whichever self you choose) the questions that you are proposing to ask your clients, becoming curious about your areas and patterns of curiosity and hypothesizing about your hypothesizing in the context of Social GGRRAAACCEEESSS. If someone seems unaware of the significance of an aspect of SG and the influence it is having in their lives, then a practitioner might initiate this in the conversation. Once the client is aware of the potential influence, then a process of relational reflexivity with the client might enable the client to a make a choice as to whether or not to discuss that influence.

Summary, reflections, and exercises

In this chapter, I have situated the Social GGRRAAACCEEESSS within the broad field of social constructionism and outlined its origins and development as a tool to influence practice at the levels of approach, method, and technique (Burnham, 1992, 1993; Roper-Hall, 1998). Different methods of presentation have been used to facilitate both rigour and imagination (Bateson, 1980). A rigorous exploration of each aspect, listed as if separate, can help to promote inclusion and avoid practitioners staying within their "comfort zone" (Wilson, 2007), or experiencing "social vertigo" (Pearce, 1989) when trying to consider too much difference simultaneously. Imaginative play in the form of a "collide-scope" invites us to explore the relational, multiple reflection aspects of SG, which hints at the depth of experience and the systemic notion that "the whole is always greater than the sum of the parts". Examples of how practitioners have used SG have been referred to. A schema for exploring differences between the SG is introduced along the dimensions of visible–invisible and voiced–unvoiced. The aesthetic abilities required to practise in each quadrant and to move between is tentatively explored.

An exciting/frustrating feature of SG as a mnemonic is the wish to add another letter, so as not to exclude any aspect of socially produced difference. While writing this, I have, prompted by workshop participants, added another G for geography, and another S for sexual orientation. Where will it end? I do not have an answer for that, except to say that no framework is ever complete, and is always emerging and developing. It is intended to be practically helpful, not theoretically definitive. Creating something like *Social GgRRaAcCCEeEeSsS* can often have a refreshing or innovative effect and lead to enthusiasm and generative practices. Eventually, what was novel might slip into orthodoxy and lose the spirit in which it was conceived. It is a pity that this happens, but is indicated when we ask people why they perform a certain practice and they answer "because that's the way we do it". Perhaps this will also happen to SG, and it will be referred to, as I sometimes have here, as "SG" for brevity, convenience, or because it is not always easy to remember. I hope not, well, at least, not all of the time, anyway. But if it does, I am sure that the spirit that promoted this invention and its extensions will emerge in other ways. When SG is practised at all levels of approach, method, and technique, it can create changes *both* within a broad philosophy *and* within the small and ordinary practices of therapy, consultation, training, and supervision. I will end with two exercises ("Paper GGRRAAACCEEESSS", and "Place a Grace") that might be useful in using the schema and maintaining a flexible approach to the ideas in this chapter.

EXERCISE 1: Paper GGRRAAACCEEESSS Show and Tell?
Enabling visible and voiced (show and tell):

Step 1 Write the name of each S G on an individual piece of paper
Step 2 Arrange them on a table.
Step 3 Tell the family/client/trainees about each one
Step 4 Invite them to organize them in ways which show the significance of each one in general/in particular to the situation they are in, the problems they are facing etc.
Step 5 Discuss the arrangement(s) in relation to the work that might be done together. Including any questions the family/client/trainees/supervisees have in relation to your arrangement

EXERCISE 2: PLACE A GRACE[4]
Place a Grace in the centre of the diagram and explore the 'Grace'
in relation to each of 4 distinctions (where might you usually put it)
in the context of each quadrant (experiment with how you think/feel/do it)

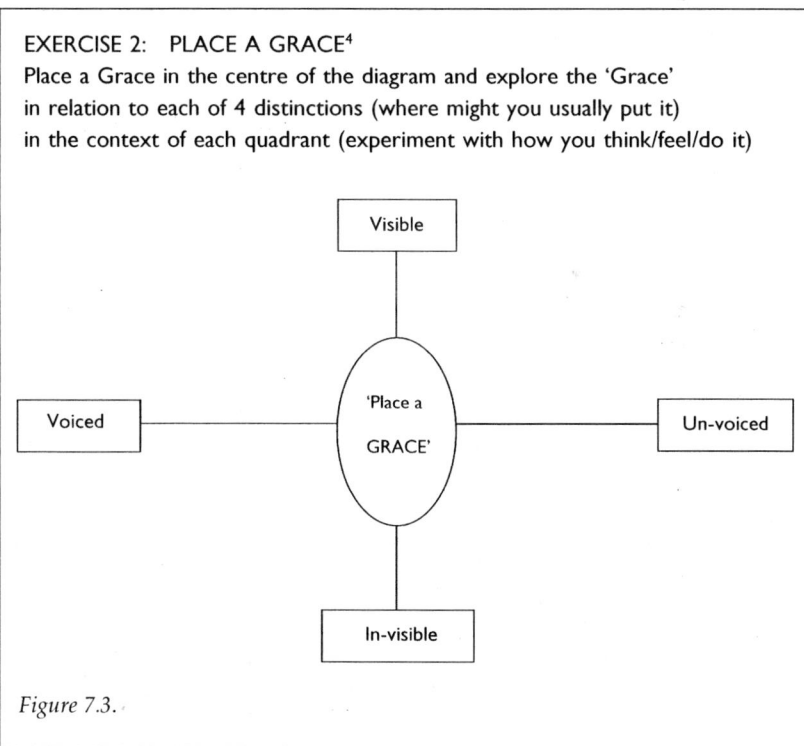

Figure 7.3.

Notes

1. I am grateful to Gail Simon, Barry Mason, Dorothy Porter, Louise Brooks, Julie Barber, and Jeanette Neden for their helpful comments and

encouragement during the writing of this chapter, especially to Alison Roper-Hall, with whom this has been developed over many years.
2. I would like to dedicate this chapter to my late father, John Burnham, who died while I was writing it. Although he never travelled widely himself, he had an openness to other ways of being and living that I continue to aspire to.
3. Roberts (2005) points out that opportunities for self-disclosure might be more limited for some therapists due to their background and their work contexts, for example, for gay and lesbian therapists.
4. Readers of drafts of this paper have suggested a family resemblance with the "Johari window" (Luft & Ingham, 1955), which some readers may wish to explore.

References

AFT website. http://www.aft.org.uk/
Amundson, J., Stewart, K., &Valentine, L. (1993). Temptations of power and certainty. *Journal of Marital and Family Therapy*, *19*(2): 111–123.
Bateson, G. (1980). *Mind and Nature: A Necessary Unity*. London: Fontana.
Burnham, J. (1992). Approach – method – technique: making distinctions and creating connections. *Human Systems*, 3: 3–27.
Burnham, J. (1993). Systemic supervision: the evolution of reflexivity in the context of the supervisory relationship. *Human Systems*, 4: 349–381.
Burnham, J. (2005). Relational reflexivity: a tool for socially constructing therapeutic relationships. In: C. Flaskas, B. Mason, & A. Perlesz (Eds.), *The Space Between: Experience, Context, and Process in the Therapeutic Relationships* (pp. 1–180). London: Karnac.
Burnham, J., & Harris, Q. (2002). Cultural perspective in supervision. In: D. Campbell & B. Mason (Eds.), *Perspectives on Supervision* (pp. 21–41). London: Karnac.
Burnham, J., Alvis Palma, D., & Whitehouse, L. (2008). Learning as a context for differences, and differences as a context for learning. *Journal of Family Therapy*, *30*(4): 529–542.
Cecchin, G. (1987). Hypothesising, circularity and neutrality revisited: an invitation to curiosity. *Family Process*, 4: 405–413.
Divac, A., & Heaphy, G. (2005). Spaces for GRRAACCEESS: training for cultural competence in supervision. *Journal of Family Therapy*, 27: 280–284.

Griffith, J. L., & Griffith, M. E. (2002). *Encountering the Sacred in Psychotherapy: How to Talk with People about their Spiritual Lives*. New York: Guilford Press.

Heaphy, G. (2000). Doing the GRRAACCES: from reflection to reflexive practice. dissertation submitted as part of the MA Systemic Practice (Teaching, Training and Supervision). University of Northumbria at Newcastle and KCC Foundation.

Hirsch, E. D. (2002). *The New Dictionary of Cultural Literacy*. New York: Houghton Mifflin.

Iantaffi, A. (2010). Working with trans youth and their families: personal and professional reflections. *Context, 111*: 30–33.

Islamic Words of Wisdom. Don't judge a book by its cover! www.ezsoftech.com/stories/mis12.asp

Karamat Ali, R. (2007). Learning to be mindful of difference: teaching systemic skills in cross-cultural encounters. *Journal of Family Therapy, 29*: 368–372.

Luft, J., & Ingham, H. (1955). The Johari window, a graphic model of interpersonal awareness. *Proceedings of the Western Training Laboratory in Group Development*. Los Angeles, CA: UCLA.

Mason, B. (1993). Towards positions of safe uncertainty. *Human Systems, 4*. 189–200.

Mason, B. (2005). Relational risk-taking and the therapeutic relationship. In: C. Flaskas, B. Mason, & A. Perlesz (Eds.), *The Space Between: Experience, Context, and Process in the Therapeutic Relationships* (pp. 157–170). London: Karnac.

Mills-Powell, D., & Worthington, R. (2007). Space for GRRAACCEESS: some reflections on training for cultural competence. *Journal of Family Therapy, 29*:364–367.

O'Hanlon, B. (2006). *Pathways to Spirituality: Connection, Wholeness, and Possibility for Therapist and Client*. New York: W. W. Norton.

Pearce, W. B. (1989). *Communication and the Human Condition*. Carbondale, IL: Southern Illinois University Press.

Petters, C. (2011). Visible voices: facilitating conversations between/deaf and hearing family members. *Context, 112*: 46–47.

Roberts, J. (2005). Transparency and self-disclosure in family therapy: dangers and possibilities. *Family Process, 44*: 45–63.

Roper-Hall, A. (1998). Working systemically with older people and their families who have "come to grief"'. In: P. Sutcliffe, G. Tufnell, & U. Cornish (Eds.), *Working with the Dying and Bereaved: Systemic Approaches to Therapeutic Work* (pp. 177–206). London: MacMillan.

Roper-Hall, A. (2008). Systemic interventions and older people. In: R. Woods & L. Clare (Eds.), *Handbook of the Clinical Psychology of Ageing* (2nd edn) (pp. 489–504). London: Wiley.

Tomm, K. (2008). Proceedings of a workshop: Ethical Postures, Birmingham Systemic Training Programme.

Totsuka, Y. (2010). "Which aspects of social GRRAAACCEEESS grab you most?": the social GRRAAACCEEESS exercise to promote therapists' use of self. Unpublished dissertation in partial fulfilment of the Advanced Diploma in the Supervision of Family and Systemic Psychotherapy, Institute of Family Therapy/Birkbeck University.

Wilson, J. (2007). *The Performance of Practice*. London: Karnac.

PART III
THERAPY AS A SOCIAL RELATIONSHIP

CHAPTER EIGHT

The personal and the professional: core beliefs and the construction of bridges across difference[1]

Barry Mason

Introduction

This is a chapter that has evolved out of practice, theory, and personal experience. It arises from a long-standing focus on the relationship between the development of my own personal core beliefs and the influence of those beliefs on my clinical work as a family and systemic psychotherapist working with individuals, couples, and families from different cultures and religions. A central question for me has become not only how I can help clients find a systemic both–and position, and how the therapeutic relationship can encompass a both–and position, but also, to what extent I can find such a position in relation to my personal beliefs and my professional task. Some of the content herein comes from a certain disillusionment with some of the more recent developments in family therapy, and could be said to be a continuation of the work that contributed to the publication of the book, *Exploring the Unsaid* (Mason & Sawyerr, 2002), which sought to encourage practitioners to take more risks in working cross-culturally. This was based on the view that interpretations of the developments in theory and practice were hindering, as well as aiding, us in creating effective clinical work. As Alice Sawyerr and I wrote in our introduction to that book, "to develop intimacy, to develop closeness of whatever kind, one has to be prepared to take chances and risk vulnerability" (p. xix). This chapter is written with that in mind.

Writing this chapter is also linked to a trend I perceive to be happening based on my role as Chair of the Advanced Programme in Supervision at the Institute of Family Therapy in London. Over the past few years, I have noticed that while therapists and supervisors are often committed, in theory, to addressing with each other the connections between their family and culture of origin issues and their professional task, many seem reluctant to explore this relationship in practice. However, it is important to make a distinction here, in that I often observe and hear about the exploration of personal–professional connections in individual, systemic supervision, but less so in group supervision. Given that family therapy has been a way of working closely associated with group work, there would seem to be a lack of fit between some aspects of systemic theory and practice in terms of the personal professional relationship.

A historical note

In some other publications (for example, Mason, 1993, 2005a,b) I have stressed the importance of the paradigm shift from a first-order to a second-order perspective in the late 1970s/early 1980s (Hoffman, 1985). In moving to a second-order perspective, there emerged a greater emphasis on "fit" and less on finding certainty. This newer perspective included the position of the therapist in the construction of reality. Hence, a second-order perspective became defined in terms of a mutually influencing relationship, that the act of observation influenced that which is observed (Heisenberg, 1962; von Foerster, 1990).

The shift from a first- to a second-order perspective embodied the view that we could no longer play the role of detached observers; we are involved in the world we observe. This implied that we needed to start asking questions of ourselves as well as of our clients. But, while a second-order perspective implied such, it was not until the late 1980s/early 1990s that the practice implications of the theory caught up with the theory itself, and that the addressing of self within systemic practice became something that could no longer remain at the margins. But, as I have noted elsewhere (Mason, 2005a), I do not want to take a stance (one often heard in the field) of first order, bad, second order, good. While I would describe my work as coming from a second-order perspective, it is plainly disrespectful (and not very second order!) to dismiss first-order ideas and practice out of hand. "The shift to a second order perspective was a development in the field, not a shift from bad to good" (Mason, 2005a, p. 159). In 1995, Hardy and Laszloffy noted that

> the content-focused approach to multicultural education overemphasises the characteristics of various cultural groups, while ignoring the importance of the trainees' perceptions of, and feelings towards, their respective cultural backgrounds. As a result, trainees are rarely challenged to examine how their respective cultural identities influence understanding and acceptance of those who are both culturally similar and dissimilar. [p. 227]

Their creation of a cultural genogram was based on the premise that "culture is a broad multidimensional concept that includes, but is not limited to, ethnicity, gender, social class and so forth" (p. 228). While this perspective is one that informs the writing of this chapter, it is also important to note that "it is difficult to be precise about what culture is" (Krause, 2002, p. 37), that in culture "there is both continuity and choice" (*ibid.*), and that there is a need for risk-taking by clinicians and supervisors (Krause, 2002; Mason, 1993, 2002, 2005a,b, 2008).

The cultural genogram paper has become a seminal one, and is probably one of the first publications that one would put down on a reading list for a systemic therapy training programme. However, I have become concerned that it is in danger of becoming an exercise at the beginning of a training programme, or work context, that is "ticked off" as completed, rather than having an ongoing life in the course of therapy and supervision. Boyd-Franklin (2002) has commented forcefully on the importance of the aspect of "the ongoing". I have similar concerns, as I have already noted, about the tendency within systemic group contexts to marginalize the self *per se*. Too often, in my experience, pre- and post-therapy session discussions within the context of group supervision, live and retrospective, tend to concentrate almost exclusively on the clients. I have suggested elsewhere (Mason, 2010) that there should be four elements that need to be kept in focus in clinical work, and a further two in terms of supervision. These are:

1. the clients;
2. the client's relationship with help;
3. the therapeutic relationship;
4. the self of the therapist;
5. the supervisory relationship;
6. the self of the supervisor.

I cannot see that calling oneself second order, but only tending to address the issues brought by clients, makes one a second-order clinician. Further, it is not helpful to talk about the importance of transparency if there is a reluctance to explore with one's colleagues the connections between the personal self and the professional task. I am not advocating personal therapy in the context of clinical work. What I am suggesting is the need, consistent with the Association for Family Therapy (UK) criteria for training and, by implication, post qualification practice (AFT, 1991) that the self is given more priority (and is lived within practice and supervision) than I think is happening. Further, I would suggest that not only is self addressed consistent with the AFT criteria, but that the story of our own core beliefs about how we should live our lives is shared with colleagues. Core beliefs (significant ideas and values to which we become emotionally attached) are not fixed; they will possibly change, be amended, over time. I believe that what our core beliefs are, and the development of such beliefs, influences who we are personally and professionally. In the next section of this chapter, I will attempt to put the ideas presented above into practice by outlining the development of my own core beliefs. This will lead on to the final section of the paper which gives some examples of how I utilize these core beliefs as part of my practice.

Because of the limitations of space, I am going to concentrate here on two particular aspects of my personal development: gender, and my relationship with religion.

The personal

Gender

I was born in Liverpool a few years after the end of the Second World War, the third son (although the brother born before me was stillborn) of a bus driver and a house cleaner. During the war, there had been mass employment of women. After the war, there was a return to the pre-war status quo. As Milkman (1987) has pointed out, society was willing to accept women working on a temporary basis due to the outbreak of war, but not on a permanent footing once the war had ended. For Freidan (1992), it was nothing more than a betrayal, a reinstitution of pre-war gender roles. Men returned to their position as being "head of the household" (a term that has tended to go out of use on official forms in the UK), as men were automatically considered to be that person by the nature of their gender. The film director, Terence Davies, born a few years before me in the same city, and within a similar white, working-class culture, has captured this time, or, at least, his memory of this time, in his films, *Distant Voices, Still Lives* (1988), *The Long Day Closes* (1992) (both highly autobiographical), and, more recently, *Of Time and the City* (2008). One scene in *Distant Voices, Still Lives* highlights the dominant position of men over women. The film shows the camaraderie, togetherness, and intimacy between women when they are single. Marriage changes this. As Dave, one of the characters, says to his new wife, Eileen (one of Davies's sisters), "You're married now—I'm your husband. Your duty's to me. Frig everyone else. Monica, Jingles (two of Eileen's friends), that's all ancient history now."

Men's dominion over women, the view (like Dave's) of ownership, was something I grew up with, although more outside of the home than within it. My father had been a disappointment to his own father in that he was not considered "manly" enough. I suspect, though, that the resentment his father showed towards him was partly because my father's mother was pregnant with him by the time they married; in the context of the time, they had to get married. Years later, when my paternal grandmother told her husband, in 1938, that my father had enlisted in the British Royal Air Force, she was met by the comment, "Perhaps that will make a man of him." My father, a quiet, gentle man tried at times to be the man he perhaps thought he should be, or his father thought he should be. He would try to be a bit bossy, authoritarian, but it did not suit him and his heart was not in it. My brothers and I, and my mother, would affectionately tease him. He was never violent, but violence towards women was only too evident—the screams and the bruises in neighbouring houses. It would have been unusual if anyone had ever contacted the police. In those days, and for a long time afterwards, a man's home was indeed his castle. Domestic violence was not a police issue; they did not intervene.

What I learnt, and this became further embedded during my adolescence and early adulthood during the social changes that occurred in the 1960s, was that men were not "above" women. There was no divine right of men, even if it often seemed like that culturally. Not only did this become a major part (perhaps the major part) of who I saw myself as being, a central aspect of my core beliefs, but my beliefs about gender and equality *per se* came to have a crucial impact on my relationship with religion.[2]

Religion

The former Bishop of Edinburgh, Richard Holloway (1999) sees the myth, as he puts it, of the eating of the forbidden fruit in the Garden of Eden as the "first example of man blaming woman for his own moral frailty" (p. 22). The account of "the Fall", he continues, "identified women as objects of temptation designed to lure men to destruction, a device employed by witch-hunters in the past and counsel for the defence in rape cases today" (*ibid.*, p. 22). The Koran has many similar sentiments, the description of paradise, for example. "I think you can say it's pretty sexist", a female Muslim colleague recently said to me; Ali (2002), among others, has expressed similar views.

Going to church as a child and a young person was something you did. It was not something you thought about doing. Attending church and believing in God was essentially culture, not religion. Church was a focal point for the community. You also had to go to church if you wanted to be in the football team and they had a good youth club; in fact, the only (Protestant) youth club on the estate where I lived. But, by the time I got into my teens, I began to actually address the beliefs. I questioned the existence of God as one might do anyway in one's teens. I became more interested in social inequalities and social justice, something, from my experience, my religion did not seem to address, although there were notable exceptions (for example, the Reverend David Shepherd in Liverpool, later its Bishop). I was not convinced that religion could do anything much to help create social change. I viewed it as something that sought to keep the status quo. Perhaps it was the arrogance of adolescence, but my belief in God waned. I valued some of the stories of Jesus, and to this day, I still love some of the hymns I used to sing. Singing might have been fine, but curiosity and asking "difficult" questions was not. Difficult questions were, for example, any that questioned God's existence, or whether the earth was created in six days, or why was God a jealous God. Curiosity, which might be seen to challenge the status quo, was seen as impolite, disrespectful, and, to some, impertinent. This, alongside my memory of such associations, that I would literally burn in hell (or as I tend to call it now—the place of religious institutionalized torture) for eternity did not exactly promote the idea of free enquiry.[3] However, when I was fifteen, a book was published titled *Honest to God* (Robinson, 1963). In it, Robinson, the Bishop of Woolwich in London, challenged many of the traditionally accepted ideas of the Christian Establishment, not least the literal interpretations of significant parts of the text. The book did not re-convert me, but it gave me permission to continue to ask "difficult" questions. Rather than showing a lack of respect, I saw my curiosity as coming from a position of integrity, although at the time it was also accompanied by anxiety.

Even in my early adulthood, calling myself an atheist was difficult. It seemed to me that atheists were akin to being considered an agent of the devil. It was safer to call oneself an agnostic in public. As I got older, I started to call myself an atheist, and later, a humanist. But, as the philosopher Peter Cave (2009) notes, "we are all atheists—to varying extents. The 'we' includes Jews, Christians, Muslims and other godly believers" (p. 6). He goes on to list a whole range of gods—Olympian, African, Nordic, Hindu, for example—that, by definition he says, have to reject each other as the true God or accept a position that there is no one true god. Such potential for conflict has led to Holloway (1999) putting forward the idea in his book *Godless Morality* that religion should be kept out of ethics: He states,

> the use of God in any moral debate is so problematic as to be almost worthless. We can argue with one another as to whether this or that alleged claim genuinely emanated from God, but surely it is better to leave God out of the moral debate and find good human reasons for supporting the system or approach we advocate, without having recourse to divinely clinching arguments. [p. 20]

As a humanist, I have a core belief in the sacredness of human life. I believe in there being only life on this earth. I have a belief that we have the capacity to make the best of this one life, and to flourish, utilizing shared human values, without recourse to a belief in a god outside of our existence. However, I also think that there is much useful morality within religion where it is similar to a humanist position: for example, to treat people as one would wish to be treated. It is just that it does not require there to be a god to behave in that way.

Indeed, most humanists, in my experience, have no problem at all with people being religious. Religion at its best is caring, comforting, empathic, and altruistic. It is concerned for the good of those who have been unfairly discriminated against, and often courageous in the pursuit of social justice. I see these traits as those of a humanist. What humanists, in particular, cannot agree with is the use of religious beliefs to oppress those who do not have those beliefs. That is why humanists cannot accept the idea of the law of God (which God?) being above, and, for some, replacing, law made by human beings. There seems to be a growing difference of perspective between those people who believe in the establishment of laws and policies based on the principles of anti-discriminatory practice and those who wish for some sort of exemption to these laws and policies based on religious beliefs. A recent example of this was Roman Catholic adoption agencies in England and Wales wanting to opt out of equality legislation to allow gay couples to adopt children. Their wish was not granted, the British government expressing the view that there was "no place in society for discrimination" (*Guardian*, 2007, p. 5). Further, it added that, "there can be no exemptions for faith-based adoption agencies offering public-funded services, from regulations that prevent discrimination" (*ibid.*).

Respect

In the development of a collaborative approach in family therapy (Anderson, 1997), I have become concerned that, in a wish to rightly acknowledge the ownership of the expertise of clients, we are in danger of being respectful in a way that might lead us to become disengaged from the possibilities of therapeutic intimacy rather than act in ways that contribute to its promotion. In just over twenty years, it seems that we have moved from irreverence (Cecchin, 1987) to respect, such that I wonder whether the use of the latter has become, at times, an unhelpful mantra. Over-respect for difference can lead, I would suggest, to not taking enough relational risks (Mason, 2005a) in therapy, supervision, and training. While I have a core belief that people are essentially decent and well meaning, and that to live harmoniously we have to be committed to finding bridges across our differences, this does not mean I respect people's ideas *per se*, nor would I expect them to automatically respect mine. In the past few years, I have changed some of the language I use. While I consider myself to be respectful towards people in the manner that I engage in conversation with them, I do not say "I respect your beliefs" when I do not. I will say, for example, "I appreciate from what you are saying that you have certain beliefs about how you should be in relation to your wife expressing her opinion about . . . such and such a matter." For, as will have become clear, I do not respect dominion of men over women in the name of culture or religion or any belief system. I do not respect aspects of the religious texts which discriminate unfairly against, or blame, women. I deplore the sexism, racism, gratuitous violence, and the rejection of the "other" because of their difference that I see as intrinsic to many religious texts. Many religious people I have met, and many religious writers whose work I have read, also do not respect the rejection of the "other" purely because of their difference. Indeed, John Shelby Spong, the former Bishop of Newark, New Jersey and now a Harvard academic, has been one of the most outspoken in condemning (as the title of his book indicates) *The Sins of Scripture* (Spong, 2006), not least in terms of gender, sexuality, and sexual orientation. I sometimes wonder how different the world might have been if all the religious texts had started with: (a) all men and women are equal and none shall be favoured over the other, and (b) that slavery is abhorrent, immoral, and illegal. The Jewish Bible, the Christian Bible, and the Koran all fail to unconditionally condemn slavery. I retain a hope that the world's religious leaders will take a lead from the present Australian Government who, on taking office, apologized to the Aboriginal people for the injustices carried out against them. A religious apology to humankind for the condoning of one of history's greatest evils is perhaps a little overdue.

The professional

In the first two sections of this chapter, I have outlined ideas about the need to address core beliefs in respect of colleagues and the therapeutic relationship, making particular reference to culture. I have then proceeded to present some of my own core beliefs, those I present to my colleagues. In this final section, I will present some specific ideas about the utilisation of some of these core beliefs in practice.

I believe that a central task of being a therapist is to engage with, and explore, the logic, or coherence, of clients' beliefs. I also adhere to the notion that for change to happen both clients and therapist need to be willing to explore uncertainty.

Exploring core beliefs—clinical examples: Avril

Avril, a fifty-year-old British Black woman, had been brought up a Protestant but said she had been put off religion by the authoritarianism of her father, who, she said, "was very much into a literal view of the Bible. He seemed to be governed by the view that to spare the rod was to spoil the child." She said she had been regularly chastised "but not abused". In her early twenties she left home, and it was then that she became a non-believer in God. I asked her what she now saw as her core beliefs about how she should live her life. She replied, "Spend time with the people you love. Value the people you love by showing them that you want the best for them. I don't believe in an afterlife but I hope there is one for my Mum." I asked her why, and she replied that "it was because she had such a tough time with my dad—she deserved something better. That must sound strange," she added. "No," I said. "I can see the logic of why you should think that." At another point in the same session, I asked her whether there were any aspects of her previous belief in Christianity that she still held on to even though she no longer believed in God. "Uhmm [short pause], to be honest I've never really thought about it but I suppose it's impossible not to hold on to something. Well [short pause], I suppose what comes to mind is, do to your neighbour as you would want done to yourself." Given that my core personal beliefs come from a humanistic and atheistic perspective, it is important that in my practice I remain consistent with one of the basic tenets of a systems theory approach, which is that there are different ways of seeing. My personal beliefs, in relation to the existence of God, had a similarity with Avril's. To try to ensure that the therapy was not potentially constrained by similarity (of core beliefs), I reintroduced religious belief back into the conversation.

John

John was a white British man in his early forties. He had been diagnosed with fibromyalgia six months prior to my seeing him in therapy. He told me he had become very depressed, not least because the pain he was experiencing was contributing to his inability to get restful sleep. His relationship with his wife was suffering and he said he had distanced himself from her. At one point he had even said to her, "Why are you bothering to stay with me?" In exploring some of his family history, I asked him to tell me the story of how his core beliefs about how to live his life had emerged. His parents were from Eastern Europe. They had emigrated to Britain when he was in his early teens. His script in coping with adversity (Byng-Hall, 1995; Mason, 2004) centred on the need to never give in, to always persist. His parents were Roman Catholic, but he had become an atheist. He did not believe in an afterlife: he believed one had to make the best of life on earth. I asked him how that view about living his life was helping him deal with his present difficulties. He took a while to answer. Eventually, he smiled, almost in an embarrassed way, and said that he had not realized until then that he was not being consistent with his core beliefs. I said, "Suppose it was OK at times to be inconsistent; what do you think the logic of that inconsistency is?" He thought further, but said he did not know what the logic might be. I said I had an idea. Would he like to hear about it or would he prefer me to hold back on my thinking for the moment (Burnham, 2005)? He said he would like to hear, so I said to him that one way of looking at it was that fibromyalgia could have the effect of making you feel very tired and drained. It would be understandable that you just feel like giving in at times. Perhaps you can give in occasionally without feeling you have given in totally, that you can be like that without being disloyal to your core beliefs about how you should live your life. He said he wanted to think about this further.

At the next session, he said that he had not been quite sure, initially, as to how to respond to my thoughts, but between sessions they had made sense to him. He said he was more positive about getting on with his life since the last session. My comments had reminded him of his core beliefs about how to live his life, to make the best of it. He had been less distant with his wife and she had commented on it. He had also joined a self-help group to help him deal with his illness. I remarked that it was as if he had decided not to give in individually (his condition) and not to give in relationally (his marriage). Further, my sense was that he was not only being loyal to his core beliefs, but also to his parents and their struggle in coping with life in a new country.

Abraham and Rachel

Abraham, thirty-five, an orthodox Jew, was referred to me by someone in the orthodox community. He acknowledged that he was having a number of difficulties, not least, a drug and alcohol problem. Because he was worried that people in his community might find out if he sought help within the community, he preferred to see a non-Jewish therapist. At the first session, I asked him what he wanted to get from therapy and he said he wanted to find the path of God. Would it not be better, I suggested, for him to see a Rabbi? He replied that he was angry with God and in his religion that was not allowed. Therefore, he continued, it would be no use seeing a Rabbi. He said he was also angry with God for choosing the woman who had become his wife eighteen months previously. He felt that his marriage was on the verge of breaking down.

Abraham became very committed to therapy, was always on time, and was eager to talk. He said he liked the fact that I challenged him even though it was sometimes uncomfortable. By the third session, a pattern emerged of him blaming his wife for the problems between them. At one point, in the fifth session, I said that I remembered that he appreciated that I challenged him and so I was going to do this in relation to him always blaming his wife. I told him that in all the years I had been practising, it was rare for just one person to be the sole cause of difficulties in a marriage. From then on, I would ask him what he was contributing to the difficulties as well as what he thought his wife was contributing. This started to bear fruit, and he occasionally volunteered that at times he could be difficult. I explored what he valued about his wife, and he said he liked the fact that she spoke her mind, and then added, except that she sometimes speaks her mind in the wrong places—in public—thus challenging his authority as a man. The emphasis in the sessions was very much on his marriage difficulties and I suggested that perhaps Rachel came to a few sessions with him. He readily agreed because, he said, he thought I might be able to change her to how he wanted her to be!

Rachel came to the next four sessions. She was a woman who was able to give as good as she got from Abraham. She was feisty and vulnerable. In getting a picture of her, she told a very sad story of being rejected within her own family. At times, she had been so depressed she had wished she were dead. She felt an outsider and found it difficult to make relationships. She said she was seen as a bit loud by women in the orthodox community—but that was how she was and she was not going to be told what to do. In the next individual session with Abraham, he said he wanted to know what to do. Although I had given him my thinking at times, he was pressing me for more specific feedback. What did I think? I had started to form an idea, a reframe, as to why God might have chosen Rachel to be his wife. The problem was that when I ran the idea through my head, I was worried that I might sound as if I was coming across as a Rabbi. I pondered it further.

An intervention

In the next session, I told him I had been thinking about his wish to hear more about what I was thinking; that I could see this was important to him. I told him that, based on what he had told me so far, I wondered whether God had chosen Rachel for him because he was someone who was sympathetic to people who were on the margins of life. (Abraham did some social welfare work in his community.) God, as I understood Abraham's religion, would be aware that while he was not someone who went to synagogue regularly and could be somewhat dismissive of those who were more actively religious than him, his heart was in the right place. Indeed, God (who was perceived to see everything) would be aware of his work with people on the margins who got into difficulties. God would be aware, also, of the extremely sad and painful life that Rachel had experienced—someone very much on the margins, an outcast. It could be seen, therefore, that there was logic as to why he and Rachel should be together. It was as if God had seen that Rachel needed someone who could empathize with her plight and would understand what it felt to be downtrodden. This is what I have been thinking, I said.

Abraham seemed fascinated and, when I had finished, he said that he had not thought about it like this before. We discussed it further, the session came to an end, and he left. When he came back for the next session, a week later, he said that my thoughts had made a big impression on him, that it had been the most useful thing that had happened in the therapy so far. He had started going to the synagogue and he felt he had been much nicer to Rachel and she had commented as such. The work continued for another few months. I saw Abraham on his own, and I also saw Rachel on her own on three more occasions. We also had two more couple sessions. There were ups and downs, but the overall improvement in the relationship Abraham had with Rachel and with God was maintained. Rachel confirmed that they were getting on much better, to such an extent that they were now thinking of starting a family.

My relationship with the intervention about the logic of God's behaviour

As I have indicated above, I was anxious about giving the intervention that in the end seemed to make a substantial difference to the therapy. Here I was, non-Jewish, not believing in God, and wondering whether I was being ethical in giving such a message. I discussed the idea with a Jewish and a non-Jewish colleague, and both of them, independently of each other, thought the idea was interesting and that I should pursue it. The message that I took away was that as long as the idea was not delivered as if from on high, then I should go ahead. My style is not to go for a blockbuster message (like the original Milan team approach) and I had no idea that it would have the impact it had. For me, it was about using my systemic skills and the non-marginalizing of my core beliefs to engage with substantial difference in such a way that I might contribute to the opening up of different, potentially useful, ways of seeing. In my intervention, I was particularly careful about the language I used, language that I felt would engage with him, yet not marginalize my own personal beliefs of not believing in a god. So I used phrases such as, "God, as I *understood* Abraham's religion . . ." Further, I said, "God, who was *perceived* to see everything . . ." In this way, I was trying to find bridges across our differences without marginalizing my own, or his, beliefs. I was trying to find a both/and position.

Training and supervision

As I indicated at the beginning of this paper, I believe that family and systemic psychotherapists and practitioners need to be more transparent in the way they talk about stories of self, their core beliefs, and their place in the therapeutic task. This transparency should include how these core beliefs might helpfully and unhelpfully influence the professional task, both at a general level and also at the specific level of particular pieces of clinical work and supervision. I believe this will help us be more consistent with the aims of the cultural genogram, be consistent with a relational, second-order perspective on self, be consistent in helping us become more adept at relational risk-taking with colleagues (Mason, 2005a), and, thus, enable us as therapists to take risks in the therapeutic work itself.

I have suggested elsewhere (Mason, 2002) seeing self in two ways: the direct expression of self, and the indirect utilization of self. In the former, the clinician may speak openly about some aspect of their own history, which they feel might be useful to the therapeutic task. In the latter they may make a connection with self, but use it indirectly, as a theme, for example, without stating personal ownership. This approach tends to be my own preference. In supervision, I think there should be more emphasis on the direct expression of self; I think this is more consistent with a peer approach. This is not to say that people should be expected to talk about personal issues that they feel are too private. However, if self is going to be consistent with the relational context of systemic supervision, there has to be a commitment to "public" discourse within the confidentiality of the group.

We are in danger of privatizing self within a relational theory and a group-based practice. Rather than tell each other the stories of our personal core beliefs and their influence on our professional task, we are in danger, sometimes due to the misplaced notion of trying to be respectful, of withholding thinking that might be potentially valuable for supervision, peer consultation, and, ultimately, therapy.

Notes

1. Acknowledgement to Peter Bruggen.
2. In the US presidential election in 1992, the Democrats had a sign on the wall to keep them focused on how to win the election—"It's the economy, stupid!" For living everyday life, my core belief has become "It's gender, stupid!"

3. Recently (May 2009), I experienced a sense of *déjà vu* on hearing the outgoing Roman Catholic Archbishop of Westminster, London, Cardinal Murphy-O'Connor, say that non-believers in God "were not totally human." He added that, "the inability to believe in God and to live by faith is the greatest of evils." This happened to be said a couple of days after the publication of the Ryan Report (2009) in Ireland, detailing the endemic abuse of children by priests and nuns.

References

AFT (1991). *The Blue Book*. Canterbury: AFT.
Ali, T. (2002). *The Clash of Fundamentalisms: Crusades, Jihads and Modernity*. London: Verso.
Anderson, H. (1997). *Conversation, Language and Possibilities: A Postmodern Approach to Therapy*. New York: Basic Books.
Boyd-Franklin, N. (2002). Foreword. In: B. Mason & A. Sawyerr (Eds.), *Exploring the Unsaid: Creativity, Risks and Dilemmas in Working Cross Culturally* (pp. xii–xvi). London: Karnac.
Burnham, J. (2005). Relational reflexivity: a tool for socially constructing therapeutic relationships. In: C. Flaskas, B. Mason, & A. Perlesz (Eds.), *The Space Between: Experience, Context and Process in the Therapeutic Relationship* (pp. 21–41). London: Karnac.
Byng-Hall, J. (1995). *Re-Writing Family Scripts*. New York: Guildford.
Cave, P. (2009). *Humanism*. Oxford: One World.
Cecchin, G. (1987). Hypothesising, circularity and neutrality revisited: an invitation to curiosity. *Family Process*, 26: 405–413.
Davies, T. (1988). *Still Voices, Distant Lives*. London: BFI Video.
Davies, T. (1992). *The Long Day Closes*. London: BFI Video.
Davies, T. (2008). *Time and the City*. London: BFI Video.
Freidan, E. (1992)[1963]. *The Feminine Mystique*. London: Penguin.
Guardian (2007). Blair: no exemption for Catholics on gay adoption. 29th January, p. 5.
Hardy, K. V., & Laszloffy, T. A. (1995). The cultural genogram: key to training culturally competent family therapists. *Journal of Family and Marital Therapy*, 21: 227–237.
Heisenberg, W. (1962). *Physics and Philosophy*. New York: Harper and Row.
Hoffman, L. (1985). Beyond power and control: towards a second-order systems therapy. *Family Systems Medicine*, 3: 381–396.

Holloway, R. (1999). *Godless Morality*. Edinburgh: Canongate.
Krause, I.-B. (2002). Uncertainty, risk-taking and ethics. In: B. Mason & A. Sawyerr (Eds.), *Exploring the Unsaid: Creativity, Risks and Dilemmas in Working Cross Culturally* (pp. 34–48). London: Karnac.
Mason, B. (1993). Towards positions of safe uncertainty. *Human Systems*, 4: 189–200.
Mason, B. (2002). A reflective recording format for the training of supervisors and supervisees. In: D. Campbell & B. Mason. (Eds.), *Perspectives on Supervision* (pp. 45–58). London: Karnac.
Mason, B. (2004). A relational approach to the management of chronic pain. *Clinical Psychology*, 35: 17–20.
Mason, B. (2005a). Relational risk taking and the therapeutic relationship. In: C. Flaskas, B. Mason, & A. Perlesz (Eds.), *The Space Between: Experience, Context and Process in the Therapeutic Relationship* (pp. 157–170). London: Karnac.
Mason, B. (2005b). Relational risk-taking and the training of supervisors. *Journal of Family Therapy*, 27: 298–301.
Mason, B. (2008). Relational risk-taking, men and affairs. *Journal of Family Therapy*, 30: 490–501.
Mason, B. (2010). Six perspectives on supervision and the training of supervisors. *Journal of Family Therapy*, 32: 436–439.
Mason, B., & Sawyerr, A. (Eds.) (2002). *Exploring the Unsaid: Creativity, Risks and Dilemmas in Working Cross Culturally*. London: Karnac.
Milkman, R. (1987). Review: gender, consciousness, and social change: rethinking women's World War II experience. *Contemporary Sociology*, 16: 21–25.
Robinson, J. (1963). *Honest to God*. Canterbury: SCM Press.
Ryan Report, The (2009). *The Commission to Inquire into Child Abuse*. Dublin: Government Publications.
Spong, S. J. (2006). *The Sins of Scripture*. New York: HarperCollins.
Von Foerster, H. (1990). Ethics and second-order cybernetics. Paper presented to the International Conference on Systems and Family Therapy: Ethics, Epistemology, New Methods. Paris.

CHAPTER NINE

Hewing out hope from mountains of despair

Archie Smith

> "With this faith, we will be able to hew out of the mountain of despair a stone of hope"
>
> (from Martin Luther King Jr's speech "I have a dream...", Washington, 1986, p. 219)

Introduction

In 1963, on the steps of the Lincoln Memorial in Washington, DC, Martin Luther King Jr, a Baptist minister and civil rights activist, shared his dream with a racially diverse cross-section of USA society. Would his speech resonate with almost everyone present? Tension and hope were in the air. National Guard troops were poised to quell a riot. It did not happen. Near the end of his "I have a dream" speech, Martin Luther King Jr said, "With this faith we will be able to hew out of the mountain of despair a stone of hope." With these words, he conjured hope for a whole nation. He pointed a way for everyone facing a seemingly intractable economic, social, and political problem (Washington, 1986).

In this chapter, I use "mountains of despair" as a metaphor for major depressive episodes. I am an African-American male, a pastoral theologian who teaches at the Graduate Theological Union in Berkeley, California, and a family therapist. A part of my task is to widen the lens for an assessment of human difficulties in the light of faith traditions and to identify grounds for hope. Sometimes, this assessment of human difficulties means crossing over into unfamiliar territory where one is a stranger and cultural outsider. I am an insider to African-American male culture, although I can only represent a small part of it, and, therefore, I might experience unfamiliar parts of my own culture as "strange". I am an outsider to the Korean Confucian–Christian culture I am about to discuss.

This chapter is an account of lectures I delivered to mainly Korean pastors and graduate students of theology at Seoul Christian University and at Yonsei University in Seoul, Korea. I was responding to an invitation from former doctoral students, who have taken their place as members of the faculty at both universities, to address issues of depression, faith, and hope. This was with reference to recent suicides in Seoul. I chose to relate this topic to Psalm 42, because depression and hope are prominent in Psalm 42, and this scripture is frequently referred to by Christians from different cultures. In the lecture, speaking through a translator, I gave an interpretation of Psalm 42 and engaged the audience in a conversation that included a listing of the kind of difficulties faced by pastors who are concerned with depression and suicide in their congregations. I then gathered privately with a few Korean graduate students and colleagues for further conversation. The fruit of that conversation is reflected in this chapter. I came away from those presentations and conversations with haunting questions and greater awareness of the complexities of depression when working across cultures and in contexts of social change. I learnt that the connections between depression, culture, power, ethnicity, and faith are often missed and/or misinterpreted. I did not come away with final answers. I raised and heard discerning questions about religious values, cultural difference, humour, and play. I came to value empathy and boundaries, the role of community, and the tapping of close relations as resources when working with depression and faith, but also the way that prayer, scriptures, and hymnody can be indispensable resources when working with depression across cultures. In this chapter, I address how one might use scripture as an aid to reflection about depression and despair, and I want to keep in mind something a colleague once said, ". . . in order to avoid colonization and imposition of a secularist discourse and to ensure anti-discriminatory practice, it is important that therapists be aware of their own ideologies" (Malik, 2007, p. 15).

Depression and the case of Choi jin-sil

Recently, a famous and well-loved Korean movie celebrity, Choi jin-sil, committed suicide in Seoul. According to one news source she was

> "the country's cinematic sweetheart... She [had] become a symbol of the difficulties women face in this deeply conservative yet technologically savvy society. Incessant online gossip appears to have been largely to blame for her death. But it's also clear that public life as a single, working, divorced mom—still a pariah status in South Korea—was one role she had a lot of trouble with. [*Time World*, 2008]

Choi jin-sil suffered a mountain of despair from depression. She was a Christian and a single mother with two young children, aged five and seven. She received much commentary and criticism, according to Korean news reports. Here is a sample of statements from one website, all relating to Choi jin-Sil's death (www.BuhayKorea.com/Choi-jin-sil-suicide/):

"I'm sad for the kids whose mother didn't want to be with them anymore."

"One way of fighting depression would be having a solid relationship with the Almighty and having people whom you could really trust to share your heartaches with ... It's better that we let others know it than keep it to ourselves but we have to choose someone who is willing to help and understand us ... I think Choi jin-sil could have made it if only she did not rely on antidepressants ... God's intervention or human interaction is better than all of those drugs that we take ...".

"We should be more understanding and accepting of the reality that life is a painful process, its not always bad though ... we have friends and family and God whom we can always turn to when problems start to overwhelm us right? Please ... NO MORE suicide ... don't ruin your life ... problems are just problems ... don't let it drive you crazy."

"I can't believe it! How could she let such a minor problem get the best of her. She had everything going for her. I am a counselor in Korea, and I heard this news at 10am and I had to come to the internet to see for myself if this is real. I really hope this is the end of suicide here in Korea. I am offering free counseling services in English and Korean to anyone who is depressed and is thinking about suicide to please go to my website for help. There is no need of this. Every problem has a solution. Trust me on this, I know."

Elsewhere it was observed that

> ... there were 12.174 suicides representing 5% of all deaths in 2007. It's also said that annual average 23.6 Koreans committed suicide out of 100.000 people in the last five years, which is one of the highest levels in the world. [*General World News*, 2008, p. 2]

> Policy makers and the general public readily admit that mental illness—even a common disorder like depression—is rarely talked about openly in the country. Koreans are very secretive about psychiatric problems ... [*Time World*, 2008]

Depression, and the many ways in which it is manifested, is not understood, especially in the context of religious faith. Rumours swirled around the celebrity, Choi jin-sil. She was divorced and a single mother in a society that shuns such women, despite celebrity status. She was a Christian. These facts, comments, and criticism took their toll. The criticisms combine to indicate a lack of understanding of a helpful relationship between depression, religious faith, and success. The criticisms revealed that a certain cultural bias operates against religious people experiencing depression, and, especially, women and single mothers in Korean culture. For Choi jin-sil, depression was something to be denied, resisted, endured, tolerated, or recovered from. But we might not always appreciate the cultural and social context out of which these sentiments arise.

The *Diagnostic and Statistical Manual* (*DSM-IV*) defines depression as a mood disorder and a general dissatisfaction with life.

> Individuals with a Major Depressive Episode frequently present with tearfulness, irritability, brooding, obsessive rumination, anxiety, phobias, excessive worry over physical health, and complaints of pain. ... The most serious consequence of a Major Depressive Episode is attempted or completed suicide. [*DSM-IV*, 1994, p. 323]

However, depression is also very common. Everyone gets depressed sooner or later. Perhaps that is why it is often called the common cold of mental illness. Millions of people struggle with it daily, the affects are cumulative, and influence one another. We learnt that on 30 March 2010, the late actress Choi jin-sil's brother, actor Choi jin-young, committed suicide. He was influenced, in part, by his sister's death (Javabeans, 2010). Former students called or wrote to tell me how sad they felt when they learnt that the former President of Seoul, Korea, committed suicide. He felt deep shame because of political scandals that were being exposed (*New York Times*, 2009). Some forms of depression are mild, some are severe, others are chronic and persistent. Some people take medication to help manage it and still others are hospitalized. For some, like Choi jin-sil, Choi jin-young, and the ex-president of Seoul, depression is like an insurmountable mountain of despair, and they commit suicide.

In USA society, depression might be interpreted as anger or aggression turned inward, or a sense of being trapped with no way to escape. This might not be the case for Korean or UK societies. In each of the societies, Korean or Western, what we call "depression" might be triggered by a host of events with different meanings: dangerous memory, loss of a valued status (e.g., loss of face or position or celebrity status), object (e.g., job, home) or relationship (e.g., divorce or other unwanted change in an intimate relationship), a move to a different place, loss of a body part (e.g., arm, leg), loss of a major body function (paralysis, speech, hearing, sight), or a change in personality. Returning war veterans know about some of this. Upon returning home from battle, they might find that things have changed significantly, and they no longer belong. They have become strangers in their own country.

Depression may result from a rumour mill, hurt, disappointment, sense of betrayal, entrapment, etc. Such events may trigger sadness, worry, and hopelessness. We might respond by displaying strange behaviour, or by playing self-negating tapes in our mind, over and again. We might distance ourselves from others and withdraw into silence or isolation, escape into drugs, mental illness, develop physical symptoms, alcoholism, or do something worse to the self. On the one hand, depression might be a response to unwanted change or loss, real or imagined, a way of coping. On the other, some expressions of depression can serve a function in a relationship. We might ask, what would happen in some relationships if the depression suddenly went away? A child, for example, might get depressed because his or her depression keeps the parents from fighting and keeps the family together.

Depression is a common experience among religious believers, but it might not always be recognized. Religious workers might not see that they have a role to play in addressing depression. They might not acknowledge a relationship between everyday life, community, faith, and depression. Cultural myths might hinder understandings of depression. Some might reason this way: "Isn't religious faith a source of happiness and well-being?"; "Does not religious faith protect one from mental illness and depression?"; "Does not the presence of mental illness or depression indicate a lack of faith?". Dismantling cultural myths and misunderstandings about the relationship between faith and depression is an important role for religious leaders and institutions. The story is told of a man who was always smiling. Some thought he was ridiculously happy. One day, in a conversation with his medical doctor, it emerged that he always smiled and acted happy because he believed that the Christian thing to do was to smile through life's hardships. That is what he did when his father died at an early age. That is what he did when his wife died. And that was what he wanted his children to do when their mother died. His children found his smiling through the death of their mother, his wife, to be a source of profound irritation and a denial of reality. His was the smiling face of depression. His depression was hard to address (Asen, Tomson, Young, & Tomson, 2004).

Three approaches to depression

Cultural approaches to depression reflect cultural outlooks on individuals and personhood as well as relationships. I think that three different approaches stand out: the individual approach (Sorajjakool, Aja, Chilson, Ramiez-Johnson, & Earll, 2008), the relational approach (Jones & Asen, 2000), and the socio-centric approach (Kwon, 2008; Shweder & Bourne, 1984).

The individual approach

Some studies on religious research define depression in terms of the lone individual. One study in particular suggested that depression creates a sense of existential despair and spiritual disconnection in the lives of individuals who struggle with chronic depression (Sorajjakool, Aja, Chilson, Ramirez-Johnson, & Earll, 2008). Here, depression is a personal, private phenomenon affecting the individual soul. The key to success, then, is through personal connections, individual freedom, increased sense of personal agency, effort, and luck. The mythic hero and image of the self-made individual, who overcomes the odds through dogged strength alone, comes to mind. This is a Western ideal. The individual soul triumphs over the forces of evil and depression through individual freedom. This ideal of the rugged individual has resonance in both USA and UK societies.

The relational approach

As an alternative, I summarize a study that demonstrates a relational approach to the understanding of depression. The title of the study is "The London Depression Intervention Trial" (Jones & Asen, 2000). The subjects for this research were seventy-seven people meeting the criteria for clinical depression and living with a critical partner. The study makes the point that depressive behaviours are primarily maintained by the various contexts of which the depressed person is part. They include partner, family, social context, and helping system. This differs from the idea that depression is something personal, private, and happening inside the individual, an implosion. The London team recognized that depression is personally felt, but it is largely a relational phenomenon. Its origins are social. With this focus, the therapists in the study were able to address a number of things: (1) identify the context of behaviour of each individual and the possible relationship mechanism that helps to maintain the depression, (2) assess the triggering events, (3) challenge the couple's ways of coping, and (4) assign appropriate alternative roles to the individual persons and coach them. The focus of this work, then, was on addressing the depressed person's difficulties in a social context.

The socio-centric approach

The relational approach, as described above, focuses on the relationships between individuals. The role of others and their interactions with the depressed person are used to illuminate a wider context in which each individual is embedded. In the socio-centric view the identification of the self is not with a single body, but with the degree to which the self is identified with others and on the value ascribed to the self in the eyes of others. "The self is most fully actualized when most deeply connected to society" (Im, 2005, p. 5). This is a Korean view of self and society. This suggests that there are different understandings of depression between Korean, UK, and USA societies. Key differences stem from cultural values and basic philosophies, understandings of selfhood, and the nature of the social bond. Generally speaking, in the UK, depression might be associated with national identity and the need or failure to "soldier on" through difficulty. In American culture, depression is typically viewed as an internal disposition of the autonomous, encapsulated individual. Depression is a private, individual affair and might result from competitive engagements where there are winners and losers. Depression results from a sense of loss and diminished self-esteem. It is the opposite of a Korean sense of "we-ness" or harmony. On the one hand, Western societies in general, and the USA in particular, highly value individual freedom, happiness, and personal well-being. They are central pursuits. On the other hand, Korea is an honour–shame based society that prizes communitarian ideals, filial piety, and inclusive family values. Koreans identify with collectivism and support mutual relationships over individualism. Accordingly, a Korean's sense of "interdependent selfhood and his or her happiness is generally realized less through the means of expressing private internal attributes than by enriching the feeling or interconnectedness with significant others" (Kwon, 2008, p. 576). The Korean term for depression is *"woo-wul-Jung"*. It is understood as a kind of mental illness, emotional feebleness, or badness. It derives from an honour–shame social system, where honour means social harmony, fulfilling one's duty or ascribed roles. Shame is the failure to do so. Depression results from departure from ascribed social expectations. It represents disharmony, a broken connection between self and others. Depression also results in a sense of collective shame. A colleague explained Choi Jin sil's depression and eventual suicide in this way: as a divorced single mother, Choi was regarded to have completely shut down her ex-husband's public life. She was too successful and famous. Her ex-husband was a famous professional baseball player. His domestic violence was the public reason for the divorce. But people still sympathized with him because the famous

Choi did not do her duty well—supporting her husband's success. Choi brought shame to the entire Korean community. After the divorce, as soon as Korean law changed, Choi changed her son's last name from his father's to hers, which brought serious criticisms and public debate. These examples sum up her situation in a Confucian, honour–shame society.

The role of faith

Faith is a confident way of knowing that cannot be justified by reason or proof. Faith means moving ahead without the assurances or guarantees we would normally expect. Faith is usually placed in someone or something that is trustworthy. Martin Luther King Jr, for example, showed faith in the future when he acted as if the non-violent society he hoped for was already here. He called those who struggled for a changed society "divine mal-discontents" or "creative dissenters". They take courage and work to transform a minus into a plus. In this way, creative dissenters are those who call their beloved community or nation to a higher destiny, to a new plateau of compassion, to a more noble expression of humaneness (King, 1968). This is a positive statement of depression and faith joined together. It might not be common and it might not always work for those who are severely or clinically depressed.

Depression, faith, and hope pose challenges for all of us (Flaskas, 2007), and in religious communities we might use scripture and sacred texts to address this.

While scripture can be an important faith or spiritual resource for those struggling with depression, there are two extremes to be avoided. One is to avoid quoting scripture without seeking to understand the complex life situations of those who turn to us for help. Scripture has been used in ways that punish or taunt people, condemn, or cause further harm. The depressed person might hear the judgement "I can't believe it! How could she let such a minor problem get the best of her!" Or, "She could have made it if only she did not rely on antidepressant drugs." The other and opposite extreme to be avoided is the neglect of scripture altogether. This can be equally unhelpful. People of religious faith tend to turn to this faith when they are at their lowest point.

Scriptures express the wisdom of a faith tradition. It is a compilation of sacred texts that have emerged over time from a community's relationship with divine mystery and presence. The Psalms are a particular genre of scripture. "Psalm" means a religious song or hymn. The Psalms are a collection of personal and communal chants, laments, petitions, prayers, and praise songs expressing the inner life of the individual and/or community (Craven & Harrelson, 2003). They were written down over long periods of time and used over and again in times of despair, joy, thanksgiving, and praise. They were often accompanied by stringed instruments and gave encouragement and voice to individuals and the faith community to move from despair and depression to thanksgiving and hope. A Psalm, such as Psalm 42, is a prayer that contains longing, lament, petition, praise. It arises from the deepest pain and distress and displays the depths of human misery, anger, and frustration, and it expresses trust and hope and continued faithfulness born of despair. Over and again, readers of this psalm have found their voices, as God's own voice joined the dialogue and as they are reminded of a sense of communitas. Turner defined communitas as that "irrefragile genuiness of mutuality" (Turner, 1969, p. 137), and further described this as an undifferentiated experience of communion, equality, openness to the other. Communitas is a spontaneous and existential experience.

I used Psalm 42 to relate issues of depression and faith to the Korean context and to help interpret the ancient and perennially existential question, "How shall we live?" The following is a rendering of Psalm 42. The text is familiar to Korean and African-Americans alike, even if it is nuanced differently across cultures. I am using the *New Living Translation* (*Holy Bible*, 1996).

[1] As the deer pants for streams of water,
so I long for you, O God.

[2] I thirst for God, the living God.
When can I come and stand before him?

[3] Day and night, I have only tears for food,
while my enemies continually taunt me, saying,
"Where is this God of yours?"

[4] My heart is breaking
as I remember how it used to be:
I walked among the crowds of worshipers,

leading a great procession to the house of God,
singing for joy and giving thanks-
it was the sound of a great celebration!

5 Why am I discouraged?
Why so sad?
I will put my hope in God!
I will praise him again-
my Savior and

6 my God!
Now I am deeply discouraged,
but I will remember your kindness-
from Mount Hermon, the source of the Jordan,
from the land of Mount Mizar.

7 I hear the tumult of the raging seas
as your waves and surging tides sweep over me.

8 Through each day the LORD pours his unfailing love upon me,
and through each night I sing his songs,
praying to God who gives me life.

9 "O God my rock," I cry,
"Why have you forsaken me?
"Why must I wander in darkness,
oppressed by my enemies?"

10 Their taunts pierce me like a fatal wound.
They scoff, "Where is this God of yours?"

11 Why am I discouraged?
Why so sad?
I will put my hope in God!
I will praise him again-
my Savior and my God!

Cross-cultural interpretation of Psalm 42

The following is my interpretation of the psalm. The psalm begins with the female deer longing for a sense of connection with God. The metaphor of moving water as living or flowing "stream", "tears", "raging seas", "waves and surging tides" is used throughout this psalm. Moving water is a multivalent symbol for searching, deep thirst, remembering, nourishment, as well as potential for chaos and destruction. The roles of the help seeker (client) and a help provider (a leader of a faith community, pastor, or therapist) are identified. The help seeker recognizes that she (or he) is in a desperate situation—a longing to overcome separation from God. The metaphor of the female deer in Psalm 42 is used to describe the desperate situation of the help seeker. The deer is beyond mere thirst. The deer is panting. That means the deer has been running from waterhole to waterhole looking for something fresh and life giving. The deer's desire is unbounded and looks for streams of living water. The deer has visited other sources of help, including dried-up waterholes. Nothing can help. A crisis situation has been reached. The deer has run out of options. This cry is spiritual as well as emotional and relational. It is a cry for the source of living water: a felt relationship with the living God. No substitute will satisfy this deepest thirst. This touches on my understanding of "spirituality". By "spiritual", I mean the human capacity to be self and other related at the same time. It is a desire to know and be known by mystery or the unknown, long for purpose, solitude, and companionship, and participate in helping to create a non-violent, just, and loving community. Spirituality includes a sense of fulfilment, meaning-making, and coming to terms with suffering and limitations. It includes a felt sense of gratitude for life itself, and a desire to give as well as to receive. It is a consequence of communitas.

In verses 1 and 2, we note a few things about the help seeker's situation that might be relevant for the therapist: help seekers, or clients, have to recognize that they have a problem. The situation is often desperate and there are limited resources. This requires some assessment. It takes courage and an openness to seek and receive assistance. The provider of help must recognize that some thirsts can be satisfied by material or chemical comforters, but the deeper thirst, in this case, is spiritual: a loss of a sense of connection and a longing for God, "I thirst for God, the living God." According to the psalmist, a vital relationship with the living God is required. "When can I come and stand before him?" Other sources of help have been tried, but the desired help has not yet been found. There might be a sense of desperation, disappointment, anger, despair, finger-pointing, and blame, panic. There is a sense that time is running out. This desperate situation, according to the psalmist, puts the help seeker in a vulnerable situation.

In verses 3–8 we get a deeper appreciation of the help seeker's situation. The help seeker (client) and the provider of help must be patient. The therapist must convey a sense of safety, show genuine interest, and ask good questions. This is important in the situation of separation, despair, and depression. A depressed person might move slowly. The therapist might ask orientating and detailed questions, "How long have you been in this situation?" "To whom do you turn when at your lowest point?" "What have you already tried?" "What do you find most/least difficult to do?" "How can those closest to you tell when help has arrived?" The client tells us that she (or he) is in such despair that even physical food for the body has not been satisfying or available. The body might be in a state of withdrawal, or deprivation and self-protection. The body is feeding upon itself. "I only have tears for food." Sometimes, the despair is so great that the desire for food has gone. Can you imagine this situation? The enemies, who appear joined in their anger, cannot imagine themselves in this isolated and desperate situation. They are too busy "taunting", hurling blame and insult. The end result of their efforts is essentially immoral. They tear down humanity, not lift it up. Therefore, the faith community is challenged to summon deep compassion and mobilize the moral strength to resist the taunting and scoffing that wears people down and destroys the resilient spirit. The therapist and/or community of faith has a helping role to play. They are challenged to hew out hope from the details that constitute the mountain of despair.

If there is body trauma, then there is also emotional trauma: taunting, ridicule, shaming, discrediting, belittling, rejecting, isolating. "I can't believe it! How could she let such a minor problem get the best of her." There are attempts to wear and tear the person down physically, emotionally, spiritually. And the perpetrators, according to Psalm 42, are not the bad folk, but the good folk of society, the upright citizens who seldom see themselves as harming or in the role of the taunting enemy. We must find out how the help seeker/client is experiencing this situation. And we cannot find out about the help seeker's plight unless we are willing to stay with them long enough to hear their full story. This might take a lot of patience. It is this determination to keep pushing that will transform the darkness of despair into the light of hope. The lost dignity of the depressed person is waiting for them in the helping acts of the accepting community. The help seeker, in this psalm, tells us something else that is important. We are not told right away, but only after we have conveyed the idea that they are safe and our interest is genuine, that they can trust going further. The help seeker tells us,

"My heart is breaking."
"I am deeply discouraged."

The help seeker/client tells us why "my heart is breaking" and why "I am deeply discouraged". It has to do with memory and remembering the tragic experiences of the past and how the past appears to be repeating itself in the present. Indeed, this is a recipe for depression, hopelessness, and helplessness: in other words, lament. The help provider, community leader, pastor, or therapist should be on high alert.

The help seeker is allowed to go deeper into their sense of despair. Despairing memories must be explored. If "God's presence is pervasive, though never predictable or one-dimensional", then "despairing memories of God must be explored and sharp words to God about divine abandonment and taunting adversaries" must be expressed (*The New Interpreter's Study Bible*, 2003, p. 788). This can be uncomfortable and frightening for both the help seeker and help provider. This is not a task for just any help provider. But it is a task for those who have the best relationship with the depressed person. The tendency on the part of the mental health provider might be to interrupt, distract, or somehow shut up the one who is telling the awful and trauma filled story. "I really hope this is the end of suicide here (in Korea) . . . I am offering free counseling services to anyone who is depressed and is thinking about suicide to please go to my website for help. There is no need of this." This is a difficult and tricky situation because it is fraught with danger! It does call for assessment and professional judgement. An appropriate question would be, "How far should the person go with their painful story?" "Is there a threshold that should not be crossed?" "Where is the point of no return?" "What is helpful and unhelpful here?" "How can we tell?" Timing and position is all important, and so is a sense of safety, trust, and competence.

Then something new happens in the Psalms. The help seeker/client is encouraged to share memories of hope. "I will put my hope in God! I will praise him again," ". . . I will remember your kindness," "Through each day the Lord pours his unfailing love upon me . . .".

We can learn another important lesson here about working with depression and faith. The help seeker/client is encouraged to "remember", to "revisit", to "review" the past in the caring present of the help provider. "I remember how it used to be: I walked among the crowds of worshipers, leading a great procession to the house of God" (verse 4).

In verses 9–11, we see that even people with a strong faith can experience the depths of despair. There is the dark night of the soul for everyone who struggles. The psalmist cried, "O God my rock, I cry, / Why have you forsaken me? Why must I wander in darkness, / oppressed by my enemies?" (verse 9). "Their taunts pierce me like a fatal wound. They scoff, "Where is this God of yours?" (verse 10). So, if relentless taunts, overwhelming despair, and subsequent depression can happen to the true and struggling believer, then it can also happen to anyone, including the one who provides help. No one is immune to existential despair or depression. So, what do we do when a strong faith seems to not be strong enough? Quoting scripture fast and often enough will not help. If we neglect scripture altogether, we might miss an opportunity. What might be helpful when despair is high? I think there are four possibilities: lament, sustaining, guidance, and thanksgiving or gratitude, all of them have cross-cultural resonance and are expressed in Psalm 42.

"My tears have been my food day and night" is a lament. My Korean sister-in-law told me about a time when she had reached the lowest point in her life. She was in despair, alone, isolated from her native land and language, abandoned in a foreign country, and with few resources. She cried for two years. Her ability to cry was her saving grace. People might need the encouragement to lament as a way to hew out hope from a mountain of despair. To sustain means to hold the line against further slippage or demoralization. Sustaining means to endure and to hope. How, then, do we enable people to express outrage, face their difficulties, and endure? What resources do we, or they, call upon? How does the community of faith do this? The community is challenged to help build networks of care and enable people to cope. The community is further challenged to use its rich and collective resources to empower a sense of agency and call forth a resilient spirit, that of communitas. People need encouragement and support to endure difficult times. Even with her celebrity status, Choi jin-sil was isolated. Guidance includes giving advice, perhaps in narrative form. It might include assigning tasks or rituals to help persons adopt certain principles, affirmations, or practices. It might be reading a text together and/or reflecting on symbols. Finally, gratitude means stimulating the attitude of thanksgiving. The help seeker might be invited to talk about the times when things were not so despairing, when there was hope. The help provider might ask, "Tell me about the exceptions to the times of deep discouragement." "What were you doing then?" The help seeker responds by reciting tradition—that is, tapping the distilled wisdom and narratives of the past by remembering times of uncommon kindness that can even come through strangers. A smile might conjure a sense of welcome and hope. According to this psalm, tradition is recalled and, in recalling it, hope is instilled. "Why am I discouraged? / Why so sad? / I will put my hope in God! / I will praise God again— / my savior and my God!" (verse 11).

Concluding thoughts

I have used Psalm 42 as a metaphor for the battle between hope and despair and also as an arena for exploring the essential and generic human bond, which Turner has referred to as communitas and which I, in my work as a pastor and a therapist, think of as faith or spirituality. In the Psalm, the help seeker's plight is acknowledged as desperate and voice is given to it. There is no attempt to minimize it. The help seeker is encouraged to go deeper by recalling the ups *and* downs, the lows *and* highs of the experience. Longing, panting, searching, and tears are noticed. The help seeker is encouraged or led to draw upon tradition and search his or her own experience for the kindness of God, who shows unfailing love even in the midst of despair. This search and experience of kindness often comes through body experiences, the natural environment, the responses of others, and the unexpected, even from strangers. The help seeker is led to recognize that we always live in the midst of nagging contradiction, that is, in the midst of praise on the one side and the accusing finger of blame, taunts, and ridicule and the asking, "Where is your God?" on the other. These rages, taunts, questions, and nagging doubts help build the mountains of despair. They are put to the help seekers. They overwhelm like a fatal wound. But they do not have the final say.

According to the psalmist, God's presence and goodness is available in the community even if we cannot see or name it for ourselves. Hope for the depressed person is waiting for them in the accepting community where God's steadfast love towards us is practised. Hope is ever possible. Even when we cannot see God's goodness or presence, or even sing our own song, there are others who can sing it for us until we get back our own voice. These are experiences shared by Korean, African-American, and UK religious communities as well as religious communities the world over. They refer to communitas, the antistructural reaction to the hierarchical and differentiated relations of the structured everyday world (Turner, 1969).

The Korean audience I addressed was encouraged to rethink the relationship between depression and religious faith and to critically address the limits of certain cultural myths. Martin Luther King appealed to his audience's sense of communitas as expressed in the dichotomy between hope and despair. I have drawn on this inspiration in order to show that it is possible to work cross-culturally if we anchor this in a sense of existing together. In a religious community, this sense of communitas might be expressed in terms of faith and spirituality, and using scriptures helps to make this tangible as well as providing a focus for the reflection and experiencing of symbols and the way they might evoke a sense of sharing. This might have a powerful healing property. However, communitas is always there, and represented through tradition and ritual, whether we are talking about individual, relational, or socio-centric understandings of persons, and in these different outlooks, ritual and tradition might provide material for the kind of journey I have sketched here through Psalm 42. To me, though, this sense of communitas is spiritual, and remembering this, we can challenge a secularist discourse on depression and discern helpful and unhelpful roles of religious faith traditions and spiritual practice in assessments of cultural expressions of despair.

References

Asen, E., Tomson, D., Young, V., & Tomson, P. (2004). Ten minutes for the family. In: *Systemic Interventions in Primary Care* (pp. 169–170). London: Routledge.

Craven, T., & Harrelson, W. (2003). *The New Interpreter's Study Bible: New Revised Standard Version with the Apocrapha*. Nashville, TN: Abingdon Press.
Diagnostic and Statistical Manual of Mental Disorders (4th edn) (1994). Washington, DC: American Psychiatric Association.
Flaskas, C. (2007). The balance of hope and hopelessness. In: C. Flaskas, I. McCarthy, & J. Sheeham (Eds.), *Hope and Despair in Family Therapy: Reflections on Adversity, Forgiveness and Reconciliation* (pp. 24–35). Hove: Brunner-Routledge.
General World News (2008). 59% of Korean teens think of suicide. 12 September.
Holy Bible (1996). *New Living Translation*. Wheaton, IL: Tyndale House.
Im, H. S. (2005). The Korean self: exploring Confucian and indigenous perspectives. Unpublished PhD dissertation, Berkeley, CA: Graduate Theological Union.
Javabeans (2010). http://www.Dramabeans.com/2010/03/choi-jin-shil-brother-choi-jin-young-commits-suicide/
Jones, E., & Asen, E. (2000). *Systemic Couple Therapy and Depression*. London: Karnac.
King, M. L. (1968). *Chaos or Community?* London: Hodder and Stoughton.
Kwon, S.-Y. (2008). Well-being and spirituality from a Korean perspective: based on the study of culture and subjective well-being. *Pastoral Psychology, 56*: 573–584.
Malik, R. (2007). Politics, Islam and therapy: beyond stereotypes. *Context, 89*: 15.
New York Times (2009). Choe Sang-Hun, Roh Moo-Hyun, ex-president of South Korea kills himself, 22 May.
Shweder, R. A., & Bourne, E. J. (1984). Does the concept of person vary cross-culturally? In: R. A. Shweder & R. A. LeVine (Eds.), *Culture Theory. Essays on Mind, Self, and Emotion* (pp. 158–199). Cambridge: Cambridge University Press.
Sorajjakool, S., Aja, V., Chilson, B., Ramirez-Johnson, J., & Earll, A. (2008). Disconnection, depression, and spirituality: a study of the role of spirituality and meaning in the lives of individuals with severe depression. *Pastoral Psychology, 56*: 521–532.
The New Interpreter's Study Bible (2003). New Revised Standard Version with the Apocrypha. Nashville, TN: Abingdon Press.
Time World (2008). South Koreans are shaken by celebrity suicide. 6th October. http://www.Time.com/time/world.article/0,8599,1847437,00.html?yd=feed-cnn-/topics

Turner, V. (1969). *The Ritual Process: Structure and Anti-Structure*. London: Aldine Transaction.

Washington, J. M. (1986). *A Testament of Hope: The Essential Writings of Martin Luther King, Jr*. San Francisco, CA: Harper and Row.

www.BuhayKorea.com/Choi-jin-sil-suicide/page 1. Korean actress Choi Jin-sil commits suicide, 2008/10/02.

CHAPTER TEN

Engaging within and across culture

Rabia Malik and Philippe Mandin

Our plan for this chapter is to describe and reflect upon clinical work with Pakistani families in the context of court mandated parenting assessments in childcare proceedings. Although court work represents only a small proportion of the family work that we have done together over the past ten years, we have chosen it as the focus in this chapter as it seems to bring to the fore some of the complex processes of working across culture and of joint working, which are more difficult to identify in purely therapeutic interventions. For example, the limitations of the "not knowing approach" often used in family therapy to access cultural themes become more visible when the process is adversarial, stakes are high, and clear recommendations are expected. The clinical example will illustrate how the court context pushes towards essentializing diversity and drawing rigid lines, which are often present in cross-cultural therapy, but which can remain unacknowledged. All cultural systems operate with assumptions and constraints that organize people's behaviour, beliefs, and emotions. Working across culture means remaining open and respectful to difference, while remembering that culture is an interactive process, not a static fixed system. As the case example will also demonstrate, cultural concepts are deeply meaningful, but also fluid, illusionary (Krause, 1998) and difficult to access. We will describe and reflect on our attempts to engage with such polarized systems in order to create a thinking space to allow alternative explanations to emerge.

The first part of the chapter briefly sets the context of our work, presents a typical referral made up of anonymous clinical material, and reflects on the authors' working relationship and background. We then use four snapshots of our work to highlight critical moments in which we found ourselves, sometimes deliberately, sometimes unwittingly, addressing different levels of communication patterned by culture. We consider the way our different cultural backgrounds influenced the positions that we took or were put into by the family or professionals, and how we used our relationship to take risks, develop trust, and build bridges, as well as challenge participants' perceptions of the situation. We do this through individual and joint reflections organized around the four snapshots/themes which informed how we worked with different cultural beliefs and helped us engage with families at different levels, moving from the personal and emotional to practical and socio-political contexts.

We argue that accessing culture is an emotional process which requires a level of reflective practice, emotional engagement, and a reworking of cultural themes by both the clinicians and the family. We reflect on the therapeutic stance that we used in the work, including systemic curiosity and "not knowing" (Anderson & Goolishian, 1992) as well as Bion's "without knowledge and desire" (1988) and Kakar's "ethical relativism" (2006, p. 28).

Our working context

The Marlborough Family Service is a child and adolescent mental health service combined with an adult psychotherapy service, based in central London and part of the National Health Service (NHS). It consists of a multi-disciplinary team with a focus on systemic approaches to psychotherapy and a commitment to engaging with community groups within its catchment area. This orientation has led to the formation of the Marlborough Cultural Therapy Centre (MCTC). The MCTC consists of seven part-time bilingual therapists who work with the aim of developing and delivering culturally appropriate therapeutic services. The agency has also developed a multi-disciplinary model for working with "multi-problem families" and for undertaking independent parenting assessments as part of court proceedings in private and public law cases involving children. This has been described by Asen (Asen, 2007; Asen, McHugh, & Dawson, 2007) and others (Fyvel & Mandin, 2003; Tydeman, 2007). Referrals are received in the form of a joint letter of instruction that provides a brief summary of the local authority's concerns and a list of questions which the parties have agreed need to be assessed. The practice in our agency is to start an assessment with a network meeting involving the parents and the professionals. The work ends with a report to the court.

The referral

The family we wish to discuss was referred by the Children's Guardian after social services had accommodated Ahmed and Amina, aged eleven and eight, respectively, with a foster family under an Interim Care Order. The request was for a parenting assessment of their grandparents, who had been caring for them on and off for most of their lives. At an earlier court hearing, their mother had been found to be unable to care for them and for her newborn son, primarily because of her substance misuse. A previous assessment of the family had recommended that Amina and Ahmed stay with their grandparents as long as they could engage in culturally sensitive and appropriate family work in their local area, "to improve their communication with the children" and "to help them balance the needs of the children with the emphasis that the family placed on honour". This work had not taken place and the relationship between social services and Mrs Chaudhry and Mr Khan had broken down. Social services were opposing the grandparents' application for residence orders on the grounds that they were not meeting the children's emotional needs and the grandfather had refused to give consent for social workers to contact suitable referees. Amina and Ahmed were said to be under-achieving in school and to have limited opportunities to participate in after-school activities, as they had to attend mosque on a daily basis. The grandparents were also refusing to recognize the existence of their baby grandson and blamed their daughter for the current crisis, which they attributed to outside forces, such as her peer group's bad influence. Mrs Chaudhry and Mr Khan are first generation migrants to the UK who seemed to have limited knowledge of the care system, in spite of long-standing involvement with social services. Their primary concerns seemed to be the preservation of the family's honour and avoiding any information about professionals' involvement leaking to their community. This raised concerns about their ability to meet the children's emotional needs while they remained unable to talk to the children to help them understand and manage the separation from their mother.

Working together

This type of scenario, when the relationship between two sets of apparently reasonable and well-meaning individuals or groups breaks down, contributing to distressing decision-making processes, is not unusual in cross-cultural work (Maitra, 2005) or in court mandated parenting assessments (Asen, 2007; Asen, McHugh, & Dawson, 2000). Our first reaction when asked to consider this referral, which was previously known to us, was anger at the apparent pain and injustice inflicted on the children through this breakdown of relationships, followed by a sense of responsibility to use our experience and position to intervene in this stuck system. We also experienced a sense of dread at the enormity of the task, given the gaps in language, in understanding each other's normative ideas and systems, as well as the potential risks involved in stepping into such a conflict-laden system. Before taking on this work, we had to consider whether we could remain curious in such a polarized context, whether we had the time, skills, and energy to invest in this complex piece of work when local agencies had not found a way of working with the family, and whether we could understand, respect, and mediate each other's difference in order to work together and support each other. This last question was probably the most significant and, over the years, we have spent time talking formally and informally to get to know each other. It is, therefore, important for us to say something here about ourselves, our relationship, and the importance of trust.

> RM: I tend to describe myself as a Muslim British Pakistani woman. I was born in Pakistan, but my family moved to London when I was

two years old. Although I have been brought up in England and consider myself British, I still feel that my roots connect me to Pakistan. My parents were economic migrants who lived under the "myth of return" until my father passed away twelve years ago. To survive and establish themselves in a new country, my parents worked incredibly hard, without the support of an extended family network. My mother suffered the consequences of migration, compounded by her limited English, in the form of social isolation and severe lack of support. They tried to make a place for themselves and us by being active participants in our schools and in local mainstream politics, as well as pioneers in establishing Pakistani community organizations. They, however, maintained a boundary around the family, through language, dress, food, friendship networks, observing religious practices, values, and expectations, so that throughout my childhood I considered myself Pakistani and was proud of my Pakistani heritage. This served as a safe space to retreat to when faced with racism. As I got older and began to challenge boundaries, becoming aware of the contradictions and restrictions within my own community as well as the racism in British society, things began to get difficult, and I felt an acute sense of estrangement—of not belonging—which lasted many years. So began a long journey to understand my culture of origin. This was complicated by the ethnocentric education that I received, which precluded other world-views and knowledge systems. Moving between these systems was disorientating at times. Eventually, my faith in Islam came to serve as an important third space that has the capacity to understand the human struggle and to introduce another dimension beyond cultural and social constraints, that of ethics and spirituality. My relationship to Islam has also involved a changing, evolving process. It was important that this third space came from within my tradition, so as to avoid the dangers of colonization, but also to challenge essentialized notions of culture. No doubt, these personal experiences and my own journey has led me to want to work with ethnic minority clients as they struggle through this social, psychological, and emotional integration process, and to create space and support for them in mainstream mental health services. Taking up this position of challenging socio-cultural structures at a macro level can, at times, risk leading to a sense of embattlement, exhaustion, and frustration, both with the mainstream system and the communities I work with. The back-up of a supportive organization and colleagues has been vital. My doctoral research on the cultural construction of depression among Pakistanis, prior to training as a systemic therapist, gave me a useful grounding in how notions of self, relationships, health, and illness are culturally constructed. Subsequently, my more informal Islamic studies have provided me with an understanding of the Islamic world-view, metaphors, language, and how these might relate to human and spiritual development.

PM: I tend to describe myself as a white, French, agnostic, middle-aged man who has been living in London longer than in France. When I researched my family of origin a few years ago, I went back 150 years in time but only ten miles in space. So, until I moved to the UK, I probably would have struggled to describe my culture other than through familiar stereotypes about food, wine, and language. Yet, local differences sometimes felt huge, especially between town and villages and in terms of socio-economic factors and aspirations. I still identify with the culture of my family of origin, although they now laugh at my accent and my father-in-law in the UK described me as an honorary Yorkshireman. When working with French-speaking families in London, I often find myself speaking French when we talk about the past, and English or "franglais" when speaking about the present. The characteristics which I now see as shaping my culture include the strong Catholic upbringing and faith I had as a child, the security afforded by long-established family roots in a rural part of France, and the place of food in social relationships. Social class also played an important part, as the working-class (or *paysannes*) values instilled by my extended family combined with middle-class aspirations of some family members contributed to conflict and divisions which, in a small community, were managed covertly. I became expert at bridging the gaps and keeping the peace, until cracks started to show in the form of mental health problems in members of my family who refused to engage with professional services. They have now recovered, but these experiences must have had a bearing on my choice of profession and interest in reaching out to "reluctant" families. This sometimes leads me to a tendency to want to rescue people, which, in cross-cultural work, risks carrying overtones of colonialism. I remember being put in my place as a social worker by a father who rightly pointed out that I was showing off my knowledge and interest in his culture instead of understanding what his family needed. It has been important for me to maintain a connection to the social work discipline, its values and practice, through teaching, writing, and court work. I also decided more recently to revisit psychoanalytic ideas which I had found helpful when I needed personal psychotherapy and which now help me complement the current emphasis of systemic thinking on language.

We have been working together for over ten years, and one piece of work post 7/7/2005 challenged and influenced our thinking. This was a referral of a Muslim family who had been caught in a racist attack as part of the backlash from the London bombings. We were faced with two unjust events bringing two communities at loggerheads with each other: both victims, both perpetrators. Taking on this work meant examining our personal and political views and our respective positions within our own community discourse and our capacity to hold, as Campbell and Draper recently described, a "both–and . . . and more" position (2009, p. xi). Through this work, we recognized in each other personal stories and positions as "bridge builders" in our families of origin. We also share a commitment to social justice and a determination to think through divisive, sometimes personal and emotive, subjects.

We now move on to describe our practice through a number of themes that we have identified during our work with Amina and Ahmed's family. After each theme, we offer our individual and joint reflections on our thoughts, feelings, and interventions. The work took place over a six-month period during which the children were returned to the care of their grandparents. This chapter focuses on the first few weeks of the work.

Theme 1: engaging polarized systems

The initial network meeting was attended by the grandparents, the Children's Guardian, her solicitor, the children's social worker, and her manager. The social worker and managers were late for the meeting. The conflict between the family and professionals soon emerged when the grandparents started to complain about social services being unreliable, while the social work manager took an official position of non-co-operation with the referral, arguing that "the department" had made a decision to place the children for adoption. The position that individuals and their organizations were taking within the proceedings and the strengths of emotions displayed in those first few moments suggested both external systemic pulls and also more or less unconscious patterns of interactions influenced by the court context, and, no doubt, memories and experiences of colonialism, racism, and discrimination.

The grandparents appeared to have positioned professionals in two camps; the Guardian as benevolent rescuer, and the social worker as incompetent and insensitive invader. Social services also appeared to take rigid positions. Phrases like "children's emotional needs" were used by social workers to build a case against the grandparents without explaining or defining them. Such labels can contribute to the essentializing of culture and a retreat to unspoken stereotypical positions which, unchallenged in the legal context, can take on the status of fact. For example, the social work intervention in this case was partly triggered by the grandparents' attempts to protect and retain the "honour" of the family from outside negative influence, but this was seen as deceptive or unco-operative and raised unspoken fears of future forced marriage.

Part of our intervention was to slow down the meeting to unpick the meaning and explore the context of such labels in order to highlight their complexity and negotiate with the parties for a timed space to reflect. We attempted to reframe participants' positions in more constructive, less blaming ways, adopting a stance of curiosity informed by our knowledge of the cultural and the professionals' systems. We used the authority of the court to keep participants on the task of prioritizing the children's welfare. This involved at times taking a challenging position, first encouraging the grandparents to think in front of professionals about what they might need to change to convince the court that the children were safe with them, then inviting professionals to explain their expectations and the decision to remove the children.

The children had become caught up in this polarized system. Amina had taken the side of her family, making allegations against her foster mother, while Ahmed reported that he had been physically chastised by his grandfather, prompting social services to cancel contact. In spite of this, the children were making obvious efforts to preserve their relationship, providing us with an incentive and model for bridge building.

Reflections

> RM: During the meeting, I felt frustrated by the lack of awareness in both the professional and family systems that they were speaking a different language and using different conceptual frameworks from

those used by the family. Things were lost in translation and a collaborative understanding was not unfolding; the distance between the systems seemed wide. It reminded me of the constant oscillating that I have done throughout my life between my family and community and wider mainstream society: managing mistrust and misperceptions and prejudices; trying to work out how to explain and articulate the differences. At times I feel tired of the struggle and the hard work required for this task, and I am mindful of how challenging it is to bring different world-views together and overcome splits.

PM: I like bringing people together, and this type of conflict tends to bring the rescuing part of me into action. But in this meeting, the emotional pulls were, at times, overwhelming. For example, my perception of the grandmother swayed from that of a controlling and emotionally abusive matriarch to that of a strong woman determined to protect her grandchildren from some of the adversity she had experienced herself. Similarly, the social workers sometimes came across as caring and protective of the children, but at other times seemed to hold judgemental cultural stereotypes and sounded rigid and bureaucratic. At times, I felt ashamed of my chosen profession, while wanting to support my colleagues. I also wanted to rescue the grandparents by using my knowledge of social work to help them manage the system to their advantage. What helped me overcome these colonizing tendencies and some of the macro social issues was the way Rabia and I used the discussion we have had about our own family and professional cultures to ask small questions to elicit more depth and more contextual information.

Our experience of living in a different culture, away from home, probably contributes to our attention to details such as smells, tastes, colours, and words that can help connect across boundaries. For example, Amina, during a discussion later on in English about her favourite food, used the Urdu term "saag"—spinach—to describe a dish her grandma used to make. Language and images can act as important symbols that keep connections to a visceral identity. But ignoring or devaluing this kind of detail can contribute to a rejection or repression of one's culture and sense of self.

Theme 2: engaging with cultural themes

During the initial network meeting, it was clear that trust between the family and social services had broken down. The social work manager had clearly stated that the grandparents were not co-operating and the family had felt a disconnection with social services as social workers kept changing and the recommendation for family therapy work had not been followed through. Consequently, they were shocked when the children were removed from them and taken into foster care. The grandparents' reluctance to disclose information about referees from their community (including Mr Khan's first wife) was seen as highly suspicious and contributed to the picture that was painted of them, but never explicitly stated, as withholding and dishonest. From Mr Khan and Mrs Chaudhry's perspective and from within the Pakistani cultural context, family honour—*izzath*—is highly valued and had an impact on the whole family's standing within the community. They were in a grave predicament, and they seemed to have a sense of *sharam*—shame—about their situation. Mrs Chaudhry had also not wanted to talk about her first marriage and the domestic violence that she and her children had experienced, as her first husband had passed away and she thought it best that the past be buried with him.

We were struck by how, throughout the work, Mr Khan had kept a detailed log of meetings and an account of who had said what. Whenever things came to a head with the different perspectives of the grandparents and social services and decisions/consequences were talked about, Mr Khan would get out the book and start defending himself and his wife and highlighting the incompetence of social services. In our second session with the grandparents, when discussing their reluctance and predicament in disclosing information about their past, we described their life story as a book which they had learnt or chosen to keep tightly closed. We suggested that in order for us to understand them better, we would like to help them "open the book" of their lives. After exploring some of the risks involved, both grandparents agreed, and the "open book" became a metaphor for a more open, trusting relationship.

Reflections

> RM: Families often assume that if the therapist is from the same cultural and religious background as themselves, they will understand them better, and it is easier in some respects to build trust. I could more intuitively connect with the family's ideas of *izzath* and *sharam* and the constraints they impose. However, I was also aware that

language and concepts do not easily translate from one cultural system to another, and that what was being required of them by social services and the legal system was to transcend these cultural constraints and disclose more intimate details in order for the system to trust them. Cultural themes can sometimes present as impasses that feed into understandable defences against what might feel like insurmountable social change and fear of colonization. So, while the family's fear of social repercussions in their communities was valid and real for them, the need for change and to push the family beyond the sticking point was also paramount, given the possible repercussions of them losing their grandchildren. In such situations, respecting the family's cultural beliefs (in this case, the notion of *izzath*) and trying to understand the real constraints it poses, rather than trying to bypass what might appear as a cultural hindrance, can help to build a trusting relationship and create a safe space where families can be encouraged to be more honest and take risks to share highly personal and intimate information. In this sense, culture can be both deeply meaningful for families and also fluid and illusory (Krause, 1998).

PM: When I started working cross-culturally, I always tried, before meeting a new family, to "find out about their culture" by talking to people or looking on the Internet. I then became attracted to the concept of "not knowing" in family therapy (Anderson & Goolishian, 1992). This contributed to the current emphasis of language in family therapy, which, as Rabia's experience, above, illustrates, does not always go far enough in making sense of people's lived experience. While Rabia could use her intuitive knowledge of cultural themes, I had to find other ways of approximating what I was hearing and feeling that would resonate with my own emotional experiences and connections. The therapeutic stance I found myself in at times had similarities with aspects of Bion's description of the analytic process. Bion (1992) argued that unconscious processes are ultimately unknowable and coined the letter "O" to describe what might be going on ("the thing-in-itself" (p. 181)). He recommended that the therapists adopt a position of listening "in the absence of memory or desire" (1992, p. 315). This is probably unachievable, but describes a state of "heightened receptivity", focusing on the here-and-now, which can act as a "container resembling the mother's reverie which gives her access to what is going on" for her infant (Schermer, 2003, p. 241). This position, combined with empathy, contributed to the development of trust and honesty and also to a sense of emotional connection with the family. Bion's theory of containment also suggests that this stance could only be sustained if I also felt contained by the trust in the co-working relationship and in our capacity to remain curious, thoughtful, and, ultimately, focused on the task of assessing and promoting the children's welfare.

Theme 3: engaging with the personal

Understanding the grandparents' cultural context and the constraints of notions such as *izzath* and *sharam*, rather than dismissing them, took us some way towards engaging with the grandparents but did not, in itself, take us beyond the impasse. "Opening the book" and hearing the stories enabled a deeper understanding and emotional attunement. Mr Khan told of how he and Mrs Chaudhry had known, and been fond of, each other as teenagers. Their families were unaware of this, and Mrs Chaudhry was taken to Pakistan by her family and was married while she was there. Mr Khan learnt of this, and soon after also married. Some years later, by chance, he went to her house to do a delivery and there they were reunited. Over time, he came to know of how Mrs Chaudhry, who by then had five children, was unhappy in her marriage and that her husband was an alcoholic and violent towards her and the children. Mr Khan started to help her out secretly. A number of years later, when Mrs Chaudhry's husband passed away, she asked Mr Khan to marry her, to afford some social acceptability to their relationship and to offer her some status and protection as a lone woman. They knew the marriage would not be recognized in the UK, but was permissible in Pakistan and within the Islamic faith, where a man is allowed to have more than one wife (although it should be noted that within Islam there is some contention about the practice of polygamy). Mrs Chaudhry said she did not expect Mr Khan to leave his first wife and live with her. However, when Mr Khan's wife found out, she was hurt and angry, and their relationship deteriorated. Mr Khan feared that if she were consulted by social services she might use the opportunity to take some revenge, and, hence, his lack of co-operation with social services.

Opening up this conversation helped us to begin to understand Mr Khan and Mrs Chaudhry on a more personal and emotional level and highlighted the complexities of their relationship. Hearing this story was critical in opening up an emotional understanding of the personal dimension underlying the cultural notions of *izzath* and *sharam*. By witnessing the sadness of their story and the dilemma they found themselves in, we were now in a more "experience near" terrain from which we could speak empathically about emotional needs and the complexities of life. "Opening the book" and a stance of curiosity enabled a more personal story, which hitherto remained hidden, to emerge and created the possibility for further open conversations. However, it also raised deeper ethical dilemmas for both of us.

Reflections

> RM: For me, this brought up questions about *izzath*, *sharam*, and ethics. I could share the sense of constraints the family had about what would be socially acceptable. One way of dealing with this can be to find ways around the rules and to hide things. This can also serve as a way of avoiding dealing with, and working through, emotional complexities. While I could relate to the grandparents' predicament regarding their relationship with one another before marriage and afterwards, when Mr Khan tried to help Mrs Chaudhry out, at the same time I was mindful of how they had not been able to accept the breaking of rules by their own daughter and how they had deceived Mr Khan's first wife. I felt frustrated by the hypocrisy and dishonesty that notions such as *izzath* can result in. Through my work over the years, I have come to recognize how family "name" and social honour can lead people to behave in ways that are otherwise ethically dishonourable. Consequently, I have tried to reframe this by exploring and teasing apart different levels of honour with clients, such as the honour in maintaining a social standing, or the honour in being honest, even when it goes against social standing. Paradoxically, however, I also found myself wanting to defend the "honour" of Pakistani culture with colleagues, as I was afraid that *izzath* would be interpreted as yet another "backward" cultural practice. All cultural systems operate constraints, but minority cultures are subject to scrutiny and judgement in a way that majority cultures are not. The scrutinizing gaze, with the added dimension of power, can carry with it colonizing and racist overtones that fix and essentialize culture and people. These double standards extend to relations not just between people within cultures, but also across cultures. Judgements can, thus, serve to close down communication and reflections within families and cultures and across cultures. It was all the more important, then, that Philippe and I could talk honestly and hold on to a "not knowing", non-judgemental position and emotional containment *vis-à-vis* the family and culture, while being mindful of our own ethical concerns and position.

PM: I sometimes had difficulties remaining sympathetic towards the grandparents. Their rigidity had, in my view, contributed to the harm caused to the children and, as a social worker, I understood social services' frustration and desire to protect the children. As a lapsed Catholic, who experienced pressure as an adolescent to attend church, I was also ready to accept the children's moans about going to the mosque too often. In some meetings with the grandparents I was beginning to feel "two-faced", as I identified more with the children and social workers on this issue. What helped me manage this, I think, were the memories of the strong faith that I had had as a child and my critical reactions at the time to people who seemed to attend church as a social duty more than because of genuine faith. This helped me understand the centrality of religion for the grandparents and connect with their beliefs while encouraging them to consider other points of view. Listening to Rabia's discomfort reminded me of the contradictions in my own culture, and of the amazing capacity of people to hold on to or tolerate seemingly paradoxical positions (what the eye does not see) that brought both frustrating and strangely fond memories of the people I cared about. The grandparents' position was not so different from my father insisting I go to church while he spent most of the service in the bar, or ignoring the fact that my grandfather held very different religious beliefs from the other side of my family.

Kakar's concept of ethical relativism has been useful for us with regard to managing competing and contradicting questions of ethics. He describes the "Indian ethical sensibility" as having developed a "pronounced ethical relativism", linked to the "Indian conviction in the existence of a higher level of reality beyond the shared, verifiable, empirical reality of the world, our body and our emotions" (2006, p. 28), which suggests that "right and wrong are relative; depending on its particular context every action can be right—or wrong" (p. 30). Although Kakar was highlighting the difference between Hindu, Islamic, and Judeo-Christian culture, this type of ethical compromise might be more prevalent and universal than one might like to accept. However, this position felt controversial, particularly in the context of court proceedings, where the truth takes such a powerful meaning. This capacity for, and stance of, ethical relativism (Kakar, 2006, p. 28) has been important in our joint work together, so as to remain open with one another and with families and to allow more complex thinking and new possibilities and positions to emerge.

Theme 4: creating new possibilities

During the assessment, and in the absence of Amina and Ahmed's mother, we tried to enlist the help of Mrs Chaudhry's other grown-up children (see Genogram, Figure 10.1). Her youngest son, Akhbar, who was also the father of two children, agreed to attend. Initially, Akhbar adopted a similar story to his parents and dealt with the emotional difficulties in the family by making a distinction between the "good family" and the bad society. Such splits can also get translated by minority families into the "good" culture they are trying to preserve and the "bad" culture outside, and also by professionals into the "good" culture they ascribe to and the seemingly "bad" and "backward" traditional culture of minority families.

When asked about his family's difficulties, Akhbar described how his younger sister had been adversely influenced by the "bad society" and had made wrong choices, getting involved with drugs and the wrong people. He felt he had been able to make the right choice by keeping away from some of his friends who are now in prison. He was initially attributing all the blame to the outside world and was

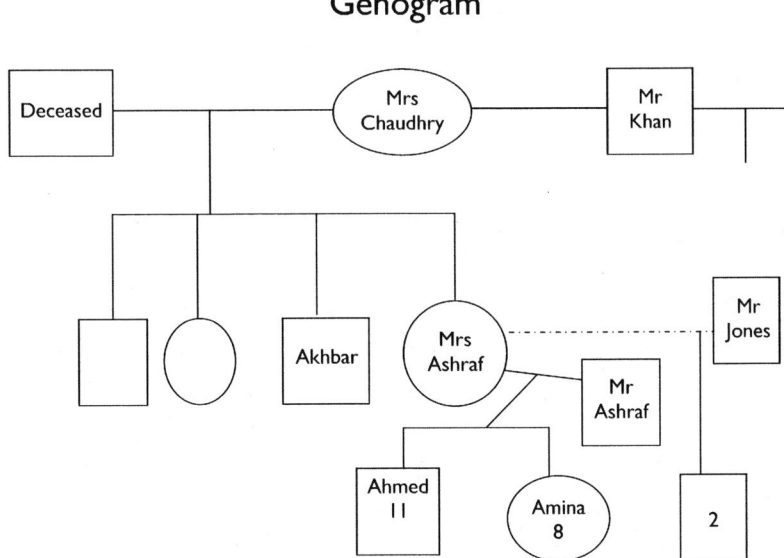

Figure 10.1. Genogram of Mrs Chaudhry and Mr Khan.

reluctant to talk about any family problems. However, when he heard about his mother's decision to "open her book", he talked movingly about his early childhood experiences. His father used to drink and take drugs, and frequently hit Mrs Chaudhry and all the children. When their father died, they were not able to talk about it as a family. Mrs Chaudhry went to Pakistan for several months and his elder siblings struggled to keep the family together. Akhbar felt that he and his siblings had been supportive to each other and that his younger sister (the mother of Amina and Ahmed) had worked hard to support their mother and the whole family until she became involved with "bad people". We talked about the very thin line between being "good" and "bad", and how, after many years of hard work to be good, one false move could lead to a completely different path. We challenged the idea that all good things are within the family and all bad things outside, and tried to encourage Akhbar to talk to his mother about some of the bad things they experienced within the family. Akhbar talked movingly in English about the lack of support he experienced from his mother and Mr Khan, which he attributed to generational differences and to his mother's own difficult experiences of domestic violence. He talked about his own way of parenting his children, how he makes links with teachers and the outside world in order to support and monitor his children. He acknowledged some of his parent's shortcomings with Amina and Ahmed, and, in particular, he thought that his mother had sometimes been too preoccupied with the family's honour and not communicated enough with professionals and with the children. However, when Akhbar was asked if he could have this conversation in Urdu with his mother, with tears in his eyes he said he could not say these things to his mother because he did not want to hurt her and make her cry. Rabia suggested that she could translate the conversation for him. Mrs Chaudhry listened attentively.

Reflections

> RM: The session with Akhbar highlighted the way in which families can make simplistic splits as a way of dealing with complex issues. It was easier to blame his sister's drug taking on the influence of "bad society" than to acknowledge the domestic violence and some of the "bad" things that the family had faced within their home. Such psychological splits might be helpful at one level and at certain times,

but can become problematic when systems overlap and when rigid divisions create absolutes that might impede greater understanding. Language can reinforce these splits and I was struck by how Akhbar was able to talk about the "bad" things that happened at home in English, but when he was asked if he could tell his mum what he had told us in Urdu, he could not, and became very emotional. For me, translating what Akhbar had said to his mother in his "mother tongue" was also difficult, and I could feel the overwhelming emotions. This is because culture and language not only pattern relationships and hierarchy, but also the emotional texture of relationships. Speaking in Urdu and being aware of the cultural respect and obedience accorded to mothers was challenging for me also, and brought my personal and professional identities into close juxtaposition. Trusting that Philippe had the patience and conviction that this was an important part of the work while remaining engaged and without feeling excluded was important to enable me to challenge the family and to carry out this intervention in Urdu .

PM: Trust played an important role in our professional relationship with one another. Being aware of how we feel about our relationship during different parts of sessions provided information about how much to push the family, and not fall into splits. During the conversation with Akhbar, I could sense by Rabia's reactions and the heightened emotional mood that something important was happening, even though I did not fully understand the content. Although I wanted to be involved, I knew that translating would have interrupted the flow and exaggerated differences between us. I felt privileged to be part of such an intimate family interaction, while, at the same time, aware of being an outsider. I think I was able to stay emotionally connected by noticing my own emotional reactions as well as commenting occasionally on the non-verbal communication, or picking up the odd English word. The physical nature of the "open book" analogy helped me maintain non-verbal connection with the family: for example, by making open or closed hand gestures (which became a joke) when I thought communication was being encouraged or, alternatively, shut down. Working across cultures, I also sometimes try to use words in the family's language, learnt from them or from colleagues, in order to connect and make an effort, which might help families feel appreciated.

End comment

Trusting interpersonal relationships were also crucial for the family. We did this partly by showing commitment, taking time to listen to their side of the story, going out of our way to offer home visits, to help them communicate with professionals and foster carers, and by accepting and appreciating their food. We tried to show that we could take their predicament seriously rather than judging it, while retaining a commitment to the idea of truth as setting people free—or, at least, opening things up again. The court context helps in this process by providing strict time boundaries within which to undertake assessments while the children's welfare is monitored. It also provides a clear focus on the children's needs. This allows us clinicians space to take risks to explore various positions in some depth, which, in a different context, might have felt too uncomfortable to sustain a therapeutic engagement. During the course of an assessment, it is not unusual for us to sway from one extreme recommendation to another as we hear opposing points of views. Our assessment is dynamic, and constantly reviewed and informed often by small but repetitive observations. For example, during home visits and observations of contact, we noticed small interactions between the grandparents and with the children that demonstrated a high level of warmth and tacit understanding between them. Sharing these observations with them helped the family to be more emotionally demonstrative in our presence. For example, Ahmed, who had been complaining that he no longer liked Pakistani food, was seen enjoying being fed by his grandmother once he had been reassured that a white person would not laugh at him in his family context.

Conclusion

Court work, with its high stakes, intense pressure, and time constraints, can bring to the fore complex processes and challenges involved in cross-cultural work. In describing this case, we hope to highlight the importance of reflecting and engaging within and across cultures. Through the four snapshots, we have tried to identify key aspects in the process of cross-cultural work by reflecting on the therapeutic stance and positions we took up. Engaging families in these highly adversarial circumstances highlights the need to engage sociopolitically with the family and social services systems, as well as with the deeply held cultural meanings that were pivotal for the family and were creating an impasse between them and professionals. Attending to these macro socio-cultural processes was essential in order to engage with and uncover hidden personal stories in a safe, containing manner and to allow new possibilities and relationships to emerge.

Engaging with the socio-political context requires an awareness of power dynamics, and how impasses can resonate with wider social issues, such as the history of colonization and assumptions about, and fears of, cultural practices, such as forced marriages. It is important for professionals to be aware of how these forces can polarize systems and to work towards negotiating a thinking space to attend to the details and particulars of the case at hand and to translate difficult concepts such as "emotional and behavioural needs", and all that it is assumed to entail, across cultures. In order to engage with, and to try to understand, the cultural constraints the family experienced and not just the requirements of the professional and legal system, we had to respect that notions such as *izzath* are deeply meaningful for families, but also are fluid and illusory and always open to redefinition and reinterpretation. Only then were we able to work with the family in a trusting and more collaborative relationship to "open the book" and hear more about their personal stories and dilemmas. Opening up in this way can expose the complexities of relationships and the contradictions, tensions, and ethics that people understandably try to avoid. This contributes to splitting on both sides, which is facilitated at a social level by cultures and a system that still struggles with integrating minority communities.

In our reflections, we have tried to highlight the challenges this posed for us as therapists and for our relationship with the clients and one another. In the face of highly charged situations, it can be difficult for therapists to sustain an open "not knowing" and non-judgemental position. We find the current emphasis on language and meaning in the systemic notion of "not knowing" limited in this regard. We have come to realize that "not knowing" is not as simple as the therapist remaining open to what the client might tell them. Rather, it is about creating a context for the therapist and client to come to "know" together. This takes us beyond language, as the case illustrates. Mr Khan and Mrs Chaudhry knew why their honour was at stake, but they knew it as something to forget. Grappling with this level of "not knowing" requires an emotional containment which we think Bion's concept of "listening without memory or desire" goes some way towards. This is not to suggest that the therapist is a blank slate, but, rather, that to get to know someone in their context, the therapist has to be aware of his/her own cultural position and hold in suspension his/her preconceived ideas. This can be especially challenging when the therapist does not speak the client's language, and requires a level of emotional engagement that is containing but also can withstand the pulls of highly opposing cultural viewpoints within the therapist and therapeutic system. Moreover, it requires the ability to remain non-judgemental and open to competing ethical questions. Kakar's concept of ethical relativism enabled us to take a more complex stance towards these ethical dilemmas rather than a privileging of truth from a linear professional and legalistic viewpoint alone, which court work tends to enforce. Only by the process of developing this kind of relationship, which required the reworking of themes, not just for clients, but also for us as clinicians, were we able to take risks and enable new conversations and relationships to develop in the family.

Amina and Ahmed were eventually returned to their grandparents' care after six months' work with the extended family and foster carers, focusing on parenting and meeting the cultural, behavioural, and emotional needs of the children and their identities.

References

Anderson, H., & Goolishian, H. (1992). The client is the expert: a not-knowing approach to therapy. In: S. McNamee & K. Gergen (Eds.), *Therapy as Social Construction* (pp. 25–39). London: Sage.

Asen, E. (2007). Therapeutic assessments. Assessing the ability to change. In: C. Thorpe & J. Trowell (Eds.), *Re-Rooted Lives: Inter-disciplinary Work Within the Family System* (pp. 39–48). Bristol: Family Law Jordan.

Asen, E., McHugh, B., & Dawson, N. (2000). *The Marlborough Model.* London: Karnac.

Bion, W. R. (1988). Notes on memory and desire. In: E. B. Spillus (Ed.), *Melanie Klein Today, Vol. 2: Mainly Practice* (pp. 15–18). London: Routledge.

Bion, W. R. (1992). *Cogitations.* London: Karnac.

Campbell, D., & Draper, R. (2009). Foreword. In: C. Flaskas & D. Pocock (Eds.), *Systems and Psychoanalysis: Contemporary Integrations in Family Therapy* (pp. xi–xii). London: Karnac.

Fyvel, S., & Mandin, P. (2003). The whole is greater than the sum of its parts. *Context, 66*: 14–17.

Kakar, S. (2006). Culture and psychoanalysis. A personal journey. *Social Analysis, 50*(2): 25–44.
Krause, I.-B. (1998). *Therapy Across Culture*. London: Sage.
Maitra, B. (2005). Culture and child protection. *Current Paediatrics, 15*(3): 253–259.
Schermer, V. L. (2003). Building on "O": Bion and epistemology. In: M. Lipgar & M. Pines (Eds.), *Building on Bion's Roots* (pp. 223–253). London: Jessica Kingsley.
Tydeman, B. (2007). Making the links – a child psychotherapy perspective within a systemic team undertaking parenting assessments for court. *Journal of Social Work Practice, 21*: 2.

Epilogue

Inga-Britt Krause

Being preoccupied with "culture" and "race" is characteristic of an era where ideology and politics are focused on identity. However, in contemporary systemic psychotherapy, as elsewhere in the current context, discrimination and racism persist and attention to "culture" and "race" can lead us on many paths, not all of them towards increasing understanding or ethical awareness. "Culture" and "race" are concepts, which categorize, but what matters is what we do with such a process. Do we use it to assist domination or to assist recognition? Do we use it to neutralize or to transcend "race" and "culture" (Amin, 2010)? What might seem like recognition to us might be experienced as domination by others, and what is aimed at transcendence at one level might help neutralize at another. The fundamental dilemma addressed by all the contributors to this volume has been when and how to recognize differences and similarities. This is, of course, a dilemma in all our practice. But what happens when these differences and similarities have cultural meanings and a local history that we cannot easily grasp? What happens when these meanings implicate aspects of our own unconscious and dominating (hi)story, or are hidden to us, or when meanings are so foreign that we lack the imagination to reach out? Yet, we find ourselves in the same physical space with our clients with assumptions about some, probably, fundamental similarities. Most pressingly, how do we carry on the therapeutic conversation in a way that does not ignore uncomfortable questions about who discriminates and who is discriminated against? As some contributors have pointed out, this requires the courage to persist, despite getting it wrong and getting it wrong again (Campbell, this volume), as well as an enquiry into the limits of our own curiosity.

Following anthropologists, we might refer to this process as "dialogical relativism" (Graeber, 2007, p. 289), and several contributors have noted the similarities in the challenges to the systemic psychotherapist and the anthropologist/ethnographer in this process. However, there are also differences due to the history, task, and method of the two disciplines. If anthropology has placed too much emphasis on "culture", systemic psychotherapy has placed too little. This has also meant that the former has tended to emphasize a pre-constituted continuity, social structure, and history, while the latter has focused on the social claims implied by utterances, voices, or dialogues, and the way a particular situation helps make and sustain such claims. The writings here suggest that we need some of both.

But we also have to do more. Our emphasis on the present and the future might articulate a wish to move away from the past, but this has also, all too often, become a denial of the past in the present. While this is a caricature of contemporary systemic clinical practice, I believe that it is a tendency that has been buttressed by the place of theory in the discipline. In a sense, practice has moved ahead of theory. This is a dangerous state of affairs as far as "race" and "culture" is concerned, both because practice without theory is practice without reflection, and because theory is a way of clarifying assumptions. Without such clarification, assumptions will hold sway and reign as if they are true. I go along with Bourdieu (1990), who argued that there is no clear distinction between theory and practice, first, because all thought is based on models and, therefore, are theories about the world, and second, because all theory is a kind of practice. Perhaps our approaches to "race" and "culture" have been constrained by the slow development of theory in the discipline. It is time to place these topics and experiences at the centre of the development of generic thinking.

We cannot address reflexivity without an idea of a "subject" or a "person". There must be a subject/person who does the reflecting. You can choose not to enquire about who is reflecting and how: her personal and professional history, experience, development, and context influence and construct the reflection. However, this poses the danger of assuming that others are just like us. At best, it will impede understanding, at worst, it will articulate and even promote domination and discrimination. The contributors to this volume have shown that, to further reflexivity, systemic psychotherapists need to think about individuals, persons, and subjects. They have demonstrated this by thinking about themselves, their own histories and experiences in relation to "the other", their clients. This is wholly in tune with an emphasis on relationships, a view of systems as relationships between relationships, and an emphasis on the meaning for those who participate. But it is important to note that the contributors, who have spoken about themselves and their clients, have also done so with reference to their own, and not only their clients', specific contexts: white Australia, white USA, African America, Pakistan, Pakistani Britain, Italy, France, England, northern England and Denmark and their numerous local variations and intersections in terms of gender, age, class, ethnicity, religion etc. Subjectivity and personhood are situated in specific contexts, which also influence the way "the other" is seen. Conversely, "otherness" is always situated in the contemporary, in the particular, in the local, and in context. It reflects the historical, social, emotional, cognitive, and political relationships between the parties concerned, and it implicates processes, which we cannot or, perhaps, would rather not, see or enquire into. These relationships come to influence and constrain the perspectives which therapists and clients have of one another and of themselves. An emphasis on "the individual", "the subject", and "the person" need be no stranger to systemic psychotherapy. Rather, attention to subject positions opens the possibility of asking a broad range of questions about the role of situated cultural resources in the constitution of experience and subjectivity. Here, systemic psychotherapy has an important contribution to make to reflexivity and transference in psychotherapy generally.

References

Amin, A. (2010). The remainders of race. *Theory, Culture & Society*, 27: 1–23.

Bourdieu, P. (1990). *The Logic of Practice*. Cambridge: Polity Press.
Graeber, D. (2007). *Possibilities. Essays on Hierarchy, Rebellion and Desire*. Oakland, CA: AK Press.

INDEX

Abu Baker, K., xx, xxiii
affect, 77, 119, 130, 185
   negative, 77, 82
   positive, 77
African, xxii, 56, 108, 126, 169
   -American, 41, 78–80, 181–182, 190, 197, 225
AFT, 139, 158, 166, 178
Afuape, T., 110
Aja, V., 186–187
Ali, T., 168, 178
Alvis Palma, D., 145, 158
Amin, A., 223, 225
Amundson, J., 153, 158
Andersen, T., xxi, xxiii, xxv–xxvi, xxxiii, 4, 6–7, 26–27
Anderson, H., xxvi, xxxiv, 4, 6–8, 11–12, 26–27, 59–60, 68, 170, 178, 202, 211, 220
anger, 43, 82, 102, 118, 120, 123, 126, 133, 174, 185, 190, 192–193, 204, 212
Ani, M., 110

anthropology, xvi, xxx–xxxi, 2–4, 9, 16–17, 25–26, 63, 120, 129–130, 132, 224
   social, 8–9, 72
Arcelloni, T., 16, 28, 128, 134
Arnkil, T., xxvi, xxxv, 14–15, 34
Asen, E., 186–187, 197–198, 203–204, 220
Association for Family Therapy, 166
Atkinson, B., 6, 27
attachment, 74, 77, 99, 101, 166
   insecure, 81
   transitional, 79
   volatile, 42
Auerswald, E. H., xxvi, xxxiv, 19, 27
Australia, xxix, 53–54, 116, 132–133, 171
   Aboriginal, xxix, 53–58, 65, 116–117, 171
   Islander, 53–54
   white, 53, 55, 65–66, 225
Ayvasian, A., 43, 50

Bakhtin, M. M., 8, 13–16, 18–19, 27, 42, 50, 104, 109–110, 130–131, 133–134
Baldacchino, J-P., 22, 27
Bales, R. T., 129, 136
Bateson, G., xxvi, xxx–xxxi, xxxiv, 1–3, 5, 16–17, 25, 27–28, 72, 74, 76–77, 83–84, 118, 121–122, 128, 134, 141, 155, 158
Bateson, M. C., 3, 28
Bean, R. A., xx, xxiii
Beavin, J., 118, 137
Bedell, T. M., xx, xxiii
behaviour, xxv, 2–3, 5, 16–17, 77, 81, 118–119, 176, 185, 187, 201, 219–220
  cultural, 25, 134
  depressive, 187
Belenky, M. F., 96, 111
Benedict, R., 121, 126, 134
Benjamin, J., 20–22, 26, 28, 47–48, 50, 80, 84, 97–99, 111
Berger, M., 2, 28
Bertrando, P., xxvi, xxx–xxxi, xxxiv, 4, 6, 14–16, 25, 28, 77, 84, 127–129, 131, 134
Bhabha, H. K., 24, 28, 104, 111
Bhavnani, K., 93, 111
Bion, W. R., xxxii, xxxiv, 202, 211, 219–220
Birdwhistell, R. L., 118, 134
Borges, J. L., 132, 134
Borneman, J., 26, 28
Borofsky, R., 78, 84
Borstnar, J., 105, 111
Boscolo, L., xxvi, xxxv, 4, 25, 28, 34, 47, 51, 63, 70, 84, 128, 134
Bourdieu, P., xxvii, xxxiv, 9, 28, 78, 84, 92, 111, 224, 226
Bourne, E. J., 186, 198
Bowen, M., 16, 28
Boyd-Franklin, N., 18, 28, 165, 178
Briggs, J. L., 120, 135
British Association for Sexual and Relational Therapy, 150
Brown, W., xviii–xix, xxiii

Buck-Morss, S., xvii, xxiii–xxiv
Burck, C., 12, 28, 96, 101, 105–106, 111
Burnham, J., xxvi, xxxi, xxxiv, 10, 28, 139–140, 145, 147, 149, 155, 158, 173, 178
Burr, V., 72, 84
Butler, J., 97, 100–101, 111
Byng-Hall, J., 72, 84, 173, 178

Campbell, D., xvi, xxix, 26, 29, 48, 50–51, 207, 220, 224
Carrier, J., 129, 135
Carstens, J., 11, 19, 29
case studies
  Abraham, 174–176
  Ahmed, 203, 207–208, 215–216, 218, 220
  Akhbar, 215–217
  Amina, 203, 207–209, 215–216, 220
  Avril, 172
  Carla, 101–102
  David, 102–103
  Donny, 55, 57, 60–62, 64–66
  Emily, 122–127, 130
  John, 173
  Lily, 57, 60–61, 64–66
  Mr Khan, 203–204, 210, 212–213, 215–216, 219
  Mrs Chaudhry, 203–204, 210, 212–213, 215–216, 219
  Nadia, 102–103
  Nina, 81–82, 84
  Rachel, 174–176
Cave, P., 169, 178
Cecchin, G., xxvi, xxxiv–xxxv, 4, 29, 34, 47, 50–51, 63, 68, 70, 84, 92, 111, 128, 135, 153, 158, 170, 178
child and family mental health service (CAMHS), 54–55
Chilson, B., 186–187
Christian, xxxii, 79, 150–151, 169, 171–172, 182–184, 186
  Baptist, 79–80, 181

Catholic, 79, 82, 170, 173, 206, 214
Judeo-, 214
Cirillo, S., 4, 35
Clarke, G., 20, 35
Clifford, J., 9, 20, 22, 29
Clinchy, B. M., 96, 111
Collier, A., 73, 85
Collini, S., 22, 29
colonial(ism), xvii, xix–xx, xxxiii, 4, 18, 56, 76, 92, 94, 206–207
Combs, G., 7, 30
conscious(ness), xxv, xxx, 1, 9, 15, 19, 22, 24–26, 54, 59, 75–76, 78–79, 81, 83, 94–95, 98, 133 *see also*: unconscious(ness)
containment, 26, 211, 213, 219
Conway, D., xxviii, xxxv
Coontz, S., 116, 135
Cooper, D., 116, 135
Cosmides, L., 118, 135
Cowley, S., 77, 85
Crapanzano, V., 13, 17, 26, 29
Craven, T., 190, 198
Crittenden, P., 77, 82, 85
Cronen, V. E., 6, 33
Csordas, T., 17, 29
cybernetics, xxi, 2–3, 6, 17, 72

Dalal, F., 20, 29
Daniel, G., 96, 101, 105, 111
Darwin, C., 118, 135
Das, V., 20, 29
Davies, C. A., 26, 29
Davies, T., 167, 178
Davis, J., 7, 32
Dawson, N., 203–204, 220
Dell, P., 3–4, 29
Dempster, C., xxviii, xxxiv
depression, xxxii, 55–56, 62, 78, 81, 107, 121, 132, 173, 175, 181–190, 193–195, 197, 205
Derrida, J., 42, 51
development(al), xxvii, xxix, 6–7, 10, 21, 47, 75, 77, 98, 106, 128, 142, 145, 148, 166, 185, 206, 220, 225
Di Nicola, V., xx, xxiv

Diagnostic and Statistical Manual of Mental Disorders (*DSM-IV*), 184, 198
discrimination, xx, xxvi–xxvii, 15, 19, 23, 97, 107, 170–171, 183, 207, 223–225
DISGRRACCE, 139–140
Divac, A., 145, 158
Doe, T., 126, 135
Donovan, M., 8, 29
Draper, R., xvi, 207, 220
Du Bois, W. E. B., 94, 111
Duarte, E., xx, xxiv
Dyckman, J., 75, 86

Earll, A., 186–187
Edwards, R., 93, 111
Ekman, P., 118–119, 121, 133, 135
Epston, D., 7, 29
Eriksson, E., xxvi, xxxv, 14–15, 34
Escobar, J., 106, 111
Ewing, K., 22, 29

Falicov, C., xx, xxiv, xxvii, xxxiv, 18–19, 24, 30, 73–74, 85, 106, 111
Fanon, F., xxvii, xxxiv, 20, 30
fantasy, xxi, 15, 17, 57, 63–65, 99
Fine, M., 7, 30
Fiori-Cowley, A., 77, 85
Fisek, G., 18–19, 30
Fishman, H. C., 4, 33
Flaskas, C., xxvii, xxix–xxx, xxxiv, 10, 30, 49, 58–59, 61–62, 68, 82, 85, 107, 111, 189, 198
Fonagy, P., 8, 30, 77, 85
Foucault, M., 10, 22, 30, 61, 71, 85, 131, 135
Frankenberg, R., xxviii, xxxiv
Fredman, G., 16, 30
Freedman, J., 7, 30
Freidan, E., 167, 178
Friesen, W. V., 118, 135
Frosh, S., 10, 31, 67–68, 74, 80, 85, 92, 96, 98, 112
Fruggeri, L., 116, 135
Fyvel, S., 203, 220

Geertz, C., 9, 31, 120, 133, 135
General World News, 184, 198
Gergely, G., 77, 85
Gergen, K. J., 59, 68–69, 73, 85, 110, 112, 130, 135
GGRRAAACCEEESSS, xxxi, 139, 142–145, 155–157
Gilligan, C., 96, 112
Gilroy, P., 94, 112
Giordano, J., xxvii, xxxv, 18, 33
Golann, S., 7, 31
Goldberger, N. R., 96, 111
Goldner, V., 6, 31
Gonzalez, A., 133, 135
Goolishian, H., xxvi, xxxiv, 4, 6–8, 11–12, 27, 29, 59–60, 68, 202, 211, 220
Gordon, C., 62, 69
Graduate Theological Union, 182
Graeber, D., 9, 26, 31, 224, 226
Griffith, J. L., 151, 159
Griffith, M. E., 151, 159
Grøenbaek, M., 26, 29, 48, 50–51
Gross, D. M., 121, 136
Guardian, 170, 178
Guilfoyle, M., 10, 14, 31
guilt, 46, 72, 126, 132–133
 -free, 76
Gutierrez, M., 18, 33

Haley, J., 129, 136
Hall, C., 22, 31
Hall, S., 95–96, 100–101, 112
Hammoudi, A., 26, 28
Hansson, A., xviii, xxiv
Hardy, K. V., xxvii, xxxiv, 18, 31, 165, 178
Harré, R., 42, 51, 129, 136
Harrelson, W., 190, 198
Harries-Jones, P., 17, 31, 72, 85
Harris, Q., 145, 158
Hastrup, K., xxvii, xxxiv, 19, 31
Heaphy, G., 145, 158
Heath, A., 6, 27
Heisenberg, W., 164, 178

Henderson, M., 24, 31
Hermans, H., 13, 31
Hermes, 13, 26
Hirsch, E. D., 150, 159
Hobsbawn, E., 84–85
Hoffman, L., 3–7, 31, 164, 178
Hoffman-Hennessy, L., 7, 32
Holland, D., 15, 32
Holloway, R., 168–169, 179
Holquist, M., 13, 32
Holy Bible, 190, 198

Iantaffi, A., 152, 159
Ifaluk, 120
Im, H. S., 188, 198
Inger, I., 20, 32
Ingham, H., 158–159
Institute of Family Therapy, 164
 Advanced Programme in Supervision, 164
intervention, 5, 45, 47–48, 77, 130, 176, 183, 204, 207–208
 therapeutic, 201
Islamic Words of Wisdom, 150, 159

Jackson, D. D., 118, 137
Javabeans, 185, 198
Jenkins, R., 19, 32
Jew, xviii, 148, 169, 171, 174, 176
Jones, E., 186–187, 198
Jurist, E., 77, 85

Kakar, S., xxxii, xxxv, 202, 214, 220–221
Karamat Ali, R., 145, 159
Kempen, H., 13, 31
Khanna, R., 22, 32
King, M. L., xxxii, 181, 189, 197–198
King, R., 43
Kitzinger, C., 20, 32, 93, 113
Klein, M., 20–21, 32
Konery, V., xx, xxiv
Krause, I.-B., xv, xx, xxiv, xxviii, xxxi, xxxv, 2–3, 6, 11–13, 16–19, 32–33,

40, 51, 58–59, 67, 69, 72–73, 75–79, 85–86, 92–93, 112, 118, 121–122, 130–131, 136, 165, 179, 202, 211, 221
Kwon, S.-Y., 186, 188, 198

Laird, J., 60, 69
Lane, G., xxvi, xxxiv, 6, 29, 50–51, 92, 111, 128, 135
Lannamann, J. W., 58, 69
Larner, G., 10, 32, 58–60, 69
Laszloffy, T. A., 18, 31, 165, 178
Lau, A., 20, 35
Lave, J., 15, 32
Layton, L., 75, 86
LeDoux, J., 118, 136
Levinas, E., xxx, xxxv, 47, 51, 100, 112
Levi-Strauss, C., xxxii, xxxv
Levy, R. I., 120, 136
life, xix, xxvii–xxviii, 8, 15, 18, 21, 55, 74, 81, 94, 103–105, 121, 129, 144–145, 151, 169, 172–175, 177, 183–184, 186, 188–190, 192, 209–210, 213
  family, 11, 18, 129
  social, 16
Lincoln Memorial, 181
London Depression Intervention Trial, The, 187
López, J., 59, 69, 73, 86
Luepnitz, D., 17, 32
Luft, J., 158–159
Lutz, C. A., 120–121, 136
Lyotard, J.-F., 73, 86

Ma'ari, S., 110
MacKinnon, C., 94, 96–97, 99, 112
Maitra, B., 204, 221
Malik, R., xx, xxiv, xxxii–xxxiii, 13, 17, 19, 33, 49, 58–59, 69, 78, 86, 183, 198
Mama, A., 93, 95, 104, 112
Mandin, P., 203, 220
Marcus, G., 9, 20, 22, 29, 34
Maslow, A., 49, 51

Mason, B., xxvi, xxxi–xxxii, xxxv, 8, 33, 42, 49, 51, 60, 69, 146, 148, 157, 159, 163–165, 170, 173, 177, 179
Mattingly, C., 24, 33
Maturana, H., xx, xxiv, 6, 33
McGoldrick, M., xxvii, xxxv, 18, 33
McHugh, B., 203–204, 220
McIntosh, P., 97, 112
McKinnon, L., 6, 33
McPherson report, 107
Mead, M., 118, 121, 134, 136
Meissner, W., 78, 86
Milkman, R., 167, 179
Miller, D., 6, 33
Mills-Powell, D., 145, 159
Milton, K., 12, 33
Mimica, J., 8, 33
Minuchin, S., xxvi, xxxv, 4, 33, 58–59, 69, 129, 136
Mocnik-Bucar, M., 105, 111
Modood, T., 24, 35
Moghaddan, F., 129, 136
Montalvo, B., 18, 33
Moodley, S., 77, 85
Moore, H., 8, 33
Morgan, A., 7, 33
mother, 14, 16, 55–56, 65–66, 78–80, 93, 98, 101–102, 107–109, 122–128, 130, 132–133, 137, 167, 183–184, 186, 188, 203–205, 208, 211, 215–217
  grand-, 81, 124, 167, 209, 218
Mouffe, C., xviii, xxiv
Muhammad Ali, T., 91, 112

Nathan, T., 126, 133, 136
National Health Service (NHS), 202
  Marlborough Cultural Therapy Centre (MCTC), 202
  Marlborough Family Service, 202
naven, 2, 16–17, 76–77, 121
Nehushtan, Y., xviii, xxiv
New Guinea, 2, 121–122
  Iatmul, 2–3, 16, 76, 81, 83–84, 121–122, 128

New Interpreter's Study Bible, The, 194, 198
New York Times, 185, 198
Northumbria University, 142
Nuckolls, C., 2, 33

Oatley, K., 121, 136
Obama, B., 41
object, xxx, 23, 26, 80, 83, 98–99, 144, 168
objective/objectivity, 3, 9, 28, 122
O'Hanlon, B., 151, 159
Orange, D., 79, 86

Pakaslahti, A., 104, 112
Pakes, K., 73, 86
Panksepp, J., 117, 136
parent(s), 54, 65, 80–82, 93, 122–127, 132–133, 152, 173–174, 177, 186, 201, 203–205, 215–216
  grand-, 53–54, 56, 67, 123, 127, 203, 207–210, 212–214, 218, 220
Parrott, W. G., 119, 136
Parsons, T., 129, 136
Pearce, J., xxvii, xxxv, 18, 33
Pearce, W. B., 6, 33, 144, 156, 159
Penn, P., 6, 31
Perlesz, A., 107, 111
Perry, B. J., xx, xxiii
Perry, R., 63, 69
Petters, C., 147, 159
Phillips, A., xviii, xxiv
Phoenix, A., 93, 111
Planalp, S., 130, 136
Plutchik, R., 119, 136
Pocock, D., xxx, 10, 16–17, 33–34, 49, 58–59, 69, 73, 76, 82, 86
Potter, G., 59, 69, 73, 86
Prata, G., xxvi, xxxv, 4, 34, 47, 51, 63, 70
projection, 61, 80–81, 83, 98, 101, 131
projective identification, 80

Rabinow, P., 8–9, 25, 34
Ramirez-Johnson, J., 186–187

Ray, W. A., xxvi, xxxiv, 6, 29, 50–51, 92, 111, 128, 135
Real, T., xxvi, xxxv, 5–7, 34
Relate Institute, 142
Rober, P., xxiii–xxiv, xxvi, xxxv, 8–9, 15–16, 34, 109, 112, 131, 136
Roberts, J., 147, 158–159
Robinson, J., 169, 179
Roper-Hall, A., 139–141, 145, 155, 158–160
Rorty, R., 106, 112
Rose, J., 99, 112
Rosenbaum, R., 75, 86
Roth, P., 39, 51
Royal Air Force, 167
Roy-Chowdhury, S., 73, 86
Rus-Makovec, M., 105, 111
Russell, B., 72, 87
Ryan Report, The, 178–179

Said, E., 20, 22, 34, 94–95, 104, 112
Sampson, E., 93–94, 97, 99, 112
Sawyerr, A., 163, 179
Schermer, V. L., 211, 221
schismogenesis, xxvi, 2–3, 16
Segal, H., 20, 34
Segal, L., 98, 112
Seikkula, J., xxvi, xxxv, 14–15, 34
self, xxvi, 8, 13–14, 20, 22–24, 59, 62–66, 74–75, 77, 79, 81–83, 92–93, 95, 97–99, 105, 131–132, 147, 150, 155, 164–166, 177, 185, 188, 192, 206, 209
  -assessment, 143
  -authoring, 15
  -centred, 124
  cognitive, 18
  -denigration, 82
  -determination, 10
  dialogical, 13–14, 18, 23
  -disclosure, 158
  -effacing, 16
  -esteem, 188
  -healing, 5
  -hood, 14, 102, 188
  -interest, 48

-negating, 185
-protection, 193
-realization, 96
-referential, 20, 25
-reflection, xxxii–xxxiii
-reflexive, xxix, 9, 24, 92, 106, 151
true, 98
Seltzer, M., xxiii–xxiv, 9, 16, 34
Selvini Palazzoli, M., xxvi, xxxv, 4, 34–35, 47, 51, 63, 70
Sen, A., 96, 113
Seoul Christian University, 182
sexism, 15, 140, 171
sexual, 73, 84, 99, 123, 150
orientation, 72, 150, 156, 171
sexuality, 72, 107, 140, 142, 150, 171
bi-, xvii
homo-, 107
Shands, H., 40, 51
Sheinberg, M., 6, 31
Shotter, J., 73, 87
Shweder, R. A., 186, 198
Simon Wiesenthal Center Museum of Tolerance, The, xviii
Singh, R., 20, 35
Sorajjakool, S., 186–187
Sorenson, E. R., 118, 135
Sorrentino, A., 4, 35
Speed, B., 58–59, 70
Spender, D., 96, 113
Spong, S. J., 171, 179
Stengers, I., 126, 136
Stewart, K., 153, 158
Steyn, M., xxviii, xxxv
Strathern, M., 2, 11, 19–20, 25, 35
subject(s), xxv–xxvi, xxix–xxx, 10–11, 13–14, 16–17, 22–25, 47–48, 75, 80, 83, 96, 101, 109, 224–225
subjectivity, xxix, 10, 13–17, 20, 23, 74–75, 79, 81, 225
inter-, xxix–xxx, 11, 47, 73–75, 77–80, 83, 98, 110

Tamura, T., 20, 35
Target, M., 8, 30, 77, 85
Tarule, J. M., 96, 111

Tatum, D., 43, 50
Tavistock Clinic, 107
Taylor, C., 26, 35
Thomas, L., 94, 103, 113
Time World, 183–184, 198
Tomm, K., xxvi, xxxv, 4–5, 7–8, 35, 146, 160
Tomson, D., 186, 197
Tomson, P., 186, 197
Tooby, J., 118, 135
Totsuka, Y., 145, 148, 150, 160
Turner, J., 7, 30
Turner, V., xxxii, xxxv, 24, 35, 190, 196–197, 199
Tydeman, B., 203, 221

unconscious(ness), xxv, xxvii, xxix, 9, 17–18, 22, 25–26, 54, 59, 61, 75–76, 78–80, 82, 134, 207, 211, 223 *see also*: conscious(ness)
University of Newcastle, 142

Valentine, L., 153, 158
van Langenhove, L., 42, 51
Verala, F., xx, xxiv, 6, 33
violence, 99, 167, 171, 212
domestic, 168, 188, 210, 216
Von Foerster, H., xxvi, xxxv, 118, 137, 164, 179

Walker, G., 6, 31
Walsh, F., 116, 137
Washington, J. M., 181, 199
Wasserman, S., xx, xxiv
Watts-Jones, D., 18, 35
Watzlawick, P., 118, 137
Weakland, J., 2, 35
Weisman, A., xx, xxiv
Werbner, P., 24, 35
White, M., xxvi, xxxv, 7, 9, 29, 35, 63, 70
Whitehead, A., 3, 36, 72, 87
Whitehouse, L., 145, 158
Wilder-Mott, C., 2, 36
Wilkinson, S., 20, 32, 93, 113
Wilson, J., 17, 36, 156, 160

Winnicott, D. W., 20–22, 36
Wittgenstein, L., 72, 87, 115, 120, 128, 137
Worthington, R., 145, 159
www.BuhayKorea.com/Choi-jin-sil-suicide/page 1, 183, 199

Yonsei University, 182
You, Y. G., 126, 137
Young, V., 186, 197

Žižek, S., xviii–xix, xxii, xxiv, 22, 36